The Welsh Terrier Leads the Way

By

Bardi McLennan

Doral Publishing, Inc.
Wilsonville, Oregon

Published by Doral Publishing, 8560 SW Salish Lane,
Wilsonville, Oregon 97070
1-800-633-5385
http://www.doralpub.com

Printed in the United States of America

Edited by Mark Anderson
Cover design by Randy Conger
Cover art by Dorothy Hardcastle
Layout by Mark Anderson

Library of Congress Card Number: 98-87267

The Welsh Terrier : leads the way / by Bardi McLennan.
    302 p. cm.
    ISBN: 0-944875-38-6 (hc)
    A history of the breed from its origin in Wales, breeding,
    showing and care of the breed. Famous breeders and dogs
    of the past and current years.
    1. Welsh terriers. 2. Dog breeds. 3. Dog shows. I. McLennan, Bardi.
SF429.W38 1998
636.7   97-67743
                                                           CIP

TABLE OF CONTENTS

PREFACE

The thing I fear most in writing this book is that I will have omitted some important dogs, some worthy persons, some notable events. However, if my worst fears should be realized, I would now—at the start of the book—beg the reader's forgiveness and indulgence. Such an omission would not be made willfully. But, on the other hand, it would be technically impossible to include every noteworthy dog and person and event ever involved in the long history of our breed between the covers of one manageable book.

Therefore, the aim has been to attempt to include all the true greats (dogs, people, events), to touch on some of the notables (worthy, but in some small ways perhaps less than "great"), and not to overlook mentions and anecdotes about what might be termed "the plebeians," i.e., the bulk of Welsh Terrier owners, fanciers, breeders, pro-moters, kennel managers, handlers, and their dogs, to whom we owe our undying gratitude for keeping our feet firmly fixed on the earth—the same terra firma for which our breed was created and which our dogs know so well.

—Bardi McLennan
Newtown, CT

The author with two Welsh Terrier pups—one obviously the more dominant!

ACKNOWLEDGEMENTS

This book would not have been possible without the groundwork, help, and constant prodding of Mrs. Walter Pangburn. Peggy became Welsh Terrier Club of America Historian in 1982 when there was barely a scrap of paper to enrich our knowledge of the club's beginnings. She did a monumental job of sourcing, collecting, sorting and cataloging articles, yearbooks, photographs, etc. There was literally nothing when she took over and a wealth of material when she stepped down in 1993. *Sine qua non* would be an understatement to describe her dedication and accomplishments. We all owe this fine lady a heartfelt vote of thanks.

Thanks also to Dan Kiedrowski of *Terrier Type* magazine for permission to use portions of the Arden Ross articles on handstripping, which originally appeared in his magazine. And to Arden Ross for writing what has become the handstripper's bible.

My thanks to Diane Hamilton Orange for her illustrated directions for a perfect Welsh Terrier pet clip, and especially for her drawings of the two delightful puppies and the standing Welsh Terrier. Thanks also to Pam Posey-Tanzey for illustrating the "almost" obedient Welsh Terrier.

An extended (overseas) thank you to Clifford L.B. "Doggie" Hubbard for a personal chat regarding source books and for his excellent work with Capt. I. Morlais Thomas on "The Welsh Terrier Handbook." And, while I'm overseas, my sincere gratitude to Drys Thomas and Gerrard Morris for a guided tour of the Rhondda Valley, the whelping box of our breed, and for all the side trips and information along the way.

A special thank you to Emlyn Snow, whose "daily reminder of Felstead" lies under my feet, and who has become a good friend and source of much history.

I hope that one day—before they are lost—the Welsh Terrier Association and Welsh Terrier Club will publish in one book, all their kennel histories that have appeared in recent yearbooks. They provide a fascinating overview of the breed as well as the people.

This acknowledgement would not be complete without mention of Sue Weiss, my "manager" who pushed, prodded, and encouraged me every time I was ready to give up. My thanks to a true friend.

—Bardi McLennan
Newtown, Connecticut

The Welsh Terrier

Leads the Way

Introduction to the Welsh Terrier

The Welsh Terrier is a handsome show dog, an intelligent and single-minded hunter, exhibiting courage and tenacity tempered with discretion. He's a sensible dog, outgoing and friendly toward people with an attitude similar to his own, good with good children, wisely cautious but not quarrelsome with his own kind. Not given to excess, he is neither overly active or needlessly noisy.

That is today's ideal. But dogs are individuals and owners are to a great degree responsible for the extent of their dog's individuality, therefore you may occasionally run across a spoiled, pampered, illiterate, undisciplined specimen, quite the opposite of the "ideal." If, however, that is precisely what the owner wants, the Welshman will be happy to oblige.

These dogs take pride in their appearance and patiently endure regular brushing, nail trimming, and teeth brushing. No matter how adept—or inept—you become at the stripping or clipping techniques, the dog will not criticize, but he'll complain mightily if you let him. They don't shed, so brushing is important to remove dead hair. For some pet owners, there is something very appealing, perhaps puppy-like, about the half-grown-out, woolly look. Keep the dog brushed, clean and trim away hair from eyes, ears and beneath the tail and he won't mind a bit being a woolly-bully.

Throughout his lifetime, the Welsh Terrier needs intelligent exercise, meaning activity with a rewarding purpose. To a Welsh, jogging takes no brains at all and a military-type march only gets you where you're going. But a brisk walk that is punctuated by frequent stops to sniff or track will suit him perfectly. If all you can offer is tossing a toy for him to retrieve so you can do it again, so be it. Chasing squirrels, crows, and cats, on the other hand, is another altogether rewarding pursuit. Speaking of cats, if raised with a cat, the Welsh will be compatible—until his sense of mischief strikes and the pair turn the house upside down.

The Welsh Terrier is a calm dog to live with; highly alert to a stranger's approach, responding with a strong voice, but not a nuisance barker. Every Welsh Terrier I've known is a "talker," or, on occasion and true to their native roots, a "singer;" not howling, mind you, but carrying on a sing-song conversation as long as you wish and, need I say it, all quite seriously as though taking a great deal of pride in his singing voice.

This brings up another aspect of the breed. They are amusing, but often it is their somewhat staid, almost Victorian demeanor that we find most humorous.

When one of my granddaughters was visiting (she was about five years old) my house dog was a very serious, no-nonsense, elderly Welsh named Samantha. The two seemed to be playing quietly in another room when Mindy called out, "Gran', come and see Samantha." There, sitting stiffly upright in the middle of a large armchair was indeed Samantha—with a scarf on her head, a string of beads around her neck, and her muzzle covered in black shoe polish topped by white-rimmed sun glasses. The scene was extremely funny, but the look of "we are not amused" in Samantha's eyes as she peered over the glasses, surpassed the joke of the get-up. She dared us to laugh—and we didn't. So I guess we should add "tolerant" to the list of breed attributes.

The Welsh Terrier is in many respects a cat-like canine, crawling along the ground when stalking a squirrel, or rearing up on hind legs to sight a rabbit moving in tall grass. They are also apt to use their paws when playing with toys, which makes them great soccer players. This, of course, is preferable to being compared to a cat, since, if a Welsh could understand the English language (and some owners would swear that they do—they just don't bother to speak it) he would no doubt take great offense at being called "cat-like." However, give a Welsh a neck and shoulder rub and he practically purrs in appreciation, and if he doesn't use his front paws to clean off his whiskers, he'll soon find a rug in your house that will do the job.

A young puppy will readily learn as much as you're willing to teach and as much as he's physically and mentally able to handle at any given stage. Consistent, good-natured reminders (and food reinforcements) are essential to the learning process of a terrier, since a typical Welsh learns quickly and sees no advantage to himself in repeating a performance over and over again once he has demonstrated to you how well he can do it. Thus he soon becomes "innovative," which in turn leads to frustration, hilarity. or perhaps the end of an obedience career, depending on how the scenario is perceived by the owner.

One obedience-trained dog (he eventually earned a utility degree) had scored well in trials until one day when he was directed to retrieve a specific glove of the three placed at the opposite end of the ring. He went smartly out, did a brief detour (looking at another glove, so his owner thought) and returned to do a perfect "sit"—with half a hamburger in his mouth! He flunked, but the owner and judge had a good laugh while the Welsh did the sensible thing and polished off the stolen burger.

Here's another example of how frustrating it can be to obedience-train a Welsh. One exercise requires the dog to go over the jump, retrieve a thrown dumbbell, return over the jump and present it to the handler. Each time the dog came back, she'd spit out the dumbbell before clearing the hurdle. Numerous training experts worked with her to no avail. Then we realized that this was a case of instinct taking precedence over training. She had not been taught as a puppy to hold anything in her mouth, but she was an avid hunter in our barn. Having killed a rat, being a sensible Welsh, she'd drop it and go after the next one. She didn't hold the kill to carry back to her owner (for which I was thankful!)

The breed, as we shall see, are natural hunters, but if you don't have access to fields and streams, it will only take a few minutes to teach a Welsh to play hide-and-seek with a toy or a piece of hot dog under a box or to find you in another room. They also take to sailing like true seafaring Welshmen, but most prefer boats (with life jackets) to ocean swimming. Pools, however, are as much fun as mud puddles.

So you see, the Welsh Terrier likes to be with people, his communications skills are unsurpassed, he has an sensible attitude toward life and invariably tries never to do the same thing the same way twice—all of which makes him a truly delightful, albeit challenging companion.

Affection for the breed is addictive. People who were raised with a Welsh Terrier subsequently want one for their own children, and then another when they reach their retirement years. It would seem the breed is all things to all people—a pal for the kids, a natural for life in the country, but perfectly content to conform to city life, and a personable companion to spark up our later life.

To this day, there is controversy over the exact origin of the dog we have known only since its inception in the stud registry of the Kennel Club in 1886 as a separate breed called the Welsh Terrier. In this respect, it is no different from the majority of breeds that evolved worldwide over many hundreds of years. The virtues of each were fine-tuned, not by random engineering, but by the land in which they worked and the special needs of the men they served. Breed names became essential only after there were stud registries.

A description of a dog fitting that of today's Welsh Terrier in coloring and purpose appears in an *englyn*, or poem, written as a thank-you note, about 1450:

"You gave me a good black and red bitch
to throttle the polecat . . ."

The conflict over origin persists because it has never been possible to prove without doubt whether this specific terrier was indigenous to Wales or was one of a family of similar small "earth dogs" common throughout the British Isles. Bear in mind that Wales once extended its boundaries to the borders of Scotland and the

Midlands of England as well as across the English Channel into Brittany. One glance at a line-up of the Terrier group today would indicate that many of them certainly had common ancestors, which is not surprising taking into account that most are of British origin, the size of the British Isles, and the need for small earth dogs by the common man. Additional terriers—the Dandie Dinmont, Bedlington, Staffordshire and Bull Terriers among them—were knowingly manufactured and are of more recent vintage.

There are two distinct schools of thought as to the Welsh Terrier's roots and both will be offered here so that you, the reader, may then takes sides and perpetuate the controversy as long as you like!

What follows will introduce you to the ancient history of the land itself—the hauntingly beautiful, mysterious, yet realistic wild Wales—as well as to some of the many people who have been instrumental in shaping the Welsh Terrier, in the hope that a knowledge of his total background will help to explain how the Welsh Terrier was molded into the very special breed we so admire today and thus to understand him more fully.

CHAPTER ONE

YESTERDAY

In recent years much has been made of people's roots or origins on the premise that who, where, and what we were define to a large extent who and what we are today. It is said that people who do not look back to their ancestry can't look forward to their posterity. With that in mind, in order to understand today's Welsh Terrier we must first examine the history, the land and the people who determined what was wanted in the original, ancestral *daeargi* or terrier.

What we know of ancient Wales is partially wrapped in mystery and at the same time bursting with well-documented history. The Welsh flag, for example, with its rampant red dragon, is thought to have derived from the purple griffon found on Roman banners and is, as such, the oldest national flag in the world.

The Welsh people tackle life with passion and purpose. Their tenacity in battling great odds to protect their "Welshness" against all comers—Saxons, Normans, English—and against all attempts at conformity, has gone on for well over a thousand years. Their contemporary connection with this history, the depth of their involvement in religion, rugby matches, mythology, poetry, singing, and the love of the land itself all attest to this intenseness that is Welsh. The Welsh are neither indecisive nor humble; they know who they are and do not find themselves lacking.

In *Pleasures of a Tangled Life*, Jan Morris points to the basics of what is aptly called "Welshness" as three separate but equal influences: First, the history of Wales, which is visible everywhere in its 8,000 square miles of mountains and ruins, with one-twentieth the population of Britain—plus six million sheep! Next, the land itself. The dramatic sheep-covered hills, purple-to-black mountains, blue lakes, green valleys, and the sea; all of which influenced the history of the land and molded the character of its people. Lastly, the Welsh language, arguably the true basis of the enigma that is Wales. It is a land full of contradictions and therefore its people (and perhaps its terriers?) are hard to pin down. Another Welsh author, Trevor Fishlock, explains the complexity well: "Just when you think you have the picture (of Wales and the Welsh) right, somebody gives the kaleidoscope a nudge and moves all the pieces."

The Language

Welsh is the oldest literary language in Europe, and there is no other nation that has continued over the centuries to celebrate its language as the Welsh do with the annual *Eisteddfod* (or "meeting of the bards," sometimes described as a Celtic picnic) where, drawn together by their ancient tongue, love of poetry, music, and the camaraderie of the *gwerin* 'ordinary people', the Welsh are revitalized.

It is not only one of the oldest, it is also one of the largest languages in the world, and undeniably one of the most difficult for an outsider to learn. It almost defies pronunciation, spelling, and rules of grammar. Whereas Irish and Scottish Gaelic were invaded by far-off foreign tongues, French and Norse, and English primarily by Latin and Saxon, the Celtic Welsh language had definitive inroads only from neighboring Cornwall and Brittany. One is easily enchanted by the sing-song melody, without comprehending one single word.

Celtic has a peculiarity called "the mutation" which it shares with Gaelic. The mutation is a mountainous stumbling block for would-be students of the language. Disliking sharp edges, the Welsh alter and soften certain consonants at the beginning of a word according to the sound of the word that precedes it.

Thus the word for Wales—*Cymru*—changes on road signs saying, "Welcome to Wales" to read *"Croeso I Gymru."*

One of our breed's foundation dogs bred by Mr. John Mitchell in 1891 was named *Cymro-o-Gymru*, even though you may see it misspelled as *"Cymru."* The English words, Wales and Welsh are derived from the Anglo-Saxon *Wealh* and *Wealeas* meaning 'foreign,' but in their own language the land is *Cymru* and the people call themselves *Cymry,* which means 'fellow countrymen' or 'comrades'. With the rise of Plaid Cymru, the Welsh nationalist group, you'll also see signs reading *"Cymru am byth"* or "Wales For Ever." Another example of the mutation is the word for father—*tad*. "My father" becomes *fy nhad*. It's easy to see the total confusion this evokes in the outside world, although it makes perfect sense to the Welsh.

And now the reason for this discourse: Don't some of these complexities—combined with complete self-confidence and self-assuredness for what is right—begin to remind you of the Welsh Terrier?

"As to its sounds . . . it can be sublimely sonorous, terribly sharp, diabolically guttural and sibilant, and sweet and harmonious to a remarkable degree." So wrote the English author, George Borrow, in *Wild Wales* (1854), about the Welsh language. Once you've conquered the pronunciation of *Cymru* as "kum-REE," you'll discover that form is correct only in South Wales. In the North, it's "kum-RU." No wonder the Welsh avidly form committees!

Mr. Borrow tells of meeting a woman on the way to Rhiwabon. He pointed to the ridge and in English asked its name. The woman just shook her head, saying, *"Dim Saesneg,"* meaning 'No English'. "Now," wrote Mr. Borrow, "I feel I am in Wales!" (Isn't this a sketch of a Welsh Terrier with its nose in the air saying the canine equivalent of *"Dim Saesneg"* in response to our repeated calls of "Taffy, come!")

Mr. Borrow makes another point about this Welsh tenacity of language:

The Welsh are afraid lest an Englishman should
understand their language and by hearing their conversation become acquainted with their private
affairs, or by listening to it, pick up their language
which they have no mind that he should know—and
their very children sympathize with them. All conquered people are suspicious of their conquerors.
The English have forgot that they ever conquered
the Welsh, but some ages will elapse before the
Welsh forget that the English have conquered them.

This became clear to me when attending the International
Sheep Dog Trials in Aberystwyth, and I thought to capture just the
music of the native tongue. Nothing stops a Welsh conversation
quicker than the proximity of a stranger! Outsiders remain outsiders to what is intrinsically Welsh, despite the depth of Welsh hospitality, warmth and friendliness; yet more strikingly similar traits
that are found in our Welsh Terriers.

From *Wales and The Welsh* by Jan Morris comes this observation of national character: "On all levels of life in Wales there is
a current of argument of a kind not found in England." There's a
saying that if you shout "YES!" down any street in Wales, a dozen
people will shout back "NO!" Again, our Welsh Terriers, or perhaps you haven't tried obedience training? First you need a committee meeting, explain what you have in mind, get the dog to
agree, and only then can you proceed successfully.

History

In the year 942, Hwyl Dda 'Hwyl the Good' ruled Wales
and codified the laws of the land, which included giving each recognized type of dog a legal value while spelling out its duties and
privileges in great detail. Of the three curs, the "House Cur" is
assumed to be the terrier, since the other two were referred to as a
"Shepherd's Cur" and a "Mastiff" or watchdog. The House Cur

was valued at four curt pence regardless of who owned it, commoner or king. All pups and kittens were worth a penny until their eyes opened. The penalties were explicit regarding the stealing or killing of dogs, and stiff fines were exacted. It was only when breeds became specialists (terriers among them) and earned individual nomenclature that our current use of "cur" came to mean a mongrel.

Morlais Thomas contended that because Wales had an indigenous Welsh Pony, Welsh Black Cattle, Welsh Springer Spaniel, Welsh Hound, Welsh Sheepdogs, two breeds of Welsh Corgi and even a Welsh Setter, it stands to reason that the Welsh would also have had their own terrier to tackle the vermin that prevailed throughout the country.

Perhaps something can also be surmised from the fact that William the Conqueror in 1066 conquered all of Great Britain except for Wales, something that had been accurately forecast in "Destiny of Britons" written in the sixth century and attributed to Taliesin:

> Their Lord they shall praise.
> Their language they shall keep.
> Their land they shall lose,
> Except Wild Wales.

Is this early warning perhaps what prompted the sound advice: "Cajole him, win him over with praise and presents, enjoy his inventive mind, but never try to conquer the Welsh Terrier"? The Welsh were good warriors yet clever and cultured. "The battered Rhondda is still, like its people, rugged, stubborn, and grand," wrote Trevor Fishlock. The Rhondda Valley, it should be noted, is considered to be the whelping box of the Welsh Terrier as we know the breed today. Now rid of its coal industry, it is lush and appropriately a green valley.

Now we come to the poetic mention of a specific breed ancestor, written circa 1450. An *Englyn Diolgarwch*, or 'poem of thanks', actually thanks the donor for "a good black and red terrier bitch." There are several versions; here is one:

> Urddasol ffon im eoesoch—gast dda
> Daeargast ddu dorgoch,
> T dag'r ffwlbart dugoch,
> Ac I ewy gor cachio coch

Translation:

> A fine big stick you gave me
> and a good black and red terrier bitch
> to choke the brown polecat,
> and to tear up the red fox.

So now we know that 500 years ago, a "good one" was three things: One, it was a working terrier; two, it was "black and red"; and three, was of sufficient worth to warrant an *englyn*. This was in no way our present handsome show dog, but it was identifiable and was valued for its working ability.

It should be pointed out that while black is black, the second color is given as red, the same as the description of the fox, and thus is differentiated from the polecat (also known as a *foumart* or ferret), which is described as brown. The terrier was not brown or "slightly lighter shades" (as changed in the U.S. Breed Standard), nor the American definition of tan as given in Webster's New World Dictionary as "yellowish-brown" nor any other color breeders were later to find acceptable because it appeared in the whelping box. The dog was red. Red as the fox was then and still is today.

The history of this fascinating land and its people is richly recorded and available to anyone whose interest has been aroused. There is a wealth of it to be found in the *Tales of The Mabinogian* in your local library, or, for the scholar, in the archives of the National Museum in Cardiff on your next visit.

Figure 1

Figure 2

Very Early Pictures

The illustrations (Figures 1 and 2) are from a Lincolnshire manuscript, *Lutrell's Psalter*, now in the British Museum and date from about the year 1340. They were chosen by Ruth Wright for inclusion in Trevelyan's *Illustrated English Social History* to represent useful, rather than the game or hunting aspects of medieval dogs.

Both of the dogs shown resemble present-day Welsh Terriers even more closely than do some of the early nineteenth century dogs pictured as progenitors of the breed. These illustrations show that the typical Welsh Terrier was well-established 650 years ago in size, coat, color, and expression. Erect ear carriage and a long tail in the fourteenth century may leave something to be desired by modern standards, but there is no trace of the white blaze and droopy expressions which are seen in some of those early nineteenth century specimens. The qualities that have come to the fore in the twentieth century—probably inadvertently—appear to be closer to the original.

More important than ear carriage or tail is the typical Welsh Terrier behavior considered by the artist to be worthy of note. The first shows a cobby little dog with the right coloring, alertly watching the man on a horse, who is bringing grain to the master's mill. The second illustration shows the dog attacking a crow as big as himself while his master is sowing grain. It is not hard to see that such an alert black-and-tan terrier, which could stand guard at the mill and drive away predatory crows from his master's valuable grain (as well as keep down mice and rats in both areas), could mean the difference between survival and starvation to his master. This is no doubt the earliest illustration anywhere of a Welsh Terrier "look-alike" dog.

According to The National Library of Wales, a national Welsh costume for women did not exist. Styles varied considerably with the age of the wearer and with the locality, although the basic full skirt and bodice were usually of heavy wool (with all those sheep, it's no wonder) and the shawl of fine wool. A thick cotton apron was a practical washable cover. In 1805 it was noted that most women wrapped their heads in a handkerchief, topped with a man's hat that resembled today's bowler. The tall, steeple-crowned hat over a white cambric bonnet did not appear until later in the nineteenth century. Whether or not it is true, this latter type of head covering and a specific national dress is said to have been invented to encourage tourism.

For a bit of Welsh-American trivia, hold up your heads and try this: Before America became a nation, there were no "Americans" and without Welshmen there might not have been a Constitution! Seventeen of the signers of the Declaration of

Lynda Sutton (left) and Ruth Prehn (above, right) appeared in versions of the Welsh "national dress" at a Specialty. And some Welsh Terriers got into the act, too!

Independence were of Welsh descent. Robert Morris was the major financial backer of the Revolutionary War; James Madison and Governor Morris were draftsmen of the Constitution; and John Adams and Thomas Jefferson were the architects of the Constitution. All were of Welsh stock. In 1987, when the United States was celebrating its Constitution, David Meade, a St. David's Society member, called the nation's attention to these roots.

Typically, perhaps, the Welsh do have the last word. About halfway up the stairs of the Washington Monument, there is a stone with this inscription:

"Fy Iaith, Fy Ngwlad, Fy Nghendel Wales—Cymru am Byth", which means 'My Language, My Land, My Countrymen—Wales For Ever.'

And, of course, you will note that "language" comes first.

CHAPTER TWO

THE "ORIGINAL"

There are two views as to the origins of the Welsh Terrier as a separate, specific breed of dog. The problems began not with the breed, of course, but with its name. The small, common working class dogs that were useful in controlling vermin and providing the odd rabbit for the dinner table, were never actually called anything other than "terriers" in the English language—*daeargi*" in Welsh. By the end of the 1700s, classes for "working terriers" began to appear at fairs and agricultural shows in Wales.

However, prior to the advent of breed standards and benched dog shows, no one really cared what any working, herding, or hunting breed looked like, or what name it went by, so long as it could do its job. "Form follows function" was the breeders' by-law. And, of course, the variety of jobs that dogs undertook, as well as the geographic location (terrain and climate), are what have given us a diversity of breeds and breed names.

It was when dogs were divided into specific breeds, each requiring a definitive name, that things became complicated for many terrier breeds that had been known primarily by locale (Scotch, Waterside, Bingley, Fell, etc.) or even by personal association, such as the Jones Terrier or the Dandie Dinmont.

In 1800 there were only fifteen designated breeds of dogs, and fifty years later there were a total of only forty. The first "dogs only" show held on June 28, 1859 drew sixty entries in two classes: pointers and setters. The "show dog" had not yet arrived, and a "pet" (or non-working dog) was *persona non grata* until elevated

"The Poachers Disturbed," oil painting by J.F. Lewis (London 1837). The original was owned 100 years later by Freeman Lloyd. Note that the spaniel is interested in the hare the ferrets have killed, whereas the terrier has its eye on the ferrets!

by Queen Victoria to royal status, at which point anyone could aspire to being part of the leisure class by owning a pet.

It should be noted here that duplicate names did not occur exclusively in Welsh Terriers. In 1851 the Yorkshire Terrier, for example, was also known as the "broken-haired Scotch Terrier" and only in 1870 began its show career as the Yorkshire Terrier. Littermates could and did turn up in both classes until agreement on one name settled the matter.

A Welsh By Any Other Name

In the 1850s, claims were made by two stalwart groups of people knowledgeable in dogs—the Welsh and the English. The latter claimed their version to be the "original" Old English Broken-Haired Black and Tan Terrier (or the Wire-Haired Black and Tan Terrier). The Welsh, in the no-nonsense, direct style of the people, named their dog the Welsh Terrier. The Welshmen quickly formed a strong club and came out the winners. But it wasn't quite that simple.

This is how the Welsh Terrier appellation came about and why I am convinced that both the Welsh roots and the name are correct. The reader is free to form his or her own opinion.

The first show with classes solely for Welsh Terriers—a specialty, if you will—was held in Pwllheli, North Wales, in

August, 1884, and was judged by two elderly Welshmen who had owned and bred Welsh Terriers for many years: Mr. Griffith Owen and Mr. Humphrey Griffith. They sat in armchairs in the middle of the ring while the dogs were brought to them one at a time. The rest of the dogs were kept leashed to pegs in the ground. This was long before the days of boxes, crates, tents, benching, and grooming areas! There were ninety dogs, and the judging went on all day. The exhibitors seemed pleased with the results, for there were said to be no complaints. An auspicious start.

At about this time at a show in the Southwest of England, two terrier enthusiasts, Lord Lonsdale and George Raper, gave the Old English Broken-Haired Black and Tan win to a dog named Crib. Crib was a cross between a bluish-black rough terrier and a full brother to Corinthian, a famous Smooth Fox Terrier owned by L.P.C. Astley. Crib was owned by Charles Waring of Cardiff and bred by Dick Harris. The dog was not only known to be of mixed heritage, he was deaf!

When The Kennel Club was founded in London in 1873, each breed had to be named in order to be listed in the stud registry and to be assigned classes in dog shows. A group of people in England had been promoting the Old English Broken-Haired Black and Tan as the original, definitive terrier. That is to say, they contended that their terrier was the taproot of just about all terriers in the British Isles, which may have prompted that cumbersome all-inclusive breed name.

But their claim was aimed in particular at discrediting the somewhat scruffier-looking, workmanlike terrier from over the border in Wales.

This presumption did not sit at all well with the Welsh, who were still smarting from defeat at the hands of the English in battles that had taken place some 600 years before. The terrier men rose up behind their red dragon and clung tenaciously to their claim to their aboriginal breed and to the name they'd given it, and they promptly formed a committee to promote this native son. (This came as no surprise, since it's a well-known quip that if you put four Welshmen in a room, the first thing they'll do is form a committee!)

To make a long story short (the dispute went on for almost twenty years), in 1885 The Kennel Club offered two separate classes, one for the Old English Broken-Haired Black and Tan Terriers and one for Welsh Terriers. At the Birmingham show on November 28, 1885, separate classes were included for Welsh Terriers for the first time. Mr. W. Lort (one of fourteen founders of the Welsh Terrier Club) judged the entry and indicated a need for improvement in conformity but cautioned breeders lest the breed lose its gameness, as had already happened in other terriers that became fashionable as show dogs and idle pets.

In 1886, the Welsh Terrier Club was formed in Bangor, with nine Welshmen (seven from Gwynedd alone) and five terrier men from England: Col. H. Platt as president and Mr. W. Wheldon Williams as secretary (neither of whom were breeders), Mr. W.A. Dew, Mr. Price O. Pugh, Mr. Cledwyn Owen, Mr. W. Jones, Mr. Edmund Buckley, Mr. W.J.M. Herbert, Mr. David Jones, Mr. W.C. Roberts, Mr. Edwin Powell, Mr. H. Field, Mr. F.H. Colmore, and the aforementioned Mr. W. Lort.

Almost all of these men already were, or soon became, dog show judges of high regard. Much later, the South Wales Welsh Terrier Breeders Association was formed, and in 1922 threw in its lot (and its funds) with the Welsh Terrier Club. The following year, the Welsh Terrier Association was formed in England. To this day, the two clubs continue to co-exist peacefully with about the same number of members in each and indeed with quite a few who enjoy membership in both clubs.

But back to 1886. The feat of speedy organization by the Welsh obviously had an impact on the final outcome, because the Old English Broken-Haired Black and Tan Terrier supporters were overcome and never did get themselves organized. (But, really, with a name like that, were they ever really destined to win?) On April 5, 1887, only seventeen months after sanctioning the two breed names, The Kennel Club dropped the OEBHBTTs from their books and retained classes only for the Welsh Terrier.

Walter Glynn, a staunch promoter of Welsh Terriers as show dogs even in those early years, discovered that all the OEBHBTTs entered in the 1885-1886 shows were of the first generation. Not a single one was by an OEBHBTT out of an OEBHBTT. My research indicates another problem with that "other" breed, and that is the name. It was variously called, "Old English Black and Tan," "Old English Wire-Haired," "Old English Wire-Haired Black and Tan," "Old English Broken-Haired," or "Old English Broken-Haired Black and Tan Terrier." It's obvious the people behind the dogs lacked the Welshmen's zeal for forming committees—they couldn't even get together on a breed name! It's just possible that The Kennel Club made their final decision quickly so as not to have to cope with such a plethora of adjectives!

It's more likely, of course, that this self-styled breed was dropped for the simple reason that it could not reproduce itself. Inter-breeding was not prohibited in those early years, but from the records kept, one must conclude that the OEBHBTT presented as a show dog was a mix of breeds put together solely for looks.

It should be noted, too, that the acceptance of the appellation, *Welsh Terrier*, was one more subtle achievement of Welsh patriotism underway at the time. David Lloyd George, the ward of a Welsh village cobbler, took his seat in Parliament in 1890; the University of Wales was established in Aberystwyth, followed by the National Library and the National Museum in Cardiff. The rise of intense Welsh nationalism no doubt played a part in the determination of the Welsh Terrier Club to be victorious. Not for one moment should you be left to wonder how our Welsh Terriers come by their mettle!

There is no reason not to believe, however, that there was at one time a black and tan terrier indigenous (or ubiquitous) to the British Isles. The facts, as we know them, surely lead to the conclusion that the so-called "Old English Etc." had been allowed to die out in England. Its final demise may have been due to the rise in popularity of the smarter-looking, more fashionable Wire Fox

Terrier. For whatever reasons, all attempts made to resurrect the OE Etc. met with failure. In the meantime, the serviceable black and tan terrier continued to flourish in Wales, where he was maintained for his attributes as an unassuming, useful working terrier (with or without a pack of hounds), and with a temperament suited to the family hearth.

As soon as a win at a dog show added to the dog's monetary value, Welsh Terrier breeders began to pay attention to the development of a more physically attractive dog. Mr. W.A. Dew wrote, "A good many owners of dogs in Wales who are not accustomed to exhibit think twice before paying a guinea entrance fee; but this prejudice will no doubt wear off when they learn the extra value placed upon a dog that takes a prize at the KC show and when a proper Standard has been fixed." (A guinea was an enormous sum of money in those days—the equivalent of about $30, or a large portion of the average yearly wage.)

Enter the Welsh Terrier as Show Dog

Fernyhurst Crab (a dog bred by Mr. Davidson and purchased by Edmund Buckley from Mr. A. Maxwell) was judged by W.A. Dew at the Crystal Palace Kennel Club show in February 1886. He gave this critique: "A nice-headed Terrier with good feet and legs and good tan; had cropped ears." There was no ruling about showing dogs with cropped ears, and it was not an unusual practice to protect working terriers from attacks on vulnerable ear flaps by enraged prey. *Crab* got his card that day, but went down in history not for that achievement, or for his cropped ears, but as the sire of the first Welsh Terrier champion dog. (Before we move on, the reader will please note the problems encountered in tracing dogs with little or no written pedigrees, with numerous changes of ownership, and even an occasional change of name!)

If there was an original OEBHBTT that was the taproot of so many British terriers, it certainly was *not* the man-made mix breed brought to the show ring. And again, if we do agree that there was one black and tan terrier as common ancestor of all, then one would have to agree that the Welsh is the only breed to have come down to us today as a direct and relatively unadulterated descendant of the original.

Mr. Colmore's *General Contour* received the first championship points (this was before the champion certificate or CC system) for Welsh Terriers, judged by Wheldon Williams. Mr. Williams, from North Wales, wrote that he was "proud of the established type of the black and distinctively tanned Terrier" from that part of the principality. (Note the use of "tanned" to emphasize the desired reddish-brown color of British tanned leather familiar to everyone at that time.)

Then, on September 16, 1887, at the Bangor Show, Mr. Colmore awarded W.A. Dew's bitch, *Bangor Dau Lliw* 'Bangor Two Colours', her championship. Thus she was the first champion Welsh Terrier. At this same show, Walter Glynn brought out for the first time his Welsh Terrier, *Dim Saesonaeg* 'No English', bred by Mr. R.O. Pugh. Five months later, in February 1888, *Mawddwy Nonsuch* (sired by the aforementioned *Crab*) became the first Welsh Terrier champion dog under Mr. H. Field.

Freeman Lloyd, writing at the time of *Mawddwy Nonsuch*, said that Mr. Edmund Buckley (Master of Otterhounds and enthusiastic Welsh Terrier supporter) of Newtown, Merioneth, paid 300

Ch. Bangor Dau Lliw This was the first Welsh Terrier to qualify as a champion, September 16, 1887. Born Oct. 15, 1885, bread and owned by W.A. Dew. Sired by Pym, out of Topsy.

Topsy, Bangour's dam, became a champion herself in 1888.

Ch. Mawddy Nonsuch, the first Welsh Terrier dog champion, with Ch. Bob Bethesda.

pounds for the dog, which was then worth $1500. This must have started a boom in Welsh Terrier stock! The dog was very popular and much admired, although doubts were raised as to the purity of his pedigree on the dam's side, since he was an "English-bred kennel dog" bred by Mr. Davidson, sold first as a pup to Mr. A. Maxwell (a Wire Fox Terrier breeder who judged on both sides of the Atlantic) and finally to Mr. Buckley.

Buckley's own dog, *Bob Bethesda* (one of the first four Welsh Terrier champions) spent much of his life on the road—literally—being shunted from one show to the next and cared for only by local show officials. It was a different world then, one where almost anyone could be entrusted to look after a valuable show dog. According to reports of the time, *Bob* was a very likable dog and a good public relations agent for the breed. Thus a worthy dog with a stable temperament marked the true beginning of the breed's entry into the show ring. Not all stories have happy endings, though. *Bob* was mistaken for an otter and killed by a pack of hounds in 1889. This is possibly the only drawback to working the Welsh Terrier; its color is too like most of its prey.

The Great "Welshman from Wales"

In December 1889, Walter Glynn's *Dim Saesonaeg* became a champion and went on to win twenty-eight champion certificates. His son, *Cymro-o-Gymru* 'The Welshman from Wales', bred by John Mitchell, out of *Blink Bonny*, won twenty-seven champion certificates and over 400 first and special prizes! *Cymro* was born in 1891 and died at the home of his then owner, Luke Crabtree, in May 1903. *The Illustrated Kennel News* reported, "He was one of the most wonderful dogs of his day, having won over 400 first and specials . . ."

In her design for the 1899 Kennel Club show, Miss Frances

. CHAMPION DIM SAESONAEG .

Walter Glynn's Ch. Dim Saesonaeg, bred by Mr. Pughe.

Fairman (a renowned canine artist of the day) selected *Cymro* as one of the fourteen breeds to grace the certificates. Judging from the photograph, *Cymro-o-Gymru* more than his sire, is of the type we would recognize today as a true Welsh Terrier.

Note the lack of furnishings on all the dogs prior to the

Ch. Cymro-o-Gymru, the "Welshman from Wales." Bred by John Mitchell in 1891.

1900s, whether in photos, paintings, or engravings. Since grooming for the show ring at that time was minimal at best, one must assume that the dogs did not grow much leg or face furnishings and, due to wear and tear in the fields, not much attention was paid to beauty in presentation. In fact, one notable judge of the early 1900s condemned "whiskers" as kowtowing to fashion and not in keeping with such a "good game working terrier."

It wasn't until the 1930s that face furnishings were "in" for the show ring and were encouraged to grow in sufficient quantity to be painstakingly trimmed for the illusion of perfection in competition. But even when apple-domed heads were a thing of the past and grooming emphasized the preferred rectangular shape, little or no extra hair was left on the hindquarters. That soon changed, and by the 1940s more leg hair became the vogue, and the basic show trim we see today was set. Whether or not it is true, it is felt that professional handlers in the United States have dictated fashion by the clever trimming of prolific furnishings to present an almost picture-perfect dog. Photographs of dogs around the world would bear this out. In terms of "picture-perfect" nothing can beat the renowned photographer, Mr. R.W. Tauskey!

Diehard terrier men agree that judicious crossings with the Wire Fox Terrier were responsible for giving the Welsh some of his present eye appeal, but there has likely been more fear than foundation as to the quantity of Wire that went into the Welsh. In America, any appearance of white on a Welsh is blamed on a Wire cross, yet from the very beginning Welsh Terriers often had white on the chest and feet. Just as they are also depicted with black on the ears, backskull, and top of muzzle. All these undesirable colorations crop up occasionally to this day as natural recurrences of bygone atavistic genes.

The Show Goes On The Road

There was no quarantine in those early days, so from the time the breed first entered the show ring, dogs were shown on the Continent. India was the first distant colonial land to import Welsh Terriers, but soon breeding stock was soon regularly being exported to Europe, the United States, and South Africa. In April 1897, W.C. Roberts of Llandudno, North Wales, sent a dog named *Sincuir* to Mr. Buckley Wells in the States. Three years later, Mr. Wells would become a founder of the Welsh Terrier Club of America. In August 1897 Walter Glynn sent a dog, *Brynhir Brand* and two brood bitches to the States, but unfortunately there is no record of the recipient nor the names of the bitches.

In Great Britain there were 217 dog shows in 1892, and by 1899 this number was up to 380, with national championship shows drawing entries of more than 2,000 dogs, often with ten or fewer judges. And what were those judges looking for one hundred years ago other than "good ones"? They had their eyes peeled for what were called "fakers"—dogs that were dyed, clipped, or plucked to give a false illusion of perfection. Some things haven't changed!

Ch. Brynhir Ballad. Born in 1898, winner of 31 CCs, and considered to be one of Walter Glynn's best Welsh.

There are still cheaters among us.

Mr. Glynn expressed his surprise that the Welsh Terrier was not more popular as a show dog, because "they are very charming terriers in every way . . . and there is no prettier team of dogs than four really sound, good-colored Welsh Terriers and frequently they have in consequence won team prizes against all other breeds." To back his claim, he repeatedly showed teams of Welsh Terriers, winning at Crufts in 1897, 1898, and 1902, thus taking the Sporting Cup outright. Today, it is rare to see even a brace of Welsh Terriers in the ring.

It didn't take long for "everyman's" serviceable working terrier from the Principality to become fashionable, chic, and a worthy competitor in the terrier show ring anywhere in the world. At the same time, he continued to win high accolades as a vermin-hunter and as a sensible family dog.

More on People

From 1887, when he bought his first Welsh Terrier puppy, until his death in 1933, it is irrefutable that Walter S. Glynn took a more active role in every conceivable aspect of the breed than anyone has since. Born in Wales, he was educated at Trinity College,

Oxford, became a lawyer, and a breeder-exhibitor under the famed prefix, "Brynhir" in Criccieth, North Wales.

An ardent club worker from 1898, he was the first public relations man for the breed (even before they realized they needed one), an elected Kennel Club member, a dog show judge, a critic, an overseas ambassador, and an able historian. As a judge, he drew an entry of 113 Welsh Terriers in 1924 at the Royal Welsh Agricultural Show—a record that remains unbroken to this day. When Mr. Glynn died in 1933, he was buried in Brookland Cemetery in Surrey, in the same grave as his son who had died in infancy. One of his daughters, Jeanette Hazel, attended the Welsh Terrier Club Centenary Championship Show in 1986 that was judged by Peter Green, another Welshman with lifetime ties to the breed.

In 1911 the Welsh Terrier fanciers of North Wales formed a committee (what else?) to raise the money to buy a dog for His Royal Highness The Prince of Wales. The surplus was used to buy a Breeder's Challenge Cup offered at North Wales shows. The dog chosen was *Queen Llechwedd* ("Gwen") bred by P. Williams, a quarryman from Blaenau Festiniog, and appropriately sired by a dog named *Dewi Sant* 'St. David', the patron saint of Wales). In 1912, His Royal Highness registered two puppies by *Ch. Just in Time* (bred by D.E.R. Griffith) ex *Gwen*. Fate seems to have had a hand in it, for the pups were

H.R.H. The Prince of Wales with "Gwen."

whelped on March first—St. David's Day.

Mr. T.H. Harris of Sennybridge, Breconshire was another whose life was bound up in the breed. His first champion, *Nell Gwynne*, was made up (i.e., earned a championship) in 1898, but he was breeding, exhibiting, and judging from 1885 for 65 years, exporting much of his *Senny* stock worldwide, including a dog named *Red Palm* that went to George Steadman Thomas in the U.S. in 1897. Mr. Harris died in 1953 having left us a legacy of foundation dogs, as well as the transcript of a BBC talk that he gave in 1946 in which he said, regarding the breed's history, "Several people now living in Wales can prove that Welsh Terriers had been kept by their ancestors over two hundred years ago. In the early part of the last century we know that there were several strains of Welsh Terriers in North and Mid-Wales. Also there was a noted strain in the Sennybridge district known as the Aberloch strain kept purely for sporting purposes . . ." That, of course, is how Mr. Harris came by his "Senny" kennel prefix.

He went on to say, "From my own experience, no gamer or

Int.Ch. Senny Tip Top. Born August 28, 1914. An excellent example of T.H. Harris's Senny line.

better sporting terrier exists for badger and for digging. He is also adept at rat hunting on the riverside (which is excellent sport on a summer's day) and quite as good at otter hunting, whilst he is a good worker with the gun for rabbiting, etc."

Mr. Harris exported the first U.K. champion to become an AKC champion, *Ch. Senny King* to Dr. F.C. Benson Jr.of Philadelphia in 1903 and it was considered to be the best Welsh Terrier in the States. *Ch. Senny Spinner* was the first Welsh Terrier to become a German champion. Oddly, this dog was then sent to America in 1914, possibly to do with the onset of World War I. He was imported by Miss Maud Kennedy and won the Grand Challenge Cup in that year without an AKC championship.

After recognition by The Kennel Club, and the acceptance of the first breed standard in 1887, the Welsh Terrier maintained large entries in the British show ring—ninety was not unusual. Even so, Rawdon B. Lee, author of *Modern Dogs of Great Britain and Ireland* (1896), was not in a rush to support the breed. He wrote of the Welsh Terrier show dog as "Our most modern introduction—unknown out of his principality until about a dozen or so years ago," which, of course, was true of many breeds prior to the advent of dog shows. However, he then refers to "the so-called Welsh Terrier" throughout his article about the breed, adding that while he is "reluctant to agree with all that has been said and done to popularize the so-called Welsh Terrier, one must give way to the majority." But with several more comments upholding the Old English Black and Tan as a "better terrier," Mr. Lee continued to downgrade the idea of an indigenous Welsh Terrier and to support the North England fanciers. (He later came around, as we will see.)

He quotes an unnamed friend as describing the Welsh Terrier to be a big dog of twenty-five pounds or more, and adds, "Points of beauty are not considered of such importance as gameness and ability to work." This statement backs up the contention that the Welsh Terrier continued to be valued for its work in rough cover. Beauty was not a consideration; that is, not until showing dogs became an acceptable and accessible competitive sport of the working man.

"Their ears are usually large and their skull is generally rounder between the ears than is quite orthodox in the modern fox terrier." "Modern" being the 1890s, remember. He does not explain why he felt the Welsh should emulate the fox terrier other than the fox terrier was his own personal preference and had become something of a model for show terriers.

He relents only with a backhanded compliment in saying that the "crisper coat and darker colour give the Welsh Terrier a more dare-devil and determined appearance than the fashionable fox terrier beauties of the present time." This is actually an accurate reflection of how many terrier men of the day felt about the somewhat scruffy dog from Wales, but it's easy to see that Mr. Lee's heart was definitely not with our breed in the beginning. But wait! The breed was not going to let Mr. Lee get away so easily.

The Dick Turpin Caper

Lee continues to compare the "so-called Welsh Terrier" with the OEBHBTT, but the fact that many dogs were originally shown in both classes brings us to the great Dick Turpin caper. Briefly stated, *Dick Turpin* was whelped March 20, 1888, by *Charlie* out of *Nellie*, a grizzle-and-tan Welsh Terrier bred by Mr. J. Wilkinson and registered by him as a Welsh Terrier. *Dick Turpin* changed owners four times and the third owner had the dog reclassified as an Old English Broken-Haired Black and Tan Terrier. In all, the dog won under Welsh Terrier judges when shown as a Welsh Terrier, and placed, but never won, when entered as an OEBHBTT! The fourth owner, Mr. H.M. Bryans (an Airedale breeder) showed him at Darlington on July 28, 1893, in Welsh Terrier classes where he took a first under Mr. Gresham, and in an Old English Black and Tan class where he went reserve under Mr. Clear.

Much was made of this episode at the time in an attempt to prove that the two separate breeds were actually one and the same, but it was not to be.

We can forgive Mr. Lee his favoritism since he himself was from North England, the "supposed" home of the "so-called" Old English, etc. And to give him his due, he does later concede upon his own further research that Mr. J.G. Williams of Dolgellau had kept Welsh Terriers for three generations and that Mr. Griffith Williams of Trefeiler, Mr. Owen of Ymwlch, and Mr. Edwards of Nanhorn Hall, Pwllheli, had all owned and bred Welsh Terriers for fifty to sixty years. Also Mr. Jones of Ynsfor was "never without a few couples running with his hounds in the wild, rough countryside around Beddgelert." True Welsh Terrier tenacity was at work on the doubting Mr. Lee.

Terriers and Hounds

To clear up this business of why terriers were running with the hounds, we go to France. In the early 1600s, Louis XIII popularized the idea of maintaining terriers with fox-hunting hounds in order to take the fox instead of merely chasing it to its den. By the end of that century, it was common practice to run terriers with the hounds in hunts throughout the British Isles. The Welsh Terriers of the day were of longer leg and easily capable of keeping up with the hounds. The breed is known to have been kept with the Glansevin Hunt and the Aberech Hunt since 1745.

Mrs. H.L. Aylmer, whose grandparents were connected with the Glansevin Hunt (and who used "Glansevin" as her Welsh Terrier kennel prefix) became the first woman judge to award champion certificates in the breed in 1907. Women were involved with dog shows almost from the very beginning. Another prominent woman in our breed was Mrs. H.D. Greene who was a breeder-exhibitor under the prefix "Longmynd."

In 1899 Lt. Col. Hugh Savage sold the bitch, *Brynafon Nellie*, to Princess Adolphus of Teck who was sufficiently charmed by the breed to join the Welsh Terrier Club and become a breeder-exhibitor.

The Welsh Terrier in the 1880s

As soon as dog shows were acknowledged as a respectable activity, many of the somewhat common-looking breeds, including the Welsh Terrier, took on a more uniform and stylish appearance through selective breeding. In the ten to fifteen years following their recognition by The Kennel Club, most of the short-wedged heads, the domed skulls, the large houndy ears, light eyes, and white feet had all disappeared to be refined into a dog that would indeed come close to what's still wanted in today's show ring.

As early as 1890, the intent of dog shows was being seriously questioned, whether the purpose was to improve a breed's ability or merely to impress a buyer with its beauty. It was generally agreed that no harm need be done to the brain in improving a breed's looks.

Eventually, even Mr. Lee (of "so-called Welsh Terrier" fame) came around to describe the Welsh Terrier as "a game, plucky terrier, smart and active on land, at home in the water, and free and kind in his disposition . . . a nice little dog of a handy size, and, having usually been reared away from the kennels, that is, brought up in the house, is affectionate, kindly and desirable as a companion, nor is he fond of fighting, and his colour is pleasing." So you see, in the end—not surprisingly—the Welsh Terrier was able to use its natural charms to win over even the doubting Mr. Lee.

Apart from color, physical attributes of the breed still had a bit further to go. Another writer of the time, Mr. Theo Marples, editor of *Our Dogs* (one of England's weekly dog periodicals), refers to "The English edition" of what he felt was correctly called the Welsh Terrier. He berated the bad fronts and short heads on the Welsh, but felt the breed excelled in body, coat, and colour. "If these two prevailing defects could be improved, we should have an ideal terrier as either a workman or a companion." Or, obviously, as show dog.

Stanley Dangerfield, in 1985, commented on changes or improvements to the Welsh Terrier as a show dog, saying, "Some breeders deny the Fox Terrier influence. Others deplore what they feel was a dishonest changing of natural type. The truth is that man has always changed the shape of dogs by introducing outside blood.

And it was the skill of the Britons in getting the right mixture into the cocktail that made us the leading dog breeders in the world. The countless different breeds we excelled in were not sent to us from Heaven. We made them!"

A 1908 print by Maud Earl of Mrs. H.D. Greene's Ch. Longmynd Chamberlain and Ch. Longmyd Enchantress.

CHAPTER THREE

EARLY YEARS IN GREAT BRITAIN

It fell to Major P.F. Brine to undertake the organization of a stud book for the breed going back to 1854 which he presented to the Welsh Terrier Club in June 1903. It was an even more daunting task than he at first thought, since he ran into 123 bitches named "Fan" and approximately the same number named "Nell"! The popularity of dog shows can at least be credited with stirring the breeders' imaginations to name their dogs for possible fame and fortune, not just for a quick response in the field. On working farms today, not much has changed. During a recent summer, I stayed on three consecutive Welsh farms and each one had a sheep-dog named Nell.

Along with definitive (and creative) names, came kennel prefixes to add a touch of class to the sport of breeding and exhibiting dogs. Among the first, and still revered, kennels were Brynhir (Walter Glynn), Penhill (A.E. Harris), Bangor (A.J. Dew), Aman (Joe Hitchings), and Senny (T.H. Harris).

Mr. Glynn is considered to be "the father of the breed as show dog and was rightly regarded as the world authority on the breed in his day. He was also an invaluable promoter of the breed at a time when it truly needed a good press. He was also an avid historian for which he gave credit to his mentor, Mr. Cledwyn Owen of Pwllheli, the breeder of a Fan shown in 1885. Glynn considered Mr. Owen to have been the most knowledgeable judge of the breed.

Type and Coat

Because of Glynn's prolific writings, we have a great deal of information about those first Welsh Terriers as show dogs. For example, he stated that the Welsh coat was never so abundant as the Fox Terrier, nor as "broken," adding that it is "generally a smoother, shorter coat, with the hairs very close together" with a dense undercoat, "for a terrier used to work a good deal in water, an ideal covering as waterproof almost as feathers on a duck's back."

Speaking in a breed symposium in Ohio, Peter Green (Greenfield) referred to the single-coated Welsh—not, he pointed out, what we commonly refer to today as a "single coat" (wire, without undercoat), but a true smooth-coated dog with an undercoat and slight furnishings. This is borne out by the old photographs and engravings and the following quote from Freeman Lloyd: "A shining, glossy black jacket was suspect—a cross with the smooth

Lassie of Cedarvale, a Welsh Terrier bred by Mr. B.S. Smith (1901), showing a typical lack of furnishings for the time.

Manchester. Thumb marks and pencil marks on forelegs were also a sign of impure blood." The coat had to be hard, "but there was very little trimming or plucking in the early days."

Mr. Lloyd felt that the crossing with Wire Fox Terriers produced a more elegant dog, which he referred to as "English," claiming that the sturdier, stronger-headed, heavier-boned dogs were truly "Welsh." It was also felt that pure black and tans were to be found in North Wales, while those with white on chest and toes were prevalent in the South.

In 1930, W.H. Brady of the Welsh Terrier Club, in commenting on "modern" versus "old-fashioned" types of Welsh Terriers, wrote, "I think most people will agree that *Ch. Bangor Dau Lliw* (the first Welsh Terrier champion) "might almost be taken for a spaniel" due to her shaggy coat. Apparently, one club member resigned due to the short-coated "modern" Welsh Terriers. He felt they should be "long-coated as they were in the olden times."

Illustrations dating back to 1801 indicate that the Welsh Terrier must have been virtually smooth, since no farmer poaching for rabbit or intent on dispatching a badger would have gone to the trouble of plucking and trimming. The Welsh Terrier's coat, and particularly the furnishings, underwent quite a transformation in texture and quantity in becoming what is recognized today as a show coat.

Another critique, this time by Mr. Glynn who commented on two "English-bred" Welsh Terriers, *General Contour* and *Ch. Mawddy Nonsuch*. They did a lot of winning, but according to Mr. Glynn "were devoid of Welsh Terrier type, and even as terriers possessed serious faults. The former was a truly awful looking specimen . . ." [and the latter] "was not a bad-looking terrier, but was what is called a "flatcatcher;" he was blue in colour, having a soft, silky coat and short of substance throughout." On the other hand, he felt that the best terrier shown in those early days was Mr. Dew's *Ch. Topsy*. "She was a sound-coated, well-made animal and her colour was very good." He also pointed out the fact that she produced well.

The "modern" Welsh Terrier as drawn by Arthur Wardle in 1903.

However, there was not, and never should be, an "American Welsh Terrier" or a "German Welsh Terrier" or an "Australian Welsh Terrier." Nor, for that matter, is there in the United States a "West Coast" or an "East Coast" Welsh Terrier. Slight variations will always occur in different lines, as one breeder concentrates a little more on one aspect or another, or as a particularly prepotent sire puts a stamp on his get. Judges also have their partialities which can occasionally cause a temporary straying from the blueprint, and there are regional (or national) preferences in trimming for the show ring. But there is only one breed standard and only one correct type.

The Breed Standard

The first breed standard was drawn up by the Welsh Terrier Club in 1895 and was not changed until April 1948, when, at a joint meeting of the Welsh Terrier Club and the Welsh Terrier Association, the desired height was raised from fifteen inches to fifteen and one-half inches. Two years later, a proposal to increase the height to sixteen inches was summarily rejected. The present standard was approved by The Kennel Club in 1985.

Disqualifications (all of which were dropped from the U.S. standard in 1984) included prick, tulip, or rose ears; an undershot jaw; black below the hocks; or white anywhere to an appreciable extent. Ears apparently were never a problem. Black below the hocks disappeared in short order, but as late as 1911 Mr. Glynn tells us that many of the most successful show dogs had white on the chest and hind toes and were not penalized for it by judges who considered the overall quality of the dogs of greater importance. He adds, "as long as it is not in a prominent position on the dog's anatomy, and is not in any way extensive, there is no need to trouble about it." In the United States today, the appearance of more than a few white hairs in the coat causes unwarranted alarm, resulting in two equally unwarranted reactions: blaming the stud dog, and/or reaching for the chalk or hair dye.

In earlier years, of far greater concern than a few fluffs of white were undershot jaws. Mr. Glynn found many puppies were born undershot, but the defect corrected itself within a few weeks or months. I myself have seen this phenomenon, where the upper jaw grew rapidly and caught up with the lower jaw in a matter of ten days to two weeks. A few months, however, would worry me.

His comments about grizzle jackets is as pertinent today as it was then: ". . . if the grizzle is of a dark hard colour, its owner should not be handicapped against a black and tan; if, on the contrary, it is a washed-out, bluish-looking grizzle, a judge is entitled to handicap," adding that an undesirable grizzle is invariably accompanied by an objectionable light tan. This latter description fit the two dogs, *General Contour* and *Ch. Mawddy Nonsuch*, which Mr. Glynn found so lacking in quality, noting, "It is a great mercy that they were either not used, or that, if they were, the results were so appalling that no one but their owners had an opportunity of inspecting them."

The Welsh Terrier Breed Standard (U.K.)

General Appearance: Smart, workmanlike, well-balanced, and compact.

Characteristics: Affectionate, obedient, and easily controlled.

Temperament: Happy and volatile, rarely of shy nature. Game and fearless, but definitely not aggressive, although at all times able to hold its own when necessary.

Head and Skull: Flat and of moderate width between the ears. Jaws powerful, clean cut, rather deep and punishing. Stop not too defined. Medium length from stop to end of nose, latter black in colour.

Eyes: Small, well set in, dark, expression indicative of temperament. A round, full eye is undesirable.

Ears: V-shaped. Small, leathers not too thin. Set on fairly high, carried forward, and close to the cheek.

Mouth: Jaws strong with perfect, regular scissor bite.

Neck: Moderate in length and thickness. Slightly arched and sloping gracefully into shoulders.

Forequarters: Shoulders long, sloping and well set back. Legs straight and muscular, possessing ample bone, with upright and powerful pasterns.

Body: Back short and well ribbed up, the loin strong, good depth, and moderate width of chest.

Hindquarters: Strong, thighs muscular, of good length, with the hocks well bent, well set down and with ample bone.

Feet: Small, round, and catlike.

Tail: Well set on, but not too gaily carried.

Coat: Wiry, hard, very close and abundant. Single coat undesirable.

Colour: Black and tan for preference, or black grizzle and tan, free from black penciling on toes. Black below hocks most undesirable.

Size: Height at shoulder not exceeding 39 cm. (15-1/2 inches). Weight 9–9.5 kg. (20-21 pounds).

Faults: Any departure from the foregoing points should be considered a fault and the seriousness with which the fault should be regarded should be in exact proportion to its degree.

Note: Male animals should have two apparently normal testicles fully descended into the scrotum.

In 1905 the Welsh Terrier Club added a points standard, which was also taken up by the Welsh Terrier Club of America. This "points" system has since been dropped in both countries, but it is still an excellent guide for appraising a Welsh Terrier. Its aim was to prevent putting too much value on any one part of the dog at the expense of any other in an attempt to keep the dog as close to its original form as possible. It is an excellent guide for breeders, not just judges.

Head and Jaws	10
Ears	5
Eyes	5
Neck and Shoulders	10
Body	10
Loins and Hindquarters	10
Legs and Feet	10
Coat	15
Color	5
Stern	5
General Appearance	15
Total:	100

When you lump together like parts, you can see how equally those parts are valued:

Head, jaws, ears, and eyes = 20
Neck, shoulders, and body = 20
, Loin, hindquarters, legs, and feet = 20
Coat and color = 20
Tail by itself = 5
General appearance = 15

A championship title has always been more difficult to obtain in Great Britain than in the U.S., so it is not surprising that from the very first champion in 1887—*Ch. Bangor Dau Lliw*—through 1985 only 340 Welsh Terriers achieved this goal, and since 1985, the average has been about ten per year. By contrast, the average number of champions made up each year in the United States is close to sixty. Every few years the debate is taken up by breed clubs, and occasionally by the American Kennel Club, to change the rules so that a six-month-old puppy cannot become a champion, reasoning that all breed standards are descriptive of an adult dog. But to date, the system remains and puppies in the U.S. can and do become champions.

The Welsh Terrier Club of America's breed standard underwent a "language" change in 1984 after eight years of committee work. Most of the changes were made in an effort to clarify the variations between British-English and American-English. Take, for example, the word "tan". In the U.K., "tan" refers to the reddish brown of tanned leather, whereas in the U.S. "tan" is defined as a yellowish brown or beige. The process of turning cowhide into leather in the States commonly involves bleaching rather than the use of tanbark, which may account for the difference in definition. A description of movement was added, and, since missing teeth was becoming a breed-wide problem, the requirement for full dentition was included.

Elaborating on color or movement in the nineteenth century, when the first standards were written, would have been stating the obvious, since the most familiar animal in town or country was the horse and its accompanying (tanned) leather saddlery. Basics were referred to in terms all understood. Mr. Glynn perhaps said it best: The Welsh Terrier is ". . . built on the lines of a powerful, short-legged, short-backed hunter . . . he is best with a jet-black back and neck, and deep tan head, ears, legs and tail; ears a shade deeper than elsewhere."

Into the Twentieth Century

It was J.F. Hitchings of Cwmaman in the Rhondda Valley who helped establish that area as the whelping box of the present-day Welsh Terrier and to whom we owe the influx of foundation stock into American kennels in the early 1900s. Mr. Hitchings began breeding Welsh Terriers about 1902 and by 1908 was showing a great deal locally. It wasn't until after World War I in 1917 that he registered his prefix "Aman" (taken from the name of his village) and became known at home and abroad for breeding, buying, and selling quality dogs, right up until his death in 1949.

Hitchings is credited with the initial development of the Welsh Terrier as we know it today. He was a professional handler of several other breeds, once taking thirteen dogs to Crufts where he won seven Best of Breeds. In 1938, he won seventeen of the twenty-four challenge certificates offered that year. He was obviously able to pick a "good one" and knew what to do with it when he got his hands on it.

Joe Hitching's house in Cwmaman. Today there is no sign of the extensive kennels in back of the house, kennels that played such a large role in the breed on both sides of the Atlantic.

George Steadman Thomas emigrated to Massachusetts, but regularly went back to Great Britain where his friends, Joe Hitchings and Sam Warburton (from Lancashire) would have a dozen or more dogs ready to return to the States with Mr. Thomas. The three made a lot of money in their overseas venture, but at the same time the trio made it possible for some excellent dogs to become the foundation stock of many American kennels. Red Palm, bred by T.H. Harris ("Senny"), and brought over by Mr. Thomas in 1898, was considered to be the first typical representative of the breed in America. Mr. Thomas became a well-respected terrier judge in the States.

Aman Accurate (bred by W. Hopkins and owned by Hitchings) was the first Welsh Terrier to go Best in Show in the U.K. (at Cardiff in 1934) and was immediately sold to Maurice Pollak ("Marlu") of New York via George Thomas. The young bitch was not a champion in the U.K. but quickly gained her title here.

Breeders of the Past

Here is a very abbreviated list of the first U.K. breeders whose kennel prefixes can be found in most, if not all, of the original American lines.

Aman	J. F. Hitchings
Bangor	A.J. Dew
Brynafon	Col. H. Savage
Brynhir	Walter Glynn
Defynog	Dr. D.T. Morgan & Lord Mostyn
Glansevin	Mrs. H.L. Aylmer
Hafren	Dr. Gee Williams
Hotpot	Mr. R.H. Compton
Longmynd	Mrs. H.D. Greene
Penhill	A.E. Harris
Senny	T.H. Harris

In 1922 a dog, *Ch. What Again*, bred by P. Cullen, was purchased by W. Ross Proctor (Brookwood) of New Jersey and was the first champion imported to the States from the U.K. This was the beginning of a virtual "Welsh Armada" of champions arriving on our shores. In 1925 and 1926, Dr. Samuel Milbank obtained *Ch. Hafren Wizard* (winner of the Welsh Terrier Club of America's Junior Challenge Cup in 1927) and a bitch, *Ch. Hafren Cheerily*.

Numerous dogs had preceded these titlists and many more followed to enter the breeding programs of the well-known breeder/exhibitors of the day. At about this time, another Englishman, Percy Roberts (a handler and judge), was well-established in Connecticut, lending his expertise to the selection of "good ones" for his many American clients.

The first record of a reverse situation—an American-bred champion being sent to the U.K.—was after the Second World War when Mr. Hugh J. Chisholm's *Ch. Strathglass Venture's Snowden* became a British champion in 1948.

CHAPTER FOUR

THE WELSH TERRIER "ARRIVES" IN THE U.S.A.

Not only were numerous dogs arriving on our shores as interest in the breed escalated on both sides of the Atlantic, but once they got here, they were making their presence felt in the show ring.

The first Welsh Terriers of record to be imported were *T'Other* and *Which* by Mr. Prescott Lawrence of Groton, Massachusetts, in 1885. They were two of the three shown at Westminster in Miscellaneous Classes that year. (The third entry being a dog of unknown origin named *Rough*.) There is no record of their sires or dams or dates whelped. The first dog show in America offering classes for Welsh Terriers was held in Saratoga Springs, New York, on August 23rd and 24th, 1888. Sadly, no record of an entry can be found.

The Welsh Terrier Club of America

By 1900 there were sufficient numbers of dogs and of breed fanciers to take the big step forward and form a breed club. A match show was held in the ballroom of the Hotel Longeret on Fifth Avenue in New York, after which eleven people were officially selected as the board of governors of the Welsh Terrier Club of America (WTCA), and the following officers were appointed:

Mr. E.S. Woodward, president.
Mr. Murray Bohlen, vice-president.
Mr. B.S. Smith, secretary and the first AKC dele-

gate. (His Cedarvale Kennels in Closter, New Jersey, emanated from the Rugby strain in England and produced among others, *Cedarvale Lass*, a big winner in her day. Mr. Smith began judging Welsh in 1902.)

Major G.M. Carnochan of Cairnsmuir Kennels, treasurer.

The first board of governors also consisted of Mr. Charles G. Hopton, (an AKC judge who, in 1897, had imported *Deawn*, renamed *Rodney Druid*; the dog was sold to Mr. R.W. Ellison of Radnor, Pennsylvania, and was a big winner as well as sire of winners.), Mr. J. Willoughby Mitchell, Mr. Rodney W. Ellison, Mr. Buckley Wells, Mr. Douglas Greene, Mr. J.F. Denton (Denhigh Kennels), and Mr. L.J. Knowles (Selwonk Kennels), who imported *Senny Princess*.

These men were already known for their social status and business acumen, which was not lost on the new sport of breeding and exhibiting dogs. Mr. Woodward was a wealthy wholesaler and pharmaceutical importer. Major Carnochan, a member of the New York Stock Exchange, owned *Field & Fancy* as well as *Popular Dogs*, a weekly in which he was able to give Welsh Terriers much positive publicity. Charles Hopton was the first breed judge of outdoor shows. Mr. Willoughby Mitchell moved from Brooklyn to Palisades, New Jersey, and finally to England.

In 1899 *Nigwood Nailer*, bred by R. Thomas in Wales, won a thirty guineas Challenge Cup for the "Best Welsh, Irish, or Fox Terrier in Show." He was promptly imported by Major Carnochan and, in 1903, this dog made history by becoming the first Welsh Terrier to be listed as a Champion of Record in the AKC Stud Book.

The Misses de Coppet

Among the first women to take an active part in the breed and in the club were those long-lived, tenacious breeder/exhibitors

Nigwood Nailer was bred by Mr. R. Thomas in 1899 in Wales and made history by becoming the first AKC champion Welsh Terrier.

and tireless workers, the Misses Beatrice and Gertrude de Coppet of Windermere fame. They were among the very first importers of Welsh Terriers, importing *Ch. Senny Dragon* and *Senny Starlight* in 1890. Although they attended the historic foundation meeting of the Welsh Terrier Club of America, and were considered to be charter members, it was 1927 before they were invited to hold office. The first time these two ladies missed a Specialty Show and an Annual Meeting would be in 1956!

In 1901 they imported *Brynafon Mab*, winning BOB (Best of Breed) with her at the Ladies' Kennel Association held at Madison Square Garden, which was judged by the noted British

Ch. Brynafon Mab, imported in 1901 and considered to be the foundation bitch of the de Coppetts' Windermere Kennels.

terrierman, Mr. George Raper. *Brynafon Mab* was the strong breed foundation of Windermere's half-century tenure as a leading show kennel in the United States. A few today may be able to recall the no-nonsense appearance of these ladies, attired in their "uniform" of white lab coats and hats, in the show ring. They handled their own dogs in all classes, including Brace and Team.

As we know it today, the WTCA yearbook was conceived and executed by Miss Beatrice de Coppet in 1928 when she held the post of club secretary. Mr. Guy Megargee was then vice president and writer of the *Gazette* breed column (the first of which appeared June 30, 1927) when Miss de Coppet suggested to him that the annual report be dropped in favor of a yearbook. He was bitter at the lack of cooperation from members for the breed column and therefore felt a yearbook would fail from disinterest as well as from being too expensive a venture.

Miss Gertrude de Coppet with a team of Windermere champions in 1919.

Not to be dissuaded, Miss Beatrice showed her terrier mettle and the first WTCA year book was printed the following year, in 1929. That was her first feat. The second victory appears in the 1930 yearbook where the treasurer's report shows the club took in two-thirds of the cost of printing in advertising, leaving a total expenditure of $21.00 for our first yearbook.. These were indeed ladies to be reckoned with!

It is most unfortunate that no copy of that 1929 yearbook exists today in the club's archives. We must assume that the 1930 yearbook (which we do have) follows the prototype . It is well-designed, informative, and established the format used to this day.

Our delightful club logo was also designed by Miss Beatrice de Coppet for the yearbook. She took the old limerick, "Taffy was a Welshman, Taffy was a thief." and changed the ending to: "Taffy came to my house and stole my heart not beef." She then added a touch of sobriety with the Latin *Sapiens Fidelis* 'Wise and Faithful'. She must have been pleased with the results, because

The official Welsh Terrier Club of America logo, designed by Miss Beatrice de Coppett.

she sent a block of the logo to the Welsh Terrier Club in Great Britain and they described it warmly in their 1931 yearbook.

There will be much more about the de Coppets through the years.

Stirrings up North

Meanwhile, Canada joined in the growing enthusiasm for the breed. Leading the way was Miss H.L. Beardmore, whose father was Master of the Norfolk Hunt of Canada. Her foundation stock came from Walter Glynn (Brynhir Kennels), in particular a dog named *Brynhir Barter*, a winner in both Canada and here in the U.S.

Back in the States

Senny Princess, the previously mentioned import, was the winner of the 1902 "Ladies Show" (as it was called). Another dog from Mr. Harris's famed kennels was *Ch. Senny King* imported by Dr. F.C. Benson Jr. He was widely considered to be one of the best Welsh Terrier in his day in America.

Color has always been a concern in the breed, and the 1906 Welsh Terrier Club of America description was: "The color should be black-and-tan. The best color is an all-tan head, all-tan legs, and jet black body. The light, washed-out tan is objectionable and should handicap."

Franklin B. Lord's team got the nod at Westminster in 1908 from none other than "the father of the breed," Mr. Walter Glynn, who was to judge here many times. However, it was the 1910 Westminster show that held several firsts for the breed. The Winners Classes were now divided, and for the first time a home-bred puppy, *Windermere Chips*, went up over many worthy imports. Then, with his kennelmate, *Windermere Winsome*, he won the Brace and Team Classes. The de Coppets were on their way! The following year, *Windermere Winsome* took the breed and Franklin B. Lord's *Landore Boy* went Best of Opposite Sex. Then in 1912, under Mr. Winthrop Rutherford, the results were reversed with *Landore Boy* taking BOB and *Windermere Winsome* BOS (Best of Opposite Sex).

The consensus at this time (pre-World War I) was that the breed was now being shown true to type, size, and color, and that a solid foundation had been established for the future. The breeders on both sides of the Atlantic were justifiably proud of their endeavors to bring the scruffy little working terrier into the elite show world—and see him equal and eventually surpass the competition.

Where the Imports Came From

Tom Harris (owner of *Senny*) of Sennybridge, Breconshire, was the honorary secretary of the Welsh Terrier Club at the time H.R.H. The Prince of Wales exhibited at the Welsh Terrier Club's show in Cardiff on December fifth and sixth, 1912. Mr. Harris held that the supremacy of the Welsh Terrier was due in large part to the gallant efforts of Walter Glynn. Harris went on to say, "The OEBTT emanated from the cleverest livestock breeders in the world. The Airedale and the Fox Terrier had most to do with his production, but several other breeds and varieties added their quota."

Mr. Harris exported many fine dogs to the States and elsewhere. His *Senny Spinner* was the first Welsh Terrier to become a German champion. As mentioned in Chapter Two, this dog was then imported to America in 1914 by Miss Maud Kennedy and promptly won the Grand Challenge Cup with him that year without his AKC championship. Miss Kennedy had won the Jr. Challenge Cup in 1913 with another Harris dog, *Senny Model,* and Brookwood Kennels won the Grand Challenge Cup in 1917 with yet another Harris dog, *Ch. Senny Tip Top. Ch. Senny Rex* was the top dog in post-World War I years with seventeen champion certificates before being exported to America, where he was a top winner and dominant sire.

In 1921 the North Wales fanciers threw in their lot (and

Ch. Senny Rex, bred by T.H. Harris, was a top-winning Welsh in the U.K. before claiming the same honor in America. He was one of many Senny dogs to become foundation stock in the U.S.

Int. Ch. Senny Ringleader, owned by Mr. W. Ross Proctor

their treasury) with the Welsh Terrier Club. The following year the South Wales Welsh Terrier Breeders' Association followed suit. Then in 1923 the Welsh Terrier Association was formed in England with Mr. O.T. Walters, Chairman and Mr. T.H. Harris, Secretary.

In the 1930s the breed was dominated by Penhill and Aman. Many of the winners in Great Britain were still being sent on to America. On both sides of the Atlantic, the parent clubs noted the increase of enthusiastic breeder/exhibitors as members.

Gerald R. Marriott, Honorary Secretary of the Welsh Terrier Club, had become involved in Welsh Terriers in the 1890s because of their individuality and because they were workmanlike terriers. Writing some forty years later, he had second thoughts: "I sometimes wonder if we are proceeding on quite the right lines . . . Welsh Terriers are shown in a much less natural condition than they used to be. Coats have suffered as a result, and it is rare now to find a coat that is really 'hard, very close and abundant' which is what the standard has always insisted upon. I do not like to see a Welsh Terrier with bald cheeks or shoulders, and possibly a lot of dead hair on his ribs to hide or draw attention to flat sides." He went on to comment on the numerous wins of Mr. A.E. Harris (Penhill) and Joe Hitchings (Aman) with *Penhill Passport* and *Aman Superb*. He awarded BOB to four dogs that then came to America: *Tawe Cymro*, *Ch. Galen Arsen* and *Ch. Galen Maltose* (of Marlu Farm Kennels), and *Singleton Latest*.

Meanwhile, Back in the States

Mr. W. Ross Proctor of New York City, served on the board and in the office of treasurer for many years. He initiated The Breeder's Cup in 1927 for the best Welsh Terrier over two years old and bred by exhibitor; the win to be decided by points earned at Westminster, Welsh Terrier Club of America Specialty, Eastern Dog Show, and Westbury. A sterling silver spoon was given to commemorate each win.

The rules for claiming the two Challenge Cups originally, in 1909, carried the restriction, "It is for Welsh Terrier dogs or bitches of any age, owned by the exhibitor for at least six months prior to the close of the entries." There is no mention of when that stipulation was deleted, but it no longer appeared after 1935. Prior to 1990, the Grand Challenge Cup was won thirteen times by Mrs. Alker (Twin Ponds), nine times by the de Coppets, eight times by the Clarks (Halcyon), and, more recently, five times by the McClungs (Wenmar). The Junior Challenge Cup had similar multiple wins, including eleven times by the de Coppets, eight by the Colts (Coltan), 7 by Mrs. Hudson (Penzance), seven by the Clarks, and five times by Mr. Chisholm (Strathglass).

The future of these Cups and the Homer Gage Jr. Memorial Award will be more difficult to record simply because so many dogs today have multiple co-breeders and numerous co-owners.

In 1929, without the support of a Welsh Terrier Club of America Specialty, the entire entry of Welsh Terriers at the first Montgomery County Kennel Club show consisted of five dogs, all from the Clarks' Halcyon Kennels, including the imports *Froth Blower* (bred by J.R. Ryan) and *Aman May Queen*, a bitch from Joe Hitchings. Percy Roberts handled a Flornell Airedale, and BIS (Best in Show) was the Wire Fox Terrier, *Iveshead Scamp.*

The England Cup, offered by the Welsh Terrier Club, was another "bred by" award, this time to the best Welsh Terrier under eighteen months to be competed for over 5 years from 1925 to 1930 at the Specialty, Westminster, Eastern and one Spring and one Fall show selected by a committee. The de Coppets won it in '25 and '27, the Millbanks in '26, Annandale Kennels in '28; the de Coppets tied with Welwire in '29, so the Misses de Coppet took home another prize. Welsh Terrier Club of America presented Welsh Terrier Club with a silver cup, known as "The America Cup" which was won outright in 1931 at the Great Joint Terrier Show by W. D. Price.

After a slight decline in entries following World War I, 1930 saw larger entries and good dogs being shown. Westminster drew thirty-one and Eastern twenty-one that year. The de Coppets' *Rowdy Boy* took Group 3 at both, plus BOB at the specialty. It was noted at the time that *Rowdy* was always shown on a loose lead. Money was tight during the Depression and entry fees ran about seventy-five cents. *Rowdy Boy*'s stud fee was all of $35.00. On the other hand, the import, *Ch. Galen Rexus of Scotsward*, sired by *Senny Rex* and owned by Mrs. C.B. Ward, commanded top dollar—$50.00. After a steady increase, WTCA membership in 1932 had dropped to thirty-seven regulars and eleven associates.

Ch. Galen Rexus of Scotsward, a Senny Rex son, imported by Mrs. C.B. Ward

Breeders' Concerns in 1930's

In 1931 the first worries were expressed about the crossing of Wire Fox Terriers with Welsh and the presence of occasional white hairs were once again sounding alarm bells. A dog shown at the Fairfield County Hunt Club Show in June carried a large white blaze and was put down a month later. There followed lengthy discussions on care in breeding to eliminate white. Since most of the leading kennels were large by today's standards (most running thirty-five to forty adults), breeding to eliminate any fault would indeed have involved "lengthy discussions." The de Coppets ran a relatively small kennel with 5 or 6 litters a year. They took great pride in this aspect of their operation as they felt strongly that dogs from a smaller kennel made better pets.

February 11, 1933 was a milestone in club history. The Welsh Terrier Club of America joined Associated Terrier Clubs in New York for a spring specialty. Mr. John G. Bates judged a large entry of sixty-one, with Mrs. Ward's *Galen Kola of Scotsward* taking BOB. Best in Show went to her dog, *Ch. Galen Rexus of Scotsward.*

Loosely referred to as "spring shows," it should be noted that February in New York City is hardly "spring," and there were to be more blizzards involved in the history of that Association and Westminster the following day than most care to recall!

In 1934 the board decided to allow associate members a voice, but still not a true vote. Ballots were sent out for the associates to select a representative who would then be able to attend the annual meeting and to cast one vote on matters put to the regular members. Percy Roberts became the first voice of the associates, a post he held for a year, after which for several years the honor went to Leonard Brumby. This was an unwritten change since it never did appear in the club rules or by-laws.

Maurice Pollak made great strides in this period with a beautiful modern kennel in New Jersey and with the prepotent sire, *Eng.Amer.Ch. Galen Arsen of Marlu* whose most notable offspring was *Ch. Marlu Magnificent.* Much of Pollak's foundation stock came from Joe Hitchings, including the BIS bitch, *Ch. Aman Accurate.* Marlu's "other" breed was Scotties, but Leonard Brumby handled only the Marlu Welsh Terriers until 1934 when Robert Braithwaite took over. Some dogs were sent to the West Coast with Arthur Duffy handling.

After World War II, Pollak imported *Ch. Senny Top Sawyer of Marlu,* of whom Mr. Harris, the breeder, said, "I've had fifty-four years of experience in showing and breeding and never saw a dog to fill my eye better." Pollak was an active WTCA member from 1934, serving as secretary until 1950 and many years as AKC Delegate. He died in 1976.

Quite a few breeders of Welsh Terriers had, as their "other" breed, either Scotties or Wire Fox Terriers. In fact, Marion Kingsland (Walescroft) of California, who joined WTCA in 1930, bemoaned the fact that there was little interest in Welsh on the West Coast—everyone wanted Scotties.

The 1936 Westminster entry was very large—fifty-two—

Robert Braithwaite grooming "Coquette" (Marlu Kennels) before the WTCA Specialty held in June 1938 at Mr & Mrs. Edward Clark's in Goshen, N.Y.

Ch. Halcyon Welsh Ideal went to the California-based Walescroft Kennels of Miss Marion Kingsland.

won by *Aman Ambition of Halcyon*, with BIS going to Marlu Kennel's *Ch. Aman Accurate.* (Joe Hitchings was obviously continuing to send over winners.)

Mrs. Ernestine ("Ernie") P. Alker of Great Neck, New York, and Leonard Brumby of Hicksville, New York, were voted in as associate members in 1937. Mrs. Alker's first yearbook ad for Twin Pond Kennels included *Ch. Aman Acquisition* and her "latest import, *Aman All Alone.*" John Goudie was her kennel manager from the start, and her foundation, like so many others, was once again Joe Hitchings' famous *Aman* Welsh.

Ch. Bodnant Eto, a bitch sired by Aman Ace ex Bodnant Crystal, was imported by Mrs. Edward Alker in 1937 to join Ch. Aman Sunflower and a son, Twin Poinds Reflection, who was sired by Ch. Aman Acquisition.

Another import from the Aman Kennels, Ch. Aman Ambition of Halcyon, joined the powerful stud force at Halcyon.

Spreading Our Wings

In 1937 Mr. Sylvester Paulter from St. Louis (owner of *Ch. Penhill Pennant*) attempted to start a Midwestern Specialty Club. Although he failed in this initial attempt and resigned, two stayers from Illinois joined WTCA as regular members the following year—Harold M. Florsheim (Harham) and the Lowenbachs (Harlow). A specialty show was held in St. Louis in 1939, which Mr. Ross Proctor judged. Ten years later there was enough interest to form the Midwest Welsh Terrier Club as an official regional club with Mr. Edward K. Metcalf, President. They held a specialty in Milwaukee January 11, 1947, with an entry of twelve. The club eventually dissolved, but was the precursor of the present Welsh Terrier Club of Northern Illinois, which is still active.

The Eastern Dog Club has held a leading show in the Boston area every year since 1912. In 1938 the entry was ten dogs, fourteen bitches, and one special. Of these twenty-five Welsh Terriers, five were owned by Miss Hinkle (Port Fortune), five by the de Coppets, four by the Warwicks (Warwell), three by the Clarks (Halcyon), and four were imports from that prolific breeder of winners, Joe Hitchings! *Aman Flash Lad* (owned by Marion Kingsland of California) was shown by Percy Roberts. Best of Breed was *Ch. Aman Superb of Halcyon*.

Another "first" for Westminster took place in 1938 when Miss Beatrice de Coppet became the first woman on their panel to judge Welsh Terriers.

In 1939 Richard Riggs (Manorvale, a kennel founded on Scotsward stock) wrote that obedience training was becoming so important to dog owners that classes were being held throughout the country and that the AKC offered "tests" at certain shows. He mentions that only two Welsh have acquired titles (but doesn't say which dogs or what titles!) He had high praise for the temperament of the Welsh as suitable for this training.

The WTCA yearbook for 1939 provided a list of judges as approved at the annual meeting. It has this opening line: "All members and associate members of the club in good standing and the following:" There followed forty-seven names, many of whom were, or would become, our mentors. Among them: Alva Rosenberg, William Kendrick, Edwin Sayres, Robert Braithwaite, John Goudie, Stanley Halle. This made a grand list of 117 people from which to select a judge. The oddity is that associate members were approved to judge our breed, but still not permitted to vote!

There were problems connected with breeding and showing, some of which we have overcome, some of which are still with us. An Irish Wolfhound being shown by the Clarks was poisoned at a show and died before reaching Halcyon Farms. Good dogs were occasionally stolen off the benches. And in 1941 there still was no prevention for that biggest of canine killers, distemper. One vaccine being tested only lasted about two weeks and became less effective the more it was given.

The World War II years presented all dog clubs and people with a variety of problems. One well-intended, albeit naive, club resolution was "to help the war effort" by saving paper and so suspended publication of the yearbooks for 1942 and 1943. Of more help perhaps was the decision to buy war bonds with the money normally spent on trophies. Many shows were canceled due to gasoline rationing and as one small way of acknowledging the seriousness of the world situation.

In the 1940s Ted Corby (Corbscot) worked in a plant in New Jersey where promotions were used to sell war bonds. When his wife, Verna, offered a Corbscot Welsh Terrier to be auctioned, the puppy raised $3,000. The Corbys followed up to be sure the pup had a good home, which he did. Mrs. Corby was a member for fifty years, having joined WTCA in 1938. Their daughter, Carol who did much of the showing and traveling with her father, is currently Welsh Terrier Club of America Co-Historian. She became a member in 1950. Corbscot Farms was the home of *Ch. Coltan Checkers*, *Ch. Tujays Brooke Butler*, and *Ch. Licken Run's Tinker Bell*, the dam of *Ch. Licken Run's Danny Boy*.

We hit another first in 1944 when *Ch. Flornell Rare-Bit* of

Twin Ponds became the first Welsh Terrier to go BIS in the United States—and did it at Westminster. *Rare-Bit* had also taken the breed the year before. He was sired by the top producer, *Ch. Hotpot Harriboy of Halcyon* (sire of fourteen champions), a dog that won the breed at Westminster in 1941 and 1942, ex *Flornell Autograph*. An exceptional male-tail line, *Rare-Bit* went on to sire twenty champions in all.

The second half of the 1940s proved very successful for Welsh Terriers. Many were winning Groups and going on to BIS victories. One notable bitch of this era was *Ch. Twin Pond Belle* who won the Grand Challenge Cup twice and the Junior Challenge Cup once.

Mrs. Edward Clark (Halcyon) died in 1946 and the club lost one of its great breeders and consistent club workers. Hugh Chisholm (Strathglass) became president for one year, followed by Mrs. Alker who was to hold that post until 1950, when Mrs. S. Sloan Colt took the reins for the next thirty years. There were now forty-nine regular and thirty-one associate members. Bill Etter was invited to be a regular.

1947 Bursts with Events

By 1947 the membership had risen by ten including some VIPs. Dorothy Hardcastle, a breeder and noted artist of all terrier

Ch. Flornell Rare-Bit of Twin Ponds made history by being the first Welsh Terrier to be awarded Best in Show at Westminster in 1944.

breeds (her oil painting of a Welsh hangs in The Dog Museum), Alex Boisseau (Monona), Ensley Bennett (Dorian), the Virgil Smiths (Jayness) of Michigan, and Nell B. Hudson (Penzance) of Virginia, who was to become club secretary from 1965–1980 and writer of the *AKC Gazette* breed column for almost as many years, a top breeder and all-around club worker.

Edwin Megargee (who died in 1958) was a well-known animal artist who gave us the timeless sketches of the ideal Welsh Terrier head. He also drew the Welsh Terrier head on our club pin. In regard to the Welsh Terrier head, Megargee wrote, "I remember years ago, a well-known breeder telling me that his concept of a Welsh head was one in which the foreface could be telescoped into the skull. I have always thought this an excellent description." As for the breed itself, he wrote, ". . . it would be a great pity if the breed should ever lose its essential character, its pluck, its compact power, its ruggedness, or, to coin a word, its Welshness." Whether or not he coined the word, it is widely used to indicate almost anything intrinsically associated with the land, the language, and the people.

Megargee judged the specialty and gave BOB to *Ch. Twin Ponds Belle*, Winners Dog to *Halcyon Best Man*, and Winners Bitch to *Aman Superb Again of Halcyon*. This was followed by an

A 1945 drawing by Edwin Megargee of what he considered to be a correct Welsh Terrier. He mentioned the distinctive head and added, "Equally important, however, is the joining of the head to the neck and the neck to the body."

A lovely head study by Edwin Megargee, which served as a model for his rendition of the WTCA club pin.

upset at Westminster where *Aman Rose Marie of Halcyon* came from the classes (see the glossary) to take the breed. The Aman-Halcyon tie-in certainly proved to be a winning combination. At the Fall Specialty, held on the Chisholm's estate, *Twin Ponds Carousel* took the breed with BOS going to the Colts' *Halcyon Masterpiece*, another good one that would prove his worth at stud.

Ch. Halcyon Masterpiece, bred by the Edward Clarks and owned by Coltan Kennels, winner of the Grand Challenge Cup in 1946 and of the Junior Challenege Cup in 1948.

At the February WTCA Specialty in 1948, with William Ross Proctor judging, Ch. Twin Ponds Belle (handled by John Goudie) was BOB and Ch. Halcyon Masterpiece (Johnny Murphy handling) was BOS. "Belle" went on to 29 Bests in Show, 41 Group Ones, and 79 Bests of Breed wins, an outstanding record at that time, especially for a bitch.

In 1947 the Welsh Terrier Club of America formed a national advisory committee to assist with out-of-town activities. Welsh Terrier Club of America was still predominantly a New York City club and regional groups that were loosely formed in other parts of the country soon fell apart. The breed itself, though, was flourishing and help was needed to guide the fanciers. Maurice Pollak, secretary, wrote in 1948, "Our club continues to progress steadily and soundly and [our goal is] to add to its membership and maintain its reputation as a club that may well be a model of harmony and good fellowship." One can only add, amen.

To encourage Midwest breeders, WTCA sponsored a specialty in conjunction with the International Kennel Club in Chicago to be judged by Mr. Proctor. (Ross was a friendly and extremely popular man who seems to have represented the club whenever and wherever a goodwill ambassador was needed.) "Easterners" promised to support the show. Much was made of the fact that the Virgil Smiths (Jayness), who lived in Michigan, had attended Morris & Essex—a trip of some eighteen hours to New Jersey, and this in the days when long car trips were not yet common! There were also reports of members traveling "from as far as the Pacific coast" to attend Westminster. The acceptance of travel to shows was given as a reason to continue the Stud Dog Class at Specialties—the more people could see, the more might come. As a further lure, free Westminster admission tickets were handed out at the Annual Meeting. Oh, yes! Those were the good ol' days!

Strathglass Kennels had the first and only team of Welsh Terriers to go Best Team in Show at Westminster in 1948. There were four handlers on four champion bitches: *Ch. Flornell Vogue,*

A win that only came once: The Strathglass Kennels' team won Best Team in Show at Westminster in 1948. Team entries were subsequently dropped at this show, so the record remains with Strathglass and an all-bitch, all-champion team Shown here are: Ch. Flornell Vogue, Ch. Aman Honeybee, Ch. Strathglass Tit-Bit and Ch. Strathglass Peggy Ann.

Ch. Aman Honeybee, Ch. Strathglass Tit-Bit and *Ch. Strathglass Peggy Ann.* This was the year, too, when Hugh Chisholm reversed the transatlantic flow and shipped *Ch. Strathglass Venture's Snowden* to England where the handsome young dog earned his championship title in three straight shows.

The year 1949 saw the Welsh Terrier Club of Southern California hold its first specialty with the Los Angeles Kennel Club on April thirtieth and May first. Bill Etter's homebred, *Licken Run's High Circuit* won the Brood Bitch Stakes that year, a much-coveted win. The Bodensteins (Bodie) also had a good year: The Specialty BIS was *Bodie's Temptation*, and *Bodie's Top Man* was both Winners Dog and Best of Winners.

Ch. Strathglass Bingo's Venture, already the sire of twenty-three champions, was at stud, but "Limited to one approved bitch per month" for a $100 stud fee. His son, the above-mentioned *Snowden*, an English American champion, carried a $50 fee and no limitations! *Ch. Raybrook's Elizabeth Fox*, an imported bitch also made Strathglass Kennels her home at this time.

More proof of the breed's increased popularity and coming of age was *Ch. Twin Ponds Belle,* who was twenty times BIS, forty-one times Group 1, and had seventy-nine BOB wins. Bodie Kennels continued to do a large share of winning with *Ch. Bodie's Top Raider* and *Ch. Bodie's Top Man* as well as with their top pro-

Ch. Strathglass Bingo's Venture, bred by Hugh J. Chrisholm (1942), was the sire of 30 champions, including the outstanding Snowden, pictured opposite.

ducing bitch, *Bodie's Top Row*.

And still the imports were winning. The Colts' *Eng.Amer. Ch. Victory Boy* (bred by Tom Eynon) and *Ch. Aman Ambassador*. On the West Coast, the Bilgers (Reglib) and the Van Hartesveldts (Vanhills) were both importing dogs from Great Britain in addition to dogs from the top East Coast breeders. Harold Florsheim (Harham) campaigned two dogs from A.E. Harris—*Ch. Penhill Perfect of Harham* and *Ch. Penhill Ploughman of Harham*.

From the array of photographs (many by the famed Tauskey) taken up to this time, all the dogs appear to be somewhat high on leg, due to the close trimming of furnishings and no filling out of hindquarters. Heads were squared off to the desired rectangle with a minimum of beard (goatees came into fashion much later).

We were not yet into the era of extreme cosmetic illusion. In trim, the Welsh Terrier more closely resembled today's Border Terrier than today's show ring Welsh. One would have to agree with the often repeated comment that Welsh Terriers looked more workmanlike in their first fifty years as show dogs than in the next fifty.

Aside from the trim of furnishings, the one noticeable change in the last fifty years has to be the preference displayed by many of today's breeders and judges for a too-short back. This

Int.Ch. Strathglass Venture's Snowden, bred by Chisholm in 1946 and the first U.S.-bred Welsh Terrier to become a champion in the U.K.

deformity—and that's what it is—results in upright shoulders with the neck crammed down between them, and shows up in movement as a lack of proper reach and drive. I call it "the wind-up toy trot." Any physical extreme in the breed is to be deplored, be it overly long, overly tall, overly short, or overly refined. But a too-short back forfeits the very function of the Welsh Terrier, which is the physical ability to work tirelessly above and below ground.

We do refer to a short back either in our breed standard or in critiquing an individual, so perhaps it is just the phrase that is misinterpreted. Breeders and judges today, rather than being side-tracked by the too-short back, should be looking for the dog with a back long enough to sustain the proper arch of neck, the correct shoulder layback and movement. It is the moderately short, strong loin that gives the illusion of squareness to the dog and which provides flexibility in our Welsh without the racy length of, say, the Irish Terrier. The Welsh is a short-coupled dog without any extremes.

CHAPTER FIVE

THE SECOND HALF-CENTURY

Some indication of the breed's growth during the '50s can be gauged by the annual AKC registration figures. In 1948, 651 individual Welsh Terriers were registered for the year, but by 1950, with a total of 777, the breed ranked thirty-fifth of all breeds. By 1956, even though there was an increase in the registry for the year, up to 987, our ranking went down to thirty-seventh. Ten years later, in 1966, there was a record set with 1,498 Welsh registered, yet the breed's ranking once again dropped, this time to forty-second, due to the population explosion of all pure-bred dogs and the over-popularity of some. The peak years in Welsh AKC registrations were from 1964 (1,214) to 1974 (1,126).

Jumping ahead to 1982, the breed was at a low of only 263 and ranked seventy-second. Since then we have remained in the 650-700 range. Just under ten percent of those registered become champions. The figure most difficult to understand is the fact that, consistently over the years, an average of two and a half dogs are individually registered for each registered litter. Since four to six pups constitute an average Welsh litter, we must assume that breeders themselves are not concerned about registration, or that pet owners don't see the need for it.

1950

The Montgomery County Kennel Club show in 1950 was held on the Frazier's estate in Pennsylvania without the participation of the Welsh Terrier Club of America. The usual laid-back atmosphere prevailed: judging began at 10:00 a.m.; everything

Three leaders of WTCA in the 1950s— Mrs. S. Sloan Colt (Coltan), Mrs. Edward P. Alker (Twin Ponds), and Miss Jean Hinkle (Port Fortune).

stopped for lunch from 1:00 to 2:00 p.m. (and a full lunch was $1.60). It seems the people involved in the Montgomery County Kennel Club have always read like a "Who's Who" in terriers, and this year brought out (in addition to the Fraziers) Eland Hadfield, Edward Doyle, Bill Etter, Johnny Murphy, Robert Brumby, Frank Brumby, Ed Sayres, Al Ayers, Robert Braithwaite, the Wimers, Seth Campbell, Robert Kendrick, Clifford Hallmark, Tom Gately—to name just a few of the legendary people who have helped maintain our breed.

Fifty years ago *Ch. Strathglass Bingo's Venture* commanded what was considered a "staggering" stud fee of $100! While his son, the *Eng.Amer.Ch. Strathglass Venture's Snowden*, rated the more normal $50. Service by the Coltan Kennels' top dog, *Int.Ch. Victory Boy*, split the difference, going for $75. Leading kennels began to advertise their stud dogs with the admonition "to approved bitches only," which was another sign of the times since quite a few breeds were becoming overly popular and the breeding out of control. One way to protect the Welsh Terrier was with this warning phrase, which openly allowed the owner of the stud dog to refuse service to a bitch for whatever reason—"lack of quality" or "not a champion"—being the ones most often given. Tacitly, of course, it had always been done by the responsible breeder. "Puppies for sale" or "Puppies always available" also changed to the more modest "Puppies occasionally." The breed had come into its own and there was no need to proselytize further, only to protect what had been established.

Hugh J. Chisholm's Strathglass Kennels was one of several spanning the '40s and the '50s representing the pinnacle of the breed. If he had never produced another dog, his *Ch. Strathglass Bingo's Venture* certainly earned him the spotlight. A typey dog of moderation in every quarter, *Bingo* (who is pictured on page 80) was the sire of thirty champions with 450 in direct line of descent and literally thousands of champions in total descended from this one great dog. (He held the Top Stud Dog position until the 1970s when he was surpassed by *Ch. Penzance Polaris* with thirty-seven, whose record, of course, has since been topped by *Ch. Anasazi Trail Boss* with sixty-six.) *Bingo*'s phenomenal record was achieved despite the fact that his services were "limited to one approved bitch per month" and the fact that bitches almost never came from any distance. However, he certainly did nick with the

On the right, Ch. Mawr Hydi, dam of the famous Bingo, and on the left, Ch. Bingo of Wyncote, his sire.

limited number of bitches that were brought to him.

Until quite recently almost every worthwhile pedigree in the U.S. carried *Bingo's Venture*, including those from all the leading kennels—Alvin Farms, Monona, Bodie, Jayness, Robb, Pool Forge, Aruel, Licken Run, and Twin Ponds. A good portion of American-bred dogs today can be traced back (given the patience to do so!) to that incredible dog. For many years his photo was used to depict the breed standard. In 1970 *Ch. Pool Forge Fast Freight* became the model.

Bingo's background was sound, but not outstanding, most of it being British or first-generation American. *Bingo* was out of an imported bitch, *Ch. Mawrhydi,* and was sired by *Ch. Bingo of Wyncote*, a grandson of *Ch. Galen Arsen of Marlu*, himself a grandson of the famed *Senny Rex*, once again proving the theory of "tail-male" dominance. *Bingo* was handled throughout his career by Frank Ortolani, who once told me that in addition to being good looking, sound, and putting a stamp on his get, *Bingo* was "an exceptionally steady, friendly dog to work with and to have around." As mentioned previously, it was this dog's son, *Ch. Strathglass Venture's Snowden,* that did the reverse trip and became the first American-bred Welsh Terrier to go to the U.K. and become a champion.

Hugh Chisholm joined Welsh Terrier Club of America in 1938 and for the next twenty-one years was continuously active in the club, serving on the board, as vice-president and as AKC delegate. Strathglass Farms in Port Chester, New York, was the beautiful site of numerous Welsh Terrier Club of America Specialties. He was a sportsman of the old school. Both the man and his dogs were held in high esteem here and abroad, and rightly so.

The Middle 1950s

Imports continued to play an important role in improving our stock. The February 1953 Welsh Terrier Club of America Specialty Breed went to *Ch. Toplight Template of Twin Ponds*, while BOS and BOW (Best of Winners) was Virgil Smith's *Quay-*

side No Regrets, both dogs imports. But Westminster, judged by William Kendrick, saw the Winners Dog, *Strathglass Admiral's Baron* take the breed and *Strathglass Lucifer's Dyma* take Winners Bitch and BOS, both homebreds. Reserve at both shows that year was Mr. Florsheim's import, *Felstead Model of Harham.*

Rolfe Bolster's Alvin Farms Kennels reached their prime with *Ch. Mephisto of Alvin Farms* (pictured on page 90)—sire of five champions including *Ch. Beelzebub of Alvin Farms,* who was the sire of seventeen—and with *Ch. Double Up of Alvin Farms,* a dog sired by *Ch. Strathglass Venture's Snowden* and himself the sire of nine champions. A remarkable record for a relatively small kennel.

1955

The Brood Bitch Stakes in 1955 had an entry of thirty-one and was won by *Strathglass Bethesda.* In commenting on the show, Percy Roberts said this huge interest "in the product of their breeding" (i.e. the Stakes) was significant to the breed's rise in popularity. "Quite the most important thing is the harmony in the running of Welsh Terrier Club of America by the officers, by the members, and the staunch loyalty to the breed by its adherents. Then there is the Welsh Terrier itself that can and does offer so much. They are still able to do the work they were bred for, but make ideal companions for either town or country as they are game without being aggressive." He also stated that due to the club members' efforts "this is one breed that needs no assistance from importation. In fact, from what has been seen in trips overseas, it could well be the reverse." This from someone who was a leading importer (or "dealer" as he liked to be called) of the breed to these shores.

It was Percy Roberts who imported a completely unknown little puppy, brought across in a convoy during World War II. Mrs. Alker bought him sight-unseen! Percy was understandably proud when John Goudie handled the dog, now *Ch. Flornell Rare-Bit of Twin Ponds*, to BIS at Westminster in 1944 over an entry of 2,510.

Ch. Mephisto of Alvin Farms was the link between the top Strathglass dogs from the 1930s and '40s to the top dogs of Pool Forge, Aruel, Tujay's and Coltan of the 1950s and '60s. Sired by Ch. Strathglass Venture's Lucifer, (sired by Bingo's Venture) ex Betti Da of Alvin Farm (sired by Ch. Strathglass Venture's Snowden) who was also the dam of Ch. Double Up of Alvin Farm.

Ch. Mephisto of Alvin Farms' Pedigree

	Ch. Bingo of Wyncote
Ch. Strathglass Bingo's Venture	Ch. Mawr Hydi
Ch. Strathglass Venture's Lucifer	
Ch. Raybrook's Elizabeth Fox	Raybrook's Stepping Along
	Ch. Raybrook's Betsy Fox
Ch. Mephisto of Alvin Farm	
	Ch. Strathglass Bingo's Venture
Ch. Strathglass Venture's Snowden	Ch. Strathglass Dyma
Betti Da of Alvin Farms	
Tymwyn Topsy	Ch. Halcyon Welsh Harp
	Windermere Memory

Ch. Mephisto of Alvin Farms was truly the union of some remarkable Welsh Terriers. Note, too, the careful linebreeding of Ch. Strathglass Bingo's Venture on both sides of Mephisto's family tree.

Ch. Double Up of Alvin Farm

Rolfe Bolster's Ch. Double Up of Alvin Farms

Ch. Hornell Rare-Bit of Twin Ponds, Mrs. Alker's record-setting dog with Best in Show at Westminster (1944).

After that history-making event, *Rare-Bit* appeared in ads for Ken-L-Biskit® dog food.

Percy handled four dogs to BIS at Westminster (1926, '27, '34, and '37), and in 1967 was asked to judge the event. Sadly, after Percy's death no one ever discovered what happened to the quantities of material he had on the history of our breed.

At Westminster 1955, with Mrs. Cyril Pacey judging, *Ch. Monona's Devil Dancer* took the breed and Winners Dog; and BOW, BOS went to *Ch. Syl-Von's Super Man*. Winners Bitch was the Pool Forge entry, *Luastra of Alvin Farms*. A relative newcomer, Mr. Vaughn Sylvester from New Hampshire, was extremely proud to have won the Junior Challenge Cup with his class dog. *Super Man* was later purchased and campaigned by Mrs. Alker.

The lovely bitch, *Ch. Monona's Devil Dancer* (bred by Alex Boisseau and owned by Hugh Chisholm), that won the Grand Challenge Cup that year was one of Boisseau's favorites. In a letter to me several years later, he wrote, "Devil Dancer was the best Welsh I ever bred. She was a real beauty in every way!" Indeed she was.

In September the Fall Specialty was held on the Colts' Long Island estate and just eleven members made up the entry of thirty dogs. Look how civilized we were: trophies were still sterling silver states the catalog states, "Judging will begin promptly at 2 p.m.". *Ch. Strathglass Bethesda* was BOB and *Ch. Syl-Von's*

Ch. Monona's Devil Dancer, winner of the Junior Challenge Cup in 1954 and the Grand Challenge Cup in 1955.

Super-Man was BOS.

The handlers were terrier men as well-known as the dogs' owners. John Goudie (Twin Ponds), Frank Ortolani (Strathglass), Johnny Murphy (Coltan), Eland Hadfield (Wyncote-Edward Doyle), Ben Brown (Reglib, from California and the only entry from out of the immediate area), Bill Etter (Betheen-Peter Devine). Etter also showed his own Licken Run dogs that day. John Goudie, by the way, also bred Welsh under his own kennel prefix, Cedar Ponds. At this time all professional handlers were associate (non-voting) members of Welsh Terrier Club of America.

More Lost Treasures

Mrs. Conrad Hatheway, a member for twenty-two years, died and left her paintings of Welsh Terriers to the Welsh Terrier Club of America. These were awarded for BOB and BOS at two specialties per year beginning in 1956. Unfortunately, there is no record of where they may be today except that we do know they were won by Mrs. Alker, Mrs. Wimer, Mr. Chisholm, Mrs. Colt, and, in 1958, by Mr. Joseph Urmston whose win for this award came from the classes with *Quayside Jolly Roger*, a handsome dog bred by Mr. G.E. Rees that had gone BIS at W.E.L.K.S. (the big show in Wales) before arriving on the American show scene. He went on to take the breed at Westminster that weekend.

*Not Justa Utility Dog,!
Winalesby Justa Bita
Pepper, UD, was the
Highest Scoring Dog in
Show thirteen times!*

Obedience Comes of Age

In 1955 Arthur Jensen, owner of *Winalesby Justa Bita Pepper, UD*, made history of sorts. *Pepper*, having earned the title Utility Dog in 1950, went on for the next five years taking Highest Scoring Dog in Show thirteen times! Mr. Jensen wrote so glowingly of the superb talents of the breed that it is difficult to understand how any-one could not train such a perfect dog! In his own words,

> Being intelligent and having a desire to please, he learns quickly and enjoys the work. Being alert and active, he enjoys the jumping exercises. Having a good sense of smell makes him a natural for the scent discrimination exercise and tracking. He is by instinct a retriever of any thrown object, and this serves him well in the retrieving exercises whether on the flat or over the hurdle. Above all, is his temperament which is ideal for the stand for examination, group examination, long sit and long down

exercises. He likes people and senses they like him. He quickly realizes that he has crowd appeal, also that a good performance brings applause and other preferred attention and is enough of a showman to make the effort to merit it."

How about that for praise!

In 1953 only thirteen spoons had been awarded (an indication that Bred By Exhibitor classes were down), but in 1954 the entries picked up and twenty-eight spoons were given out. The Bolsters (Alvin Farms) won eight, and Mrs. Alker and W.H. Etter won six spoons each. In 1956, twenty-five were awarded. Mrs. Alker and Harrison Frazier each took five. Three went to the Bennetts (Dorian) and two spoons each to the Bolsters and Bill Etter. The same few breeders consistently entered the Bred By classes and took home the spoons.

The names of six judges had been sent to the regular members with a request to select one judge for the 1956 Fall Specialty which Mr. Edward Doyle suggested be held in conjunction with Montgomery County Kennel Club, an invitation which was promptly accepted. The judge selected was Mr. James A. Farrell, noted Fox Terrier breeder under the Foxden prefix. He put up *Ch. Syl-Von's Super-Man* for the breed, and Pool Forge's *Ch. Luastra of Alvin Farms* for BOS.

Morris & Essex

This era cannot be complete without a mention of Giralda Farms, home of Mr. and Mrs. M. Hartley Dodge, which was the site of some of the most memorable dog shows from 1927 to 1957. The leading judges of the time helped to make it the largest outdoor dog show of the day in the States, with between two and three thousand entries. It was the social event of outdoor dog shows. Then there were the prizes. In 1933, for example, there were 136 large sterling silver plates plus special awards (also sterling silver) for Groups

Ch. Syl-Von's Super Man, handled by John Goudie, awarded the breed at the 1956 Specialty at Montgomery County Kennel Club under James A. Farrell, the noted Wire Fox Terrier breeder. Mrs. Colt, WTCA President, presented the trophy.

and BIS. Every BOB winner received a silver trophy offered by Geraldine Rockefeller Dodge, but in the name of the judge. Forty to fifty rings allowed judging to begin at the very civilized hour of 10:00 a.m. with a catered lunch under tents for four to five thousand dog fanciers!

In 1953 Mrs. Alker's *Ch. Toplight Template of Twin Ponds* (U.K. bred, by *Daneside Debonair* ex *Toplight Tearose*), winner of the Grand Challenge Cup in 1951 and 1954, was BIS at Morris & Essex. A striking stallion of a dog, but one that did not leave his mark on the breed, siring only five champions, none of them of note. Best of Winners at the last Morris &Essex show was *Strathglass Robin Hood*, owned by the Corbys.

St. Hubert's Giralda today is an unsurpassed animal shelter and learning center and was Mrs. Dodge's final gift to the people of

Mrs. Edward P. Alker's Ch. Toplight Template of Twin Ponds, winner of the Grand Challenge Cup in 1951 and 1954 and, even more notably, Best in Show at Morris & Essex in 1953.

New Jersey along with innumerable works of art, many of which are now in The Dog Museum.

1956

The February 1956 Specialty was judged by William Ross Proctor of Brookwood Kennels, an active Board member from 1935 to 1976 and a judge for whom breeders had the highest regard. He gave BOB to the Bolsters' *Ch. Beelzebub of Alvin Farms*, BOS to Florsheim's *Ch. Felstead Model of Harham.* A few days later, *Ch. Licken Run's Panic*, owned by Strathglass Kennels, took the breed at Westminster, with Mrs. Alker's *Ch. Syl-Von's*

Ch. Licken Run's Panic (owned by Hugh Chrisholm) took home the Grand Challenge Cup in 1956.

Super-Man going BOS. The compact, solid *Beelzebub* was purchased by Mr. and Mrs. Charles Marck of California where he continued to win, and ended his career having sired a grand total of seventeen champions.

The Marcks later added *Ch. Strathglass Trim Maid* to their Chancrest Kennels where she became the dam of five champions, one of which was *Ch. Max of Tremenhov.* I mention this dog only because when staying with the von Hemerts, *Max* was in residence. A handsome, well made (albeit over-sized) dog who exuded a great deal of charm, but what really set him apart was his role in the family. He is the only Welsh I've ever come across to have a hired baby-sitter come in whenever his owners left the house for more than a few minutes. He had it made, knew it, and wasn't about to mess up!

This was the year the Gaines Award for Good Sportsmanship was initiated and it went jointly to the Misses de Coppet.

1957

The Washington State Welsh Terrier Club was granted permission to hold their first specialty in Seattle and Welsh Terrier Club of America donated a silver trophy.

The Fall Specialty was held once again on the estate of Mrs. Alker rather than with Montgomery County and was judged by Seth Campbell who put up *Ch. Strathglass Admiral's Gwalia* for BOB and *Ch. Syl-Von's Super-Man* for BOS. (That dog was plagued by bitches taking the breed over him! He may have been the "best" BOS ever.)

The February Specialty was judged by Board member Mrs. Justin Herold, who was the sister of Delphine McEntyre, club secretary from 1953 to 1959. Mrs. Herold's BOB was *Ch. Strathglass Bethesda* and BOS was Mrs. Alker's *Kismet of Reglib* from the classes. (Some thirty years later Mrs. Herold, to our mutual delight, judged a Glyndwr Welsh Terrier Club match near her home in

Scarsdale, New York.) The Brood Bitch stakes were still in full swing and were won by Jean Hinkle's *Port Fortune Sea Patrol*. Twenty-two more spoons were awarded.

1958

February this year brought out some new dogs. At the Specialty, judged by Mr. Thomas Keator, BOB went to Mr. Urmstrom's *Quayside Jolly Roger* (from the classes) and BOS to the Colts' *Ch. Patty's Fancy Lady of Dorian*. The Reserve Winners Dog was the soon-to-be champion and eventual sire of eight champions—Licken Run's *Rock and Roll*.

Westminster brought George Hartman to judge. *Quayside Jolly Roger* again went up from the classes with the Licken Run dog going Reserve. *Ch. Patty's Fancy Lady of Dorian* was again BOS. Mr. Urmston died in August of that year and *Jolly Roger* was afterward kept in the ring by his widow.

Once again Montgomery County was passed up in favor of holding the Fall Specialty at Strathglass Farms, judged by Robert Kendrick. Despite the numerous comments about the excessive heat for October 3rd, *Ch. Licken Run's Rock and Roll* (now owned by Mr. Harold Florsheim) was described as a "frisky black-and-tan" and took the breed. *Ch. Strathglass Admiral's Gwalia* was BOS. Winners Dog was *Felstead Revelation* owned by the Colts,

BOB went to Quayside Jolly Roger (left), handled by Jimmy Butler at the 1958 Westminster Show. Ch. Patty's Fancy Lady of Dorian (right), handled by Johnny Murphy was Best Opposite.

a sound typey dog that was soon to be an English-American champion.

After years of having only two committees—nominating and show—this year a third was added, chaired by William W. Brainard Jr. (Downsbragh), to discuss the objectives sought by the membership. A questionnaire was sent out asking for suggestions and ideas. It would be fascinating to know what the members wanted for their club at that time, but no reliable record of the results could be found. But the committee idea certainly did catch on. By 1996 we were up to thirty-six committees for a club of 320 members.

Only nine silver spoons were given out in 1958, signaling a strong decline in the Bred by Exhibitor entries, but apparently members saw the warning signs once again and the following year the Club gave out twenty-six silver spoons after which this award was apparently discontinued and the Penzance and Port Fortune annual trophies (for Bred-by bitch and dog) were awarded instead.

Among others joining the Welsh Terrier Club of America this year were Robert and Alice Masson (Montrose), who were also to become stalwart Welsh Terrier Club of Southern California supporters, and Louise Patterson (Birr Kennels) of New Mexico. "Pat" as she was known, founded the Welsh Terrier Club of the Jemez and kept it an active regional club until her death in 1970. She will also be remembered for offering the Birr Obedience Trophy—the first trophy to recognize obedience—and open to anyone with a Welsh Terrier earning a top score in Obedience.

1959–1960

It would seem a trend developed over the years with a bitch so often winning the spring Specialty and Westminster, and males taking the BOS win. The February Specialty in 1959 was judged by Mr. George Hartman who put up *Strathglass Trim Maid* from the classes and BOS to *Ch. Licken Run's Rock and Roll*. Thomas Keator made the same selections two days later at Westminster.

Ch. Licken Run's Rock and Roll, bred by W.H. Etter and owned by Harold Florsheim, won the Junior Challenge Cup in 1959.

People, Places and Things

This was a very sad winter for Welsh Terrier Club of America as we lost three of our leading breeders, best club workers, and long time members: Jean Hinkle in November, Hugh Chisholm in December, and Gertrude de Coppet in February. Port Fortune, Strathglass, and Windermere Kennels had all come to an end. If not the end, it certainly was the beginning of the end of an era of the large, beautiful estate kennels.

Jean Hinkle was active in the Welsh Terrier Club of America, the breed ring and as an AKC judge. Her ultimate judging assignment came in 1951 when she did BIS at Eastern Dog Club's show in Boston. *Ch. Port Fortune Patriot*, a homebred, was the sire of six champions including Dorothy Hardcastle's *Ch. Mrs. Brown of Birchwood*, a bitch featured in several of Dorothy's paintings, including the one now at The Dog Museum.

Windermere Kennels

After a long illness, Beatrice de Coppet had died in 1956. Her 50+ years of dedication to the breed included serving as president, secretary, a member of the board of governors, as well as taking on any job she was asked to do. The minutes for the annual meeting read: "Her code permitted only that which was fair and forthright—and the Welsh Terrier Club of America has been enriched by her presence." There was no obituary in the Pennsylvania papers where the sisters lived for half the year.

Hmm . . . Look familiar? An oil painting by Dorothy Hardcastle of her bitch, Ch. Mrs. Brown of Hardcastle, which was donated to the Dog Museum.

When her sister, Gertrude, died in 1960 these two hard working Welsh Terrier breeders, promoters, club founders and supporters—whose kennel prefix, Windermere, was synonymous with the breed—were scarcely acknowledged beyond the confines of the club. After winning the stakes, and taking two other dogs into the ring at the February Specialty, Gertrude dropped dead in the ring surrounded by her friends and the dogs that had been her life. On her death, the obituary was given to The New York Times by her chauffeur.

The dogs were left to Jean Hinkle whose death, however, had preceded Gertrude de Coppet's. The lawyer, and a doctor in whose care the dogs were alternatively left, refused to have anything to do with them. The matter went to court in Rhode Island (the de Coppets' summer home) and a judge declared that the $100,000 trust fund set up for the care of the dogs would go to the American Society for the Prevention of Cruelty to Animals in New York who were instructed to find good homes for the dogs. The ASPCA could spend up to $10,000 a year to care and feed any dogs not re-homed. The unused portion of the trust went to a Rhode Island hospital. There were thirty-eight Welsh Terriers and one Irish Wolfhound in need of new homes. Oh, that our Welsh Terrier Club of America Rescue service had been in place twenty-five years earlier!

The 1960 Specialty was won by Mrs. Urmstrom's *Ch. Quayside Jolly Roger*, handled as always by Jimmy Butler. Winners Dog and BOW went to Mrs. Colt's new "favorite" house dog, "Jimmy," also known as *Ch. Drakehill Dinky*, handled by Johnny Murphy. We all have had a favorite dog, but "Jimmy Colt" was an imported country-kennel-raised dog brought to live in a posh New York apartment! Obedience was not in his make-up so

Ch. Drakehill Dinky, a.k.a. "Jimmy Colt."

he was sent to Thelma Cottell (a long-time Welsh Terrier Club of America member and assistant to Johnny Murphy) for lessons in gentility. He was returned to the Colts an obedient Welsh gentleman, but in no time at all he had Anne Colt completely under his charms and the two-way admiration ended only when, as a very old dog and cradled in Anne's arms, he was kindly put down.

"Jimmy Colt," age four, having his obedience training tested by Johnny Cottell (also four) and a pet rabbit. Johnny's mother, Thelma, trained the Coltan housedogs—after which Anne freely admitted to spoiling them.

The Media Influence

The Welsh Terrier suddenly caught the eye of the media and we can only be eternally grateful that it happened in the '50s and '60s rather than today when such popularity is only a dollar sign in the eyes of the irresponsible backyard breeder.

Breeders may have winced, but two sprightly Welsh puppies in a pet shop window graced a full-color ad for Rheingold beer. Another 1953 ad in Life for the same company featured Skitch Henderson and his Welsh, "Lady". Skitch and Lady appeared daily (predawn) on WNBC. When Lady became lost outside the studio in Manhattan, Skitch announced his dilemma on the air, and the radio station was flooded with calls of sympathy, encouragement, and advice. Lady was found and returned the next day, but until the Welsh Terrier became a *cause celebre*, NBC executives had no idea of the extent of the show's popularity. A recent visit to the Hendersons' Connecticut farm proved Skitch's attachment to the breed. A Welsh was in residence.

Sherman Billingsley, owner of the famed Stork Club in New York City, had a fifteen-minute television talk show to interview the celebrities who frequented the nightclub. On many occasions he was accompanied by his Welsh Terrier. He had a small kennel at one time, all started (he maintained) because he needed a dog that would kill snakes on his Westchester property. True story or not, his Welsh became a TV star.

In 1954 Hayes Blake Hoyt, the top Poodle breeder and judge, was invited to do a TV series on dogs for the popular coast-to-coast "Arlene Francis Home Show." She asked Anne Colt to lend "Tony" (*Int. Ch. Victory Boy*) to represent the terrier group. Anne was flattered, but a bit dubious as to how Tony would behave himself. She

Eng.Amer.Ch. Victory Boy, a top winner, stud dog, and best house dog, "Tony" was also one of the best ambassadors for our breed.

needn't have worried. The Welshman came through in true style. One look at the TV cameras and he turned into Anthony Hopkins "What a perfect darling is your Tony. One of the sweetest and best behaved Terriers I have had the pleasure of knowing. And so beautiful in type!" came the rave review from Mrs. Hoyt.

Not to be outdone, Tony's litter brother, *Ch. Bachgen Glan of Harham*, made the cover of Dog World in March 1955. Originally brought to the U.S. by Harold Florsheim, "Monte" was now nine years old, retired, and living in Dallas, Texas.

Johnny Murphy appeared in national advertisements for Dash dog food with Tony. Johnny also appeared in ads for Camel cigarettes with *Ch. Coltan Equipoise.*

Johnny Murphy posing with Coltan Equipoise for a Camel Cigarette ad in April 1947.

Tom Eynon, the breeder of Tony and Monte, who were sired by *Aman Supreme*, had died in October 1953 at his home in the Rhondda Valley. For thirty years he was a highly respected breeder, competitor, and judge. He was also an active club member and a past president of the Welsh Terrier Association.

Welsh Terrier as Diplomat

New York Magazine published an article by Susan Jacoby describing the '50s lifestyle in Moscow, complete with a photo of the author taken on a snowy Moscow street walking her Welsh Terrier.

In the '60s there was the very well-known White House Welsh named "Charlie." President Kennedy's doctor had prescribed swimming to help his ailing back and Charlie accompanied his master daily in the White House pool. Few people knew that JFK was highly allergic to dogs. Since the sight of a doctor running in and out of the White House might raise the nation's concern, Dr. Paul de Gara, the allergist, used to stride into the White House carrying the necessary medication in an ordinary attache case and looking like any ordinary politician in D.C. No one was any the wiser. Except, perhaps, a most appreciative Welsh Terrier named Charlie. In July 1962, Charlie was featured with young Caroline Kennedy on the cover of *Woman's Day* magazine. He also appears on the cover of a new book, *First Dogs—American Presidents and Their Best Friends* (Algonquin Books of Chapel Hill 1997) by Roy Rowan and Brooke Janis.

And in Writing

In 1959 The Welsh Terrier (*Daeargi Cymraeg*) Handbook was published by Nicholson & Watson of London. Written by I. Morlais Thomas, President of the Welsh Terrier Club and Vice President of the Welsh Terrier Association, this book instantly became a "bible" for the fancy. Up until then, there was no other collected history of our breed. Like every researcher or author who has come along since, I owe much to this work and want to add my sincere appreciation for the encouragement I received from his widow.

Elizabeth Fryman (a Welsh Terrier Club of America member 1956-'71) had a regular column in Popular Dogs and in 1961 wrote a small paperback, How to Raise and Train a Welsh Terrier, which contained many photographs of dogs from the Frymans' Druidel Kennels. In 1993 I wrote a 32-page summary of the Welsh Terrier for the same publishers as part of their breed series, in which the final two-thirds of each book shared the identical text.

Precious little else has been written about the breed except for occasional magazine articles here and abroad. It would seem the well went dry after Walter Glynn

Anne Weld Colt

Anne W. Colt (she was Mrs.Allan McLane Jr. at the time) joined the Welsh Terrier Club of America in 1930 after having *Halcyon Bugle Boy* literally forced on her. He was not shown, but he determined her future in dogs. In 1945 she married S. Sloane Colt, and together they began Coltan Kennels. Mr. Colt served the club as treasurer for many years. Anne held the presidency of the Welsh Terrier Club of America from 1949 until 1980. No one in the history of the club, before or since, has held that office longer. She was very competitive and put some very good dogs into the ring. A brief two years after resigning, Mrs. Colt died, ending the extremely successful Coltan Kennels.

Over a period of forty-plus years, Anne imported many dogs, among them the aforementioned *Eng.Amer.Ch. Victory Boy* and *Ch. Drakehall Dinky* (son of *Eng.Amer. Ch. Felstead Revelation*), *Ch. Abar Broadcaster, Sandstorm Cedewain Craig, Eng.Amer.Ch. Tawe Rosebud, Ch. Ronvale Supreme, Eng.Amer.Ch. Cedewain Caredig* (another bought sight unseen from her breeder, W. Egerton), *Ch. Groveview Goldleaf, Ch. Groveview Typesetter* and *Ch. Groveview Jake*. In addition to these, she purchased a

Ch. Taew Rosebud, bred by Tommy Evans and imported by Coltan Kennels in 1964.

number of dogs here in the U.S., including *Ch. Halcyon Masterpiece*, *Ch Strathglass Viceroy*, and *Ch. Tujays' Brooke Butler*. Perhaps the best known by today's breeders was *Amer.Can.Bermuda Ch. Tujays' Jubilee* ("Jubee"), purchased in 1970 from Jim Edwards and Jack Kimmel. He became a top-producer, siring over twenty champions. If Jubee were to be faulted at all, it might have been for his ears, which he carried "flat" and

Eng.Am.Ch. Cedewain Caredig, puchased sight unseen by the Colts in 1967.

Ch. Strathglass Viceroy, bred by Hugh Chisholm and owned by the Colts. He sired 10 champions.

Ch. Ronvale Supreme.

Ch. Groveview Goldleaf

Ch. Coltan Spitfire, sire of 9 champions, whose pedigree contains many top dogs of the time. Ever get the feeling you were in the presence of royalty?

Ch. Bingo of Wyncote

Ch. Strathglass Bingo's Venture

Ch. Mawr Hydi

Ch. Bodie's Top Raider

Ch. Bodie's Tommy Tucker

Bodie's Top Row

Bodie's Tambo

Ch. Coltan Spitfire

Thet Kimro of Glencoe

Ch. Halcyon Masterpiece

Halcyon Bronwen

Ch. Coltan Honey Bun

Ch. Bingo of Wyncote

Ch. Strathglass Bingo's Venture

Ch. Mawr Hydi

Ch. Coltan You Said It

Ch. Flornell Rare-Bit of Twin Ponds

Rose of Tralee

Little Miss Muffit

therefore lacked as alert an expression as one might like, but he made up for it in being soundly put together, of correct size and temperament.

With so many dogs from Coltan being shown and bred, it's no wonder that several made the Top Producers list. The leading bitch was *Ch. Groveview Typesetter* with eight champion get, sharing top honors with *Bodie's Top Row* who had held the record alone for some twenty years. All eight were sired by *Jubilee*. *Typesetter* (sired by Mr. Pickering's prolific sire of good ones, *Eng.Ch. Groveview Valley Lad*) was an excellent mover, with a nice reach of neck and of solid Welsh type, but perhaps a bit big for a bitch in the States. Another top dog, the homebred *Ch. Coltan Cuantro* (by *Ch. Coltan Cameo* ex *Ch. Strathglass Ballard*) was the sire of ten champions

This entire lifetime of breed dedication and accomplishment was remarkable by any standard.

The Handlers and Kennel Managers

The primary handler for Coltan was Johnny Murphy, one of three brothers from Scotland, all in dogs. John was perhaps best known for the Scottish Terriers which he handled throughout his career. At one time he handled for Maurice Pollack (Marlu) who had both Scotties and Welsh. (When in his 80's, their father was still raising Scotties just outside Glasgow and exporting good ones to the States.) John's brother, Jim, also handled Scottish Terriers, and Harry, the youngest, managed an estate-kennel of whippets on Long Island. Harry's son, Desmond Murphy, handled many breeds from the time he could walk and is now an AKC judge. Johnny eventually retired from the hectic life of handling to become an AKC judge. He was well-liked, highly respected, and his opinion was sought both in and out of the ring.

Robert Fisher was the Coltan handler who had the honor of showing Jubilee, among others. However, his kennel was in Maryland and after a time the Colts wanted to have their dogs nearer home, so Robert Clyde took over the kennel's final years. (Bobby Fisher is now judging.) One of Bob Clyde's favorites to show was *Ch. Coltan Carey*, a sweet little bitch exuding femininity. In 1977-78, she was one of a record three Welsh Terrier bitches to be in the Top Ten All Terrier charts, a record unbroken to this day. The other two were *Ch. Copperboots Wee Blaste* and *Ch. High Flyer Top Star*. It was "the year of the bitches." (This author remembers it well because with three top bitches in competition at Montgomery County Welsh Terrier Club of America Specialty, the best any male could hope for was a BOS and my *Ch. Bardwyn Bronze Bertram*, breeder handled and owned by Mrs. Allen Howard Jr., garnered that award.)

The Wimers of Pennsylvania brought Peter Green and his young family from Wales to Pool Forge Kennels in 1964. He had handled *Flight of Fancy* (by *Ch. Sandstorm Swordsman* ex *Buttes Lass*) to the Bitch Challenge Certificate at Crufts in 1958. It has become a joke here that Peter is related to just about every Welsh Terrier breeder in South Wales, mostly cousins or uncles. It's a joke that is based in truth, since Mervin Pickering (Groveview) was indeed Peter's uncle, Norina Evans (Pendevour) his cousin, and so on. As a terrier handler, Peter's reputation is founded in fact, taking the breed at Montgomery County (between 1965 and 1977) seven times! He showed top dogs for Mrs. Wimer, Mrs. Alker, and Mrs. Allen Howard Jr., who had been primarily a Smooth Fox breeder and active in Montgomery County Kennel Club.

Squiring many famous terriers to BIS at Montgomery and Westminster, Peter gave one lesson in handling that stands out as a classic. Peter was showing the Lakeland, *Special Edition*, in a crowded ring. The judge had placed all the bitches to one side, which had the predictable but undesirable effect on all the handlers of dogs to jockey for position—holding tails, jerking up fronts, and pushing their dogs under the judge's nose. Peter stepped away from the fracas, allowing "Mike" to show himself to perfection, fantasizing of being stud dog to all those bitches!

The Greens' Greenfields Kennels became the mecca for

overseas visitors year 'round, and was filled to capacity in October due to its proximity to the Montgomery shows. Gaynor disliked going into the ring, but raised all the numerous litters of terrier puppies (and entertained all those dog people) and is now entering the ring to judge. Their son, Andrew, is following the family tradition as a terrier handler.

Nell Benton Hudson's Penzance prefix was on several dogs that left their stamp on the breed, but *Ch. Penzance Polaris* was the highlight of the line that began with *Ch. Tawe Telstar* in the mid-1960s, a dog with a beautiful head and neck who sired twenty-seven champions. One of which was *Ch. Penzance Telstar Satellite*, another good one—although perhaps a little long cast—who sired the Polaris dog known as "Buddy."

In 1967, at ten months of age, Buddy was Winner's Dog at Westminster and went to the West Coast to become the foundation sire of Tujays Kennel. He was shown extensively for only eighteen months, but he was not a fancy dog and his show career was a great deal less than spectacular. He never won even a Group. However, what he lost in the ring, he more than made up for in his impact on the breed. He nicked equally well with domestic and imported bitches, and produced among his thirty-seven champions, *Ch. Tujays Jubilee* and *Tujays Rhett Butler*.

Jack Kimmel said, "Buddy was an extremely sound dog, possessing a very strong rear, good tail set, short back and a very good headpiece. He was not a 'modern' Welsh and I feel he came the closest to the breed standard of any dog I've ever owned. I think the key to his outstanding stud record is the fact that there was more right about him than wrong."

This was the very beginning of the "overdone," "modern," "cosmetically enhanced," or whatever you prefer to call it, Welsh Terrier being seen in the show ring and Jack was right: Buddy was sound, strong, and typey, but not a flashy showman.

In 1974, when Buddy was eight years old, he came back East to live with Nell Hudson at Penzance Kennels in Virginia and to sire several more champions. He is behind many a dog in the

Ch. Penzance Polaris—bred by Nell B. Hudson, and owned by Jim Edwards and Jack Kimmel (Tujays)—was the sire of 37 champions, yet a glance at his pedigree shows how few were behind him. "Buddy" was definitely one of our greats

		Hanson Simon
	Ch. Tawe Telstar	
		Tawe Peach Blossom
	Ch. Penzance Telstar Satellite	
		Penzance Paladin
	Ch. Penzance Bebe	
		Penzance Peachie-Keen
Ch. Penzance Polaris		
		Ch. Lenisto of Alvin Farms
	Ch. Pool Forge Catastrophe	
		Pool Forge Havoc
	Penzance Promise Kept	
		Penzance Private Stock
	Ch. Penzance Promise of Rocarie	
		Just Butch

ring or whelping box today coast to coast.

Wilbert H. Etter

Bill Etter, of Quakertown, Pennsylvania, is a man who has became a legend in his own time. But first we need to clear up his kennel prefix. "Licken Run" did not come from a dog's idea of playing tag. A creek (or "run") called Licken Run went through Bill's property, between the house and the kennel. But somehow the mischievous other meaning suited the breed well.

Bill got into Welsh Terriers via the one-thing-led-to-another route. As a child, Bill bred and exhibited show poultry with great success. That hobby eventually led to breeding and training standard-bred horses and training quarter-horses at a local track. The horses brought dogs into his life—hounds for hunting fox, raccoon and rabbit, and competing in field trials with Pointers and Setters.

In 1939 he swapped some exhibition chickens for a Wirehaired Fox Terrier, which became the turning point. That dog was not a show dog, but Bill's mind was made up to get into terriers. He haunted Associated Terriers, Westminster, and Morris & Essex shows trying to decide on a breed. Then, in 1944, he saw *Ch. Flornell's Rare Bit of Twin Ponds* go BIS at Westminster and his

Ch. Licken Run's Top the Rock, a typey Welsh with a beautiful head and neck.

mind was made up. Next, he set out to find the right foundation bitch.

His first two were the requisite top quality and line-bred, but didn't produce what he wanted. When Mrs. Clark died and Halcyon Kennels was closing, Bill purchased a daughter of the top-producing bitch, *Ch. Raybrooks Elizabeth Fox.* He named her *Licken Run's Foxy Beth.* She produced three champions of the sort he was after—and he was on his way. It was some years before he bothered keeping a stud dog, the first one being *Beau Ideal* (from Ed Doyle), a son of the great *Ch. Strathglass Bingo's Venture.*

Sticking with inbreeding and line breeding, Etter's Licken Run dogs soon put a stamp on the breed. He bred and sold ten or eleven BIS dogs. The dogs he himself considered outstanding (both at stud and in the BIS category) were *Ch. Licken Run's Rock & Roll* (sire of eight champions) and his son, *Ch. Licken Run's Top the Rock* and the great bitch, *Ch. Licken Run's Panic.* All three won either the Grand Challenge or Junior Challenge Cups. Aside from *Rock and Roll* as a favorite dog, most of his pleasure came from *Ch. Licken Run's Two Pence Sam* because he was the first one Bill handled himself to Group wins, a BOB at Westminster, two Specialty breed wins ('73 and '74) and on to BIS in 1974 (Bill's first). By

"Sam" (Ch. Licken Run's Two Pence Sam) winning the WTCA Specialty in 1973 under Johnny Murphy, and Mrs. S. Sloane Colt presenting the award.

Ch. Felstead True Form ex *Licken Run's Samantha*, bred by this author, *Sam* was one of four in the litter to become champions and went on to become a top producer, siring twenty-nine champions.

A son of Sam, *Ch. Licken Run's Danny Boy*, also garnered a BIS in 1975 at age two, breeder-owner handled, a rarity then and unheard of in Welsh Terriers today.

Having joined Welsh Terrier Club of America in 1942, Etter served on the board of governors from 1962 to 1984, as well as chairing numerous committees. He is best-known and possibly best-remembered as the friend and defender of the breed and of his peers, and as the mentor to every novice breeder/exhibitor who sought his advice. At the age of seventy, Bill Etter said he was "thinking about" going for a judge's license. Not one to regret a hastily-made decision, fifteen years later he decided against the idea.

Licken Run's Samantha (my foundation bitch) while never a champion herself, excelled in producing them, beginning with the above-mentioned litter. Her descendants were almost as strong in top-producing females as males. In her lifetime (1967–1981) close to 200 champions could be directly traced to this sound, typey, closely line-bred Licken Run bitch. Many present-day kennels go back to her, especially through her son of that first litter, *Ch. Licken Run's Two Pence Sam*.

1960s

Many imports made headlines in the '60s, among them: *Ch. Caradoc Llwyd of St. Aubrey, Ch. Dewi of St. Aubrey, Ch. Tawe Superb of Twin Ponds, Ch. Felstead True Form* (owned by Mrs. Alker); *Ch. Jokyl Miss Limelight* and *Ch. Jokyl Karlstar Coquette* (Pool Forge Kennels), *Ch Goldview Goldleaf* (Mr. and Mrs. Colt); *Ch. Felstead Flora of Reglib* (Mr. Bilger); and *Ch. Tawe Sweet Song* (Mrs. Nell Hudson).

Quite a few of these went on to be top producers and record-holders of Specialty wins, but two dogs of this era stand out. First,

Ch. Pool Forge Fast Freight, bred and owned by the Wimers of Pennsylvania, was handled to the top by Peter Green. This dog was the model for the breed standard and visualization in the 1970s.

Ch. Pool Forge Fast Freight (handled by Peter Green), who was winner of three consecutive Grand Challenge Cups. *Fast Freight* took over from *Bingo's Venture* as the model for our breed standard visualization. Second, *Ch. Felstead True Form* (also handled by Peter Green for Mrs. Alker), who was winner of the Grand Challenge Cup for 1968 and 1969 and whose son, *Ch. Twin Ponds Plaid Cymru* won it in 1970. Interestingly, this dog's win was voided in 1971 due to Mrs. Alker's death and a change of ownership, but, undaunted, he came back to prove his worth by winning the Cup in 1972 and 1973. The *True Form* dog, who was known as

Ch. Felstead True Form, the best-known stud dog in recent times to have come to the U.S. from Snow's kennels.

"Danny," sired twenty-three champions, and ended his days at Licken Run Kennels.

Another First

Mrs. Prescott Gustafson drew a great deal of local attention with her Welsh Terriers, *Strathglass Storm, CD* and *Strathglass Tide Rip, UD*, who were put through their paces as an Obedience Brace at a Rhode Island show. Anyone who has shown a brace in the conformation ring will understand what a great achievement it is to work an obedience brace. Even if you haven't, think of it this way: Most dogs can be a handful out on the leash when you go for a walk, this in territory he—and you—are familiar with. Now imagine putting two dogs through their paces in front of hundreds, even thousands of spectators.

Pictures For Posterity

No one person did more to preserve our breed visually than the magician behind the camera, Rudolph W. Tauskey of New Jersey. Whether self-appointed or not, he bore the title "Official Photographer of the American Kennel Club" and no one would dare dispute it. He knew dogs and he "shaped" every one of his subjects to be as close to the breed standard as possible. His tricks for the camera were the fodder of many a discussion about a particular dog. He used fishing line to hold up a tail "just so," a crated cat to hold true terrier attention. It was said many a handler learned the nitty-gritty of grooming and showing from studying Tauskey photos. He shortened bodies, leveled toplines, tidied toes, lowered hocks. In other words, Tauskey gave his clients what they saw when they looked at their dogs! But he also captured expression, even attitude. These were not show pictures, but portraits and they have left us with a thirty-year legacy of classic pictorial history.

Regional Clubs

Regional clubs were springing up, another indication of the breed's increasing popularity. For many years (from 1920 on) Miss Marion Kingsland was the only Welsh Terrier Club of America member from California. Her Walescroft Kennels had many fine dogs, including *Ch. Aman Flashlad.* She worked hard at popularizing the breed on the West Coast.

Ch. Aman Flashlad, imported by Miss Kingsland's Walescroft Kennels of California in 1938.

The Welsh Terrier Club of Southern California was the first regional breed club to spring up. According to some records, "the Welsh Terrier Breeders Club of Southern California was formed on December 29, 1934, in Los Angeles" and was sanctioned by Welsh Terrier Club of America and the AKC. In 1937, Mrs. Edward Clark, President of Welsh Terrier Club of America, judged their specialty at Golden Gate, a clear indication of their existence and acceptance at that date. However, in 1947 the club was reorganized by Mr. Francis Van Hartesveldt and the word "Breeders" was dropped from the name. A written history of this organization states that they were founded in 1930 and do not consider themselves a "regional" club, but an independently AKC licensed Welsh Terrier club, with Welsh Terrier Club of America looked upon as the "national," not the "parent" club. However, this discrepancy was laid to rest in time.

This West Coast group has always been comprised of people willing to work hard for the breed and its welfare. The Bilgers (Reglib), the Marcks (Chancrest), the Massons (Montrose), von Hemerts (Tremenhov), Jack Kimmel and Jim Edwards (Tujays), Van Hartesveldt (Vanhills), Holtzmans (Chayna), and the Tebbetts (Johnel) were among the many avid breeders who built it into a strong outpost. They have for many years held their specialty in conjunction with The Great Western Terrier Specialties, which has now grown in stature to be billed as "the Montgomery of the West." In June 1995 the first Great Western All-Terrier Group Show was won by *Ch. Anasazi Billy the Kid.* He did it again in 1997 and his son, *Ch. Tujays' Gunsmoke*, won the first puppy Best in Show offered at Great Western. In 1998 *Gunsmoke* (ex *Ch. Tujays' Fanfare*) was Best of Breed.

Not to be outdone by California, the State of Washington Welsh Terrier Club was founded in 1948 by Mr. Edgar Smith and has remained active, though small. Helen Hansen Miyoshi was an early member who worked hard to keep the club organized through trying times. Peggy Hewes, Barbara Decker, and the breeder/handler, Denis Springer, have all done their utmost to keep this small club afloat. In 1988, the Fortieth Anniversary Specialty brought out Bob Clyde to judge Sweeps, and Eric Catherall (Serenfach) from Wales to judge a record entry of fifty-four. Their recent joint venture with the Pacific Northwest Terrier Circuit will no doubt give the club a boost.

It wasn't until 1948 that a Welsh Terrier Club of America committee was formed to consider offering floating specialties in other parts of the country to stimulate interest of members outside the eastern portion of the States. It took another thirty-five years (under C. Freeman Ayers, President) before a general meeting of Welsh Terrier Club of America was held outside New York City, hosted by Welsh Terrier Club of Southern California in Los Angeles.

In 1947 there had been a Midwest Welsh Terrier Club founded by Edward Metcalf. They held a specialty that year with an entry of twelve dogs. Carl Neumann fell in love with the Welsh in 1937 and purchased a granddaughter of the famous *Ch. Senny Rex*, which began twenty-five years of breeding under the Carlano prefix.

In 1962, the Welsh Terrier Club of Northern Illinois came to life with a large contingency of Welsh Terrier owners and breeders already in place. Most notable was the Florsheims' Harham Kennels of Welsh, Wires, and Airedales. "Mac" Bell managed the kennels and Thomas Gately was their handler. The dogs were shown extensively in the East. Another kennel known not only for their dogs, but for their top terrier second-generation handler, George Ward, was the Virgil Smiths' Jayness Kennels in Michigan.

Some of the kennels more recently associated with the Midwest area are Janterrs, Counselor, Colwyn, Carlano, Chances R, Trudiot, Cardigan, Jenasis, and Edinrose. Several of these breeders have served as officers or on the board of Welsh Terrier Club of America, including Don Koski (Phildon), treasurer; Norbert Savage (Colwyn), who was president from 1988-1992; Steve Chamides (Shomar), treasurer; Helen Chamides, secretary; Bridget Gierahn (Jenasis), secretary, and Diane Orange (Counselor) board member.

Several other regionals have tried and failed. The Welsh Terrier Club of the Jemez, mentioned earlier, was founded in 1968 by "Pat" Patterson and lasted a few years. They held a specialty in 1969, which was judged by Anne Colt. The Welsh Terrier Club of the Potomac, started in 1969 by Nell Hudson, was short-lived and only lasted till 1975. For a very short time, there was a Welsh Terrier Club of Greater Houston, but they disbanded when all their "meetings" could take place at the breakfast table!. The Welsh Terrier Club of Greater Denver was founded in 1968 and held its first specialty in 1975. They also sponsored successful terrier trials. Members numbered about twenty, but show entries were 0-2 and the club ran out of steam. There is currently a new Colorado group, the Rocky Mountain Welsh Terrier Club, which is reactivating Welsh Terrier owners in the Denver area. The Welsh Terrier Club of Greater Cincinnati was the newest kid on the block, founded in 1992, but disbanded in 1995 due to serious problems with irresponsible breeders in the area. They hope to re-group soon.

In 1977 the Glyndwr Welsh Terrier Club was founded by five Welsh Terrier Club of America members (Ayers, Cottell, McLennan, Pelzman and Weiss) and for most of its twenty years the membership has remained just over 100, although it ranges geographically from Maine to Pennsylvania with a few retirees in Florida. This extended region has to date precluded AKC acceptance. However, the club was accepted by the parent club, hosted several annual meetings in New York and has very close ties with Welsh Terrier Club of America. The Glyndwr rescue group was the precursor of Welsh Terrier Club of America Rescue. The club boasts three past presidents of the parent club: C. Freeman Ayers (Welshire), Bardi McLennan (Bardwyn), and Elizabeth Leaman (Hapitails).

Apart from the successful, show-giving California and Illinois clubs, it would seem those relying too heavily on breeder/exhibitor membership suffer an early demise. The longevity of the Glyndwr club may be due to the fact that pet owners have always played a large part in the club, with the emphasis on activities and education for these people and their pets, a fair portion of whom become involved in showing.

The annual matches have served as a unique learning experience for AKC judge applicants—Charles Foley, Kenneth McDermott, Jennifer Moore, Ed Keenan, and Robert Naun, among others. Whereas a prospective judge at an average show would see two to six Welsh Terriers, the Glyndwr match brings out about forty dogs—pets, pups, finished champions, and performance-titled dogs all go in the ring—offering a broad hands-on education.

"The Strathglass Five" by Edwin Megargee (1953), was used on a Christmas card from Hugh Chisholm in 1955. Unfortunately, the dogs are not identified on the card, although they may be on the original painting.

Not to be outdone, Mrs. Colt commissioned Dorothy Hardcastle to paint "The Coltan Five" in the 1970s. Clockwise from top left: Ch. Coltan Carey, Ch. Groveview Typesetter, Ch. Tujays Jubilee, Ch. Coltan Calcutta, and Ch. Coltan Coastal.

CHAPTER SIX

MOVING ON — 1970s TO 1980s

The Welsh Terrier Club of America 1970 yearbook was a good indication that things were indeed looking up for the breed and the club. Almost all of the new articles—covering such topics as advice for the prospective owner, discipline, training and general care of the dog—an important update of the Welsh Terrier Club of America history, plus a photographic "how to" for docking tails, were all written by Mrs. Nell Benton Hudson, our hard-working secretary and *Gazette* columnist.

Nell was not only successful in her work for the club. Her Penzance Kennels at that time boasted: *Ch. Tawe Telstar*, an import and the sire of twenty champions; his son, *Ch. Penzance Telstar Satellite*, sire of ten; and his son, *Ch. Penzance Polaris*, who sired a record-setting thirty-one champions! It was a noteworthy "tail-male" threesome with a total of sixty-one champion get—and that's without the record sixteen of Polaris's son, *Ch. Tujays' Jubilee*! There were also the bitches, such as *Ch. Tawe Sweet Song*—who won the Junior Challenge Cup in 1969 and 1970—plus the home-breds. Nell was always quick to point out that any kudos for these accomplishments went equally to her Penzance partner, Ann Marie Everett.

During the '70s and '80s, the membership was spreading out across the States, including the Bruce Melloys (Bryherlee) in Nevada, the Bjorklands and McQueens (Robb's) in New Mexico, Mrs. Enoch Brown (Lisbrun) in Tennessee, Adeline and Bill Fox (Cadno) in Mississippi, Wilby and Robert Kidd (DoubleK) in Colorado, and the Mills in Anchorage, Alaska.

The breed and the club suffered an enormous loss with the death of Mrs. Alker in July 1970. She was an avid participant in dog shows, loved showing her own puppies in Sweeps, was competitive yet always approachable and friendly. All that and a renowned breeder. "Ernie" Alker joined the Welsh Terrier Club of America in 1936. Two years later she was elected to the board, a post she maintained until her death. She won the Grand Challenge Cup with *Ch. Bodnant Eto* in 1938, the first of a total thirteen times that she would win that Cup! Plus seven times winner of the Junior Challenge Cup. And the Homer Gage? Of course. She took it four times. In 1947 she became club president, a post she held until her friend, Anne Colt, took over two years later. Mrs. Alker stayed on as chairman of the Bench Show Committee.

I am especially grateful that the day before she went into hospital (and died soon thereafter) I had the opportunity to show her part of a litter sired by her recently acquired *Ch. Felstead True Form*. He had been little used until then and she seemed most pleased with his latest offspring. Four of the young pups she saw that day went on to become champions, and three became top producers. In 1972 a homebred son of *True Form*, *Ch. Twin Ponds Plaid Cymru* (bred and handled by Peter Green) won the third leg of the Samuel Milbank Memorial Challenge Cup, thus retiring that trophy. Fittingly, the dog also won the Mrs. Edward P. Alker Memorial Trophy that same year. In all, *Plaid Cymru* won the breed at Westminster for four consecutive years and the N.Y. Specialty for three.

The 1970s saw several more imports making breed headlines, dominated by M. R. Pickering's Groveview line. Anne Colt's

Mrs. Edward P. Alker diead at the age of 80, only a few months after the death of John Goudie, who had managed her kennel and handled all of her dogs. They were a terrier team of the "old school"—always gracious, friendly, and helpful—spending 45 years together in the careful breeding of Welsh Terriers.

Ch. Twin Ponds Plaid Cymru ("Ianto"), winning the Southern California Specialty in 1971 under judge Vincent Perry with Peter Green handling.

Ch. Groveview Jake (tightly linebred to the great producer, *Ch. Groveview Sirius*) and *Ch. Groveview Goldleaf*, James Smith's *Ch. Groveview Dictator*, Peter Green's. *Ch. Gunslinger of Groveview* and *Ch. Swanzee Sky Lord*, Nell Hudson's two bitches, *Ch. Tawe Sweet Song* and *Eng.Amer.Ch. Jokyl Sonoma Sweet Chimes* and C. Freeman Ayers' *Ch. Pendevour Purdy*.

On the West Coast, *Ch. Philtown Protocol* (bred by Drys

Terrier man, John Marvin, awards Best of Breed and the Grand Challenge Cup to Ch. Groveview Jake, handled by Robert Clyde, at the 1975 Westminster Kennel Club.

Thomas) was doing some nice winning for Bruce Schwartz (Bruhil). He was a nicely balanced dog with a beautiful head and neck. Many of our dogs in this period were lacking that "arch of neck" called for in the standard. A son of *Eng.Am.Ch. Rhymney Recruit* (ex *Philtown Peony*) one of several Rhymney dogs that also came over to the States, *Protocol*'s most notable offspring among his many champions owned or bred by Bruce were *Ch. Tujays' Touchdown* and *Ch. Bruhil's Concordat*. *The Sweet Chimes* bitch, also sired by *Rhymney Recruit* went out to join Bruce in California.

Ch. *Rhymney Rambler* sired many champions for the McQueens (Robb) of New Mexico. Two dogs of note were imported from Holland. Nyle Layman and James Koss leased *Ch.*

Ch. Philtown Protocol, imported by Bruce Schwartz from breeder Drys Thomas in Wales, became a top sire and a top winner on the West Coast.

Murthyn's Crackshot from breeder F. Heerkens-Thyssen. He took the breed at Montgomery in 1976, BOS at the February 1978 Specialty, and did a great deal of winning in the Midwest. Mrs. Allen Howard's *Ch. High Flyer's Top Star* (breeder Jan Albers) was BOB from the classes at Montgomery in 1977, the breed at the February Specialty and at Westminster in 1978. Both of these Welsh were considered to be on the tall side for what was generally being shown in the States, but the *High Flyer* bitch in particular was beautifully proportioned and sound with excellent coat and color.

But it was not all imports. In the East, *Ch. Bardwyn Diawl* o *Baradwys* (by *Ch. Bardwyn Jolly Sixpence* ex *Coltan Conversation Piece, CD*), owner-handled, was the Number One Welsh Terrier bitch in 1974 (although I freely admit *Sweet Chimes* was our nemesis in the show ring!). *Ch. Licken Run's Two Pence Sam* had sired *Ch. Licken Run's Billy Joe* and then came *Ch. Licken Run's Danny Boy*, winners and top producers all.

By the mid seventies, even relatively local travels with a few show dogs was now down to a fine art, with handlers taking strings of dogs by plane or motor-home coast-to-coast. Show sites bragged of providing "hook-ups

Ch. High Flyer's Top Star ("Susie"), owned by Mrs. Allen R. Howard Jr., bred by Jan Albers, and handled in the U.S. by Peter Green. Shown here winning BOB at the 1978 WTCA Specialty in New York under breeder-judge Frank Bilger Jr. Susie returned to Holland in whelp by Bardwyn Bronze Bertram.

and black-top parking" for the RVs crowding the show grounds. The steady increase in the number of dog shows, plus the swell in entries, had a side effect as more and more motels put up "No Pets" signs. The sport of showing dogs was rapidly becoming a gypsy caravan existence. The change manifested itself into the type of camaraderie that exists today. Gone are the slower-paced shows where one passed much of the day sitting at ringside (or around the benches) exchanging a few brags, establishing friendships and, more importantly, listening and learning from the terrier mentors and gurus

Today all is a rush. A rush to get to the show. A rush to get a parking space. A rush to get back and forth from the RV or the jam-packed grooming tents to the rings. At the end of the day, spending the evening sitting in a macadam parking lot with hundreds of RVs (generators running and barbecues smoking) does not seem as conducive or as connected to the sport of dogs as were the shows of yesteryear. Now, even the owners only get to the show in time to see their dogs professionally handled, and more often than not leave the minute the judge hands out the ribbons. One has the queasy feeling that one day soon dog shows will all be done on internet!

In 1971 *Ch. Golden Oak Jim Royal, CD* (owned by the Edward Fitzwilliams and handled by Dora Lee Wilson) took the coveted title of Top Terrier All Systems with the most Group wins and a record seventeen Bests In Show. Sired by *Ch. Harham's Roll Call*, he was a showy dog with a cobby body, and one glaring fault: round, light eyes. He was shown mainly in the Midwest, only once coming East, but did so in style, winning BOB at the 1972

Dora Lee Wilson handling Ch. Golden Oak Jim Royal, taking the breed under breeder-judge Nancy P. Smith. Jim broke Welsh Terrier Bests in Show records.

Ch. Coltan Cuantro, bred by the Colts and owned by Mr. and Mrs. James Edwardson, sired 8 champions, including Florrie Edwardson's favorite, Ch. Edwardson's Digymar Eto.

Montgomery Specialty. He sired twelve champions.

Montgomery 1973 was won by Etter's *Ch. Licken Run's Two Pence Sam.* He had already won the specialty in February, won it twice again down the road in addition to the breed at Westminster in '74. This was the first year that the Welsh Terrier Club of America had a Veterans Class, which was won by the James Edwardsons' *Ch. Coltan Cuantro.* There has been very little breed competition in the Brace class; Barbara Richards won one year, the Blairs another, and in 1976 Sue Weiss won with her homebred

You just can't start too soon to practice for the Brace Class!

brace, *Ch. Su-Tops Peppermint Flash* and *Ch. Su-Tops Bit-O-Honey.* Every now and then someone is strong enough to persevere with the training, and brave enough to enter the Brace class at our terrier mecca! It is far easier to put together two Welsh that look alike than it is to get two to do a synchronized trot around the ring and end up in a perfect stand-stay for the judge. The most recent multiple BIS Brace winners were Betsy Adams' litter sisters, *Ch. Xxtra Sunspryte of El-Fr-Ba* and *Xxtra Charge of Xxcitement.*

In 1974 almost all the stars came from California to win at Montgomery County. *Ch. Tujays' Touchdown,* co-owned by Bruce Schwartz and handled by J. Wood Wornall Jr., won the breed. (He would come back in February to repeat this win at the N.Y. Specialty as did the BOS winner.) Best Opposite was John Tebbett's *Ch. Valoramor's Gala Dulce* handled by Daisy Austed. Bred by Virginia Dickson, *Gala Dulce* produced a number of champions, perhaps the best-known of which was *Ch. Johnel's DD of Redondo Beach,* another West Coast dog that made his mark.

Winners Bitch and BOW was the Masson's bitch, *Chayna Laird's Lady* (Holtzmans, breeders) a lovely headed bitch albeit a bit masculine in body. Even the Reserve Winners Bitch came from the West— Schwartz's *Witan Wistful.* Montgomery is

Ch. Johnel's DD of Redondo Beach, handled in the show ring by Ray Perry, puts on another kind of show for the camera. Owned by David Jacob and Don Cortum MD, bred by John and Elizabeth Tebbetts, all of California.

always recalled in terms of the weather and that show will be remembered as one of the hottest on record. When *Bardwyn Turnaround Look At Me* took Winners Dog, it may have been because the "California sun" wasn't bothering the Connecticut Yankee. A solidly built dog, he went well in type with the Winners Bitch. In years to come *Rounders* would sire thirteen champion get. Reserve Winners Dog was from Canada—Barb and Ross Pirrie's *Wil-Wag's Singapore Sling*.

Dogs were routinely being flown coast-to-coast to catch the major shows and thus rack up a record of more wins than there had been shows a few years back. *Valoramor's Jolly Rogue*, owned by Virginia Dickson, came from California to go BOW at Montgomery in '76, and came back a champion the next year in February to take the breed at both the Specialty and the Garden.

The combined terrier specialties have grown to give Terrier Group a whole new meaning. Montgomery County Kennel Club was the first sanctioned by the AKC to hold a Group Show, and stood alone until quite recently. Great Western Terrier Association held its first Group Show in 1995, won by the Welsh, *Ch. Anasazi Billy the Kid*. The Terrier Association of Oregon held its first Group Show in January 1996, and the Garden State Terrier Association (New Jersey) made its Group debut the day before two elite Eastern shows, Bucks County and Trenton, in May 1996. *Ch. Kirkwood Top Brass*, handled by Gabriel Rangel for Frank Stevens, took BOB at the "Garden party" as the New Jersey show is appropriately called. Northern California has currently opted for the cluster show (three or more clubs using the same venue on consecutive days) which, combined with seminars and other activities, should increase their entries. (The canine gypsy caravans like the idea, too.)

Ups and Downs of the Bred-By Classes

As we have noted, awards for bred-by-exhibitor dog and bitch have been given by Welsh Terrier Club of America since those classes came into being, but for too many years the entries were minimal—often meaning one or none. In 1969 there was no dog and only one bred-by bitch award was made. The following year there were two bitches, but still no dog. By 1971 there were all of two dogs, and in bitches there were first- and second-place awards with a six-way tie for third place! It is a reflection of our priorities that the bred-by class is utilized almost exclusively at specialties. At all-breed shows, bred-by is considered the kiss of death, indicating (erroneously or unfairly) a non-professional handler on the lead with a less-than-worthy dog in tow. So the open class gets the entries and the bred-by gets ignored. Sad, because the emphasis switches from pride in breeding to what amounts to a cover up. The brag in saying a dog finished from bred-by is no longer based on competition in the bred-by classes, but on the determination of the breeder to take the points from the open class winner. It's hard to determine whether the solution (or the problem) lies with the breeders or with the judges.

The Year of the Bitch

Then we come to the Year of the Beautiful Welsh Bitches, oddly enough taking place on both sides of the Atlantic. The year 1978 saw three bitches vying for top place in the States: *Ch. Copperboots Wee Blaste* (by *Ch. Vagabond of Reglib* ex *Langwood's Aurora Sadora*), plus the previously mentioned Dutch

Ch. Copperboots Wee Blaste, a multiple BIS Bitch. Owned by Dr. and Mrs.O.W. Mc-Clung of Virginia, and handled by Clay Coady. Here shown winning the breed at a 1979 WTCA Specialty under William Brainard, longtime WTCA officer and highly regarded terrier man.

import, *Ch. High Flyer's Top Star*, that took the breed at the Specialty the year before, and *Ch. Coltan Carey* (by *Ch. Tujays' Jubilee* ex *Ch. Groveview Typesetter*, the record-holding dam of nine champion get). *Carey* was one of the most appealing, if not the best overall, of homebreds from the Coltan line. A small bitch, she was sound and typey with a lovely feminine expression. *Wee Blaste,* handled by Clay Coady, owned by Dr. O.W. "Mac" and Marge McClung, for size was "the one in the middle." (And it must be noted that *Wee* was Mac's favorite house dog, bar none!) She quickly topped the record of wins set by *Jim Royal* with nineteen Bests in Show in one year and then went all the way to BIS at Montgomery in that "year of the bitches." She thus joined an elite group of Welsh to do so. *Ch. Toplight Template of Twin Ponds* did it back-to-back in 1952 and '53, followed by two more dogs owned by Mrs. Alker: *Ch. Caradoc Llwyd of St. Aubrey* in 1961 and *Dewi of St Aubrey* in 1962. The latest Montgomery BIS award went to *Ch. Anasazi Billy the Kid* in 1996.

In the U.K., the "Dog of the Year—All Breeds" for 1978 was also a bitch, *Ch. Groveview Jubilee*. Out of twenty-six all-breed championship shows, she won half the Groups offered, five Best in Show wins and three Reserve Bests, plus the National Terrier Show. Bred by Mervyn Pickering, *Jubilee* was sired by his great stud dog, *Ch. Groveview Valley Lad.* She had the true stamp of Groveview about her and was handled by the renowned terrier handler, Ernie Sharp. All legends in their time.

Ch. Caradoc Llwyd of St. Aubrey (by Breconian ex Barre Bessie), handled by John Goudie for Mrs. Alker, won the breed at four WTCA Specialties—Feb. '61, Oct. '61, Feb. '62, and Oct. '64.

Some of the dogs in the limelight as top sires or in the show ring around this country during this period were *Ch. Wiredot Welsh Prince, Ch. Murthyn's Crackshot, Ch. Carlano Catch the Rock, Ch. Merthyr's Hyperian, Ch. Aruel Alphabet, Ch. Tujays' Touchdown, Ch. Valoramor's Jolly Rogue, Ch. Norlake's Bachelor,* and *Ch. Bryherlee The Executioner.*

By 1979, the three bitches were still at the top, but the dogs were led by a newcomer, *Ch. Secwynn I'm a Cool Li'l Dude* (breeder-owner handled by Mary Seck who was to become Welsh Terrier Club of America President in 1984). *Dude* was little more than a puppy when he went from BOW at the February Specialty to BOW and BOS at Westminster two days later, and then went right on to take the breed at Montgomery in October. Sired by *Ch. Bardwyn Turnaround Look At Me*, he was out of *Ch. Bardwyn Penny Wise, CG.* "Smarty" as the dam was aptly called, was the first Welsh Terrier (dog or bitch) to earn a Certificate of Gameness from the American Working Terrier Association.

Ch. Merthyr's Hyperion, a typey son of Ch. Murthyn's Crackshot (breed by Thyssen), was imported by Norma Apprahamian to start Chaos Kennels.

In what may well be termed the achievement of a lifetime, Mary Seck (within a matter of weeks) put a Companion Dog Excellent title on *Ch. Secwynn's Dudley Do Right*, a Utility Dog on *Ch. Kanga Roo Pooh* (an Airedale, and the first in that breed to earn a Utility Dog title) and still another Utility Dog on *Ch. Raykiln Raquel* (a Welsh). Surely the obedience "hat trick" of the year!

Show photographs during the late seventies, reveal a grooming "improvement" taking place: Long face furnishings combed straight forward to extend well beyond the nose, along with a pronounced goatee on the lower jaw. However it originated, whether to create an illusion to compensate for a short head or just as a flight of artistic fancy, is not certain, but it is difficult to rationalize this soft touch of "salon elegance" on an otherwise workmanlike terrier.

The Eighties

New dogs were making their presence felt in the show ring, and as many new names were doing so in the Welsh Terrier Club of America. Imports continued to be very much with us, but *Ch. Merthyr's Show Master* for example, was owned by a newcomer, Mrs. Louis Aprahamian of Maryland and Edward Jenner from Illinois, who was long in dogs, but new to Welsh. These were followed by many more under Norma's own kennel prefix, Chaos. Also making their presence felt at this time were: *Ch. Johnel's DD of Redondo Beach*, who was eventually owned by a consortium— D. Cortum and D. Jacob, the breeders, who were out of California, and Dr. & Mrs. O. W. McClung of Virginia; *Ch. Hasbet Terrific Taffy* owned and bred by Haskell and Betty Cohen of Wyoming; *Ch. Rushwyn's Sweet Sioux,* owned and bred by Jewel and John Rush of Oklahoma; *Ch. Counselor Wildfire* (and all the "Fire" offspring) whose breeder/owner was Diane Orange of Illinois.

By now there were many kennel prefixes throughout the country that would remain active for the next ten or fifteen years and increasingly become involved in terrier activities beyond the conformation show ring and the whelping box. Some of these include, in addition to those already mentioned: Czar (Charlene Czarnecki), Bryn Hafod (Trevor Evans, a Welshman but, alas, better known for Airedales), Ledge Rock (Ernest and Ruth Prehn), La Sierra (R.C. and Karen Williams), Sunspryte (Robert and Carole A. Beattie), Gregmar (Hank and Julie Marsh), Calkerry (Doris and Tony Tolone), Colwyn (Norbert Savage), Hapitails (John and Elizabeth Leaman). Most of the above kennels garnered Specialty, Group or Best in Show wins, and have bred some of our top producers. Sadly, some, such as Hank and Julie Marsh, and Tony

Tolone have already left us.

And the Winner Is . . .

Fifty-two champions were made up in the breed in 1981. This figure rose to an astonishing seventy-seven in 1992, before coming back to a more normal fifty-five the following year. The "year" for these stats runs from the beginning of June of one year to the beginning of July of the next in order to have all the figures tallied in time for the awards which are given out the first weekend in October at the annual dinner. This task has long been in the capable head and hands of Pamela Price (Shorlyne).

Ch. Coltan Coastal took the breed over a record entry of seventy-five Welsh at the Montgomery Specialty in 1980. He was another from this famous litter by *Ch. Tujays Jubilee* and out of *Ch. Groveview Typesetter*. Five from one litter finished their championships in 1980, a record in itself.

We also gained "star" status. Bill Cosby had been a physical therapist in the U.S. Navy in the 1960s and Jean Heath was his commissioned officer. They remained friends and when Jean retired and began breeding show dogs, Cosby, whose career as an entertainer had skyrocketed, got involved in the Blackwatch kennels. Their top-winning Welsh bitch, *Ch. Anasazi Annie Oakley* (bred by the O'Neals) twice placed in the Group at Montgomery in 1984 and 1985. In all she racked up forty Bests in Show, 106 Terrier Groups and was the top-winning Welsh Terrier at that time.

When Bill Cosby, *Annie*, and her handler, Clay Coady, were being interviewed on television after winning the breed at Westminster in 1984, Bill quipped that he was glad to meet her at last. "She's on the road four days out of five," Clay explained.

Stud Dog Achievements

It was a remarkable period for the breed's top stud dogs, with *Polaris* having sired thirty-one champions, *Merthyr's Super Man* thirty, *Licken Run's Two Pence Sam* twenty-nine, *Rushwyn's Black Hawk* twenty-seven, and *Tujays Jubilee* twenty-three. Hot

CH. ANASAZI ANNIE OAKLEY
WELSH TERRIER

Ch. Anasazi Annie Oakley, bred by the O'Neals of New Mexico, and owned by Heath and Cosby, was one of our "winningest" bitches.

Ch. Rushwyn's Black Hawk by Ch. licken Run's Cochise ex Rushwyn's Kachina. Bred by Jewel and John Rush, owned by the McClungs. He is one of our top winners and sires. Hawk looked this good when shown at 12 years of age in Veteran's class.

on their heels—and soon to overtake them all—was *Ch. Anasazi Trail Boss* with a record sixty-six champion get.

Mike and Nancy O'Neal of New Mexico have bred three record-breaking Welsh Terriers. The other two are *Annie*'s all-time record for bitches, and *Ch. Anasazi Billy the Kid* with over one hundred fifty Group Firsts. *Billy the Kid* is a true legend and closing in on a target of one hundred Bests in Show.

Ch. Tujay's Jubilee, a sound, sturdy Welsh who was rightfully a top-winning dog and stud dog. This picture shows the extended face furninshings that were in vogue at the time.

Betty Anshutz, a longtime WTCA member from Indiana, with Ch. Coryridge Ruddy-My-Beard, CD (sired by Ch. Licken Run's Two Pence Sam) and Coryridge Mali Jones at 4 -1/2 months.

In 1956, when Clement Atlee, the former Socialist Prime Minister, was elevated to an earldom, he was granted "supporters" for his coat of arms and chose his favorite pets—a pair of Welsh Terriers—and "Labor omnia vincit" or "Work conquers all." What better phrase to put with two working terriers!

CHAPTER SEVEN

THE WORLD OF WELSH

Since the United Kingdom is the source of the breed world-wide, it is the obvious place to begin this chapter, and even more specifically of course, in Wales itself.

The first club for the newly named breed, the Welsh Terrier Club, was formed in 1886 in Bangor. As we've seen in Chapter Two, one of the founders, W.A. Dew, was from Bangor and immortalized it as his kennel prefix when his *Bangor Dau Lliw* became the first Welsh Terrier champion of record. The South Wales Welsh Terrier Breeders Association came along much later and in 1923 threw in their lot (and funds, it is always gratefully noted) with the Welsh Terrier Club. One year later, the Welsh Terrier Association was formed with Mr. O.T. Walters, chairman, and Mr. T.H. Harris, secretary. These two clubs have since co-existed peacefully with many enjoying membership in both clubs. Their steadfast dedication to the breed has been paramount to any club rivalry.

A case in point: No championship shows were held during the two World Wars. In the first World War, one was held in 1917, none in 1918 and two in 1919. But in 1946 after World War II, the breed clubs were allowed to run such shows and the first championship show was run by the Welsh Terrier Association at Cardiff on September 12th with Mr. O.T. Walters, judging. As an indication of Club and Association mutual support, he drew an all-time record of 117 entries in ten classes. (The record of 113 dogs was set at the Royal Welsh Agricultural Show in 1924 with Mr. Glynn judging.)

The Open Dog Championship Certificate was Hitchings' *Aman Airman* and the Open Bitch Championship Certificate and

Best in Show was Mr. H. Simpson's Felstead-bred *Greetland Primrose*. On October. 24th that year, Mr. Tom Harris (Senny) judged eighty-four entries at the Welsh Terrier Club Show at Carmarthen. Best Veteran in Show was Hitchings' *Aman Supreme*, Open Dog was Hitchings' *Aman High Flyer* and Open Bitch was *Aman Mermaid*. A clean sweep!

On July 11, 1934 at the Cardiff Show, *Aman Accurate*, a bitch bred by Joe Hitchings, was awarded the bitch CC (Championship Certificate), Best of Breed, and went on to become the first all-breed Best in Show Welsh Terrier. She then went immediately to Mr. Maurice Pollak in New York without completing her U.K. title. An American championship was not long in the making. Mr. Hitchings' 1938 record—winning seventeen champion certificates out of a possible twenty-four—has not been surpassed, nor equaled. He was a mighty force in every aspect of the dog fancy.

A change in the breed standard was made at a joint meeting of the Welsh Terrier Club and Welsh Terrier Association in 1948 when it was decided to raise the desired height from 15 to 15-1/2 inches. Sixteen inches was suggested, but rejected. A good thing, too, or by now, in this bigger-is-better era , we might have Welsh approaching the size of Airedales!

The Kennel Club in the 1950s and '60s showed a steady number of about 300 dogs registered, topping out in 1963 with 408. In 1991 there were 356 registered with The Kennel Club and 896 with the AKC. The current figures hover around 300 and 700 respectively. I couldn't find stats for the U.K., but the AKC figures indicate that approximately one-quarter of all Welsh shown in the classes in a year become champions.

Crufts

Charles Cruft managed the first Allied Terrier Show in 1886 and the rest, to use an overdone but in this case accurate phrase, is history. No Best in Show was awarded prior to 1928 and although

Mr. Cruft died ten years later, he lived to see "Crufts" take its place as a premier world dog show. The Kennel Club took it over in 1948. The recent change of venue from London to Birmingham (and from February to March) has been deemed sacrilege by some, and just keeping up with the times by others.

The first Welsh Terrier to garner a Best in Show at this prestigious event was *Twynstar Dyma-Fi* in 1951, owned by Captain and Mrs. I.M. Thomas and bred by T.M. Jones. In 1959 *Ch. Sandstorm Saracen*, owned by Mesdames Leach and Thomas was next to do so, and there followed a long dry spell until 1994 when close to 20,000 entries were topped by the Welsh Terrier bitch, *Ch. Purston Hit and Miss From Brocolitia* owned by Mrs. A.J. Maughan and bred by Michael Collings.

A Few of the People Who have Made a Difference

Ch. Twynstar Dyma Fi, bred by T.M. Jones of Dowlais in 1948 and owned by Capt. and Mrs. I. Morlais Thomas. Handled by George Barr, "Trixie" made history in 1951 by becoming the first Welsh Terrier awarded Best in Show at Cruft's over entries of 11,265! Eight years later, Ch. Sandstorm Saracen repeated this feat for owners Thomas and Leach, handled by Phillip Thomas.

Without the luxury of running over into several volumes, we can only highlight a very few of the breeders whose dogs have put a stamp on the breed, and who themselves have been the leaders, mentors, and supporters of those who then carry on as future stewards of the Welsh Terrier. One such person was W.A.E. Egerton whose Cedewain dogs were highly regarded at home and abroad in the early years. Margaret

Thomas (Sandstorm), in referring to a puppy she was about to show, wrote, "He is by *Ch. Cedewain Cedrys*—the dog of my life!"

A.E. Harris of Cardiff, another who began breeding Welsh Terriers at the turn of the century, had many excellent dogs, the best known perhaps being the two bitches, *Ch. What's Wanted* (from her photo, a bitch I'd take home today) and *Ch. Gyp-y-Mynyod*. After many years in Canada, and serving in the army in the first World War, Harris returned to Cardiff. It was not until about 1930 that he took the prefix, Penhill, but prior to that his dogs carried memorable names in addition to championships: *What's Wanted, What Again, Take Care, Hold Tight* and *Excuse Me!* are all names that rank up there with a personal favorite—*Turith Uno Who*.

Tommy Davis was considered by his peers to be a "real terrier man" in the early 1900s. His son, Bryn Davis, bred *Who's About* sired by *Dundare David* (a leading stud dog bred by Mogg Hopkins). *David* also sired *Ch. Baglan Straight*, "a good one" bred by Gerrard Morris, who was better known in the States perhaps, for his Wires.

Harold Snow, of Felstead fame, founded a family dynasty in addition to that of his Welsh Terriers. Born in 1897 in Neath, South Wales, he remained there his entire life. (He died in 1979.) Snow began breeding Irish Terriers in 1913, and after World War I added several more breeds—Scotties, Lakelands, and Wire Fox—before settling on the "native son" acquired through his friendship with Joe Hitchings, who had exported some of Snow's Irish to America. The affix Felstead was granted in 1928, the same year Snow accepted his first judging assignment, which was the forerunner of his judging numerous open and championship shows including Crufts.

Snow's first Welsh Terrier champion was *Ch. Felstead What's Up*, whelped in 1934 when the kennel held about ten dogs. But consistent success in the breed led to expansion, and eventually the kennels housed roughly fifty Welsh Terriers, mostly bitches and, in his words, "nine top stud dogs" because he was totally dedicated to line breeding. *Felstead Endeavour* was an early stud dog,

Just a few of the Felstead greats!

Ch. Felstead Filmstar

Ch. Felstead Fascination

Ch. Felstead Fine Mist, awarded a CC under U.S. Judge, Sue Weiss at the National Terrier Show in 1995.

Emlyn Snow and Ken Moran outside Felstead's new facility in a park-like setting.

Ch. Felstead Spitfire

but *Ch. Felstead Futurist* (who earned his title at the same show as an *Endeavour* daughter, *Ch. Felstead Spitfire*) was thought by many to be the best and most dominant sire of his day—a sire of what was then the "modern" look. The breed was by now a smart, good-looking terrier with face furnishings to complete the rectangular head, expressive ears,and tails set high. Gone were the domed skulls, drooping ears, and tails at half-mast. The Welsh Terrier now looked at the world with self-esteem, something lacking at the start of its show career. And the show world noticed. *Futurist* sired eleven English champions in the late '40s and '50s. The first Sandstorm champion was *Ch. Sandstorm Society* by *Futurist* ex *Spitfire.*

There's a story about *Spitfire*, which brings us to Harold's son, Emlyn, who has been a part of Felstead since the age of six when he was old enough to clean out kennels. *Spitfire* was whelped in 1946, won seven champion certificates in 1948 and proceeded to have five litters. When Emlyn returned from service in the army, he brought her out again and won two champion certificates in 1955 when she was *nine* years old! Not many dogs of any breed can match that, and I've never heard of a bitch even approaching such a feat after five litters.

There followed so many dogs of note in such rapid succession that it's easy to miss a good one—*Felstead Famous*, *Felstead Footprints* (and *Footsteps*, and *Footnote*), *Flypast*, *Furious*, *Furious Again*, *Highflyer*, *Trade Secret*, *True Form*, and on and on. Down through line-breeding came the one dog both Snows, father and son, ranked as the "best of Felstead." He was *Ch. Felstead Flashaway*, handled by Ernie Sharpe to BIS at the South Wales show in 1959. This handsome "no fault" dog would win over any Welsh Terrier out today. His precursor, the above-mentioned *Futurist*, was another one favored by Emlyn, but he modifies that by adding that today we would term him an "old fashioned type Welsh." Few dogs, it would seem, span the years without being tagged "modern" or "old fashioned." In any case, these dogs all had that head, expression and entire frontpiece that are the Felstead stamp.

Felstead Highflyer (a grandson of *Flypast*) was the sire of twelve English champions and down from that line came *Felstead Trade Secret*, another top sire. Both of these dogs appear in pedigrees of the recent past.

It was not all stud dogs. In addition to the likes of *Spitfire*, there was *Felstead Helen's Girl*, a top producer and also the Snow's house dog. There followed many more including *Felstead Dreamer* who in turn produced two champions in her first litter, one of which was *Ch. Felstead French Fry of Purston*, sold to Michael Collongs (Purston), who in turn was the dam of *Ch. Purston Hit and Miss from Brocolitia*. Another of the "best of Felstead" was *Felstead Fair View* sold to Lore Eggerking in Germany and, confirming Emlyn's high opinion of her, finished a world champion.

The Felstead kennels are no doubt one of the largest and

most venerable Welsh Terrier kennels anywhere in the world today. The dogs are kenneled in a beautiful new facility in a park-like setting and most ably run by Ken Moran, Emlyn's longtime partner and kennel manager who also wears the judge's badge. Dogs about to be shown are kept at the house where Emlyn has easy access to them for grooming and conditioning. Emlyn judges open and championship shows and there is probably no one in the ring today with more expertise in our breed.

To say that Welsh Terriers run in this family is an understatement. Harold Snow started it; both his sons, Glen and Emlyn, became involved; Glen's son, Lynn Snow, is now a breeder and professional handler; and a nephew, Peter Green (after his aged ten stint at cleaning Felstead kennels and a tour in the RAF), brought the Felstead tradition with him when he came to America in 1963, although Felstead dogs had preceded him by many years.

A quick observation of any portion of Welsh history reveals a paucity of surnames, so it is no wonder that the pursuit of breeding Welsh Terriers is not only familial, but appears to be name-oriented. There is Mr. A.E. Harris (Penhill), Mr. Tom Harris (Senny), and Mr. Arthur Harris (Ronvale).

Mervyn Pickering was a barber by trade and became involved in terriers by way of two working Wires that were sent after badger. He bought a Welsh Terrier bitch from Harold Snow and on Boxing Day at the Ammanford show, Peter Green showed one of her puppies, *Groveview Show Girl*, to Best in Show. She was then sold to Hubert Arthur. With Peter still handling, she was the youngest Welsh Champion ever—at 7-1/2 months, an achievement not possible today due to The Kennel Club's rules change. A dog must get at least one CC after it is one year of age to become a champion.

Pickering was a consummate breeder, particularly keen on good color and teeth. At its prime, the Groveview kennels only maintained about a dozen dogs and the kennels were away from the house, down by a canal. Pickering was convinced that feeding canal water corrected snow nose. Whether or not it worked, we will never know for certain. Pickering was an active Welsh Terrier Association member and officer, and a championship judge.

The Groveview name and its stamp on the breed live on worldwide. A great one, *Ch. Groveview Valley Lad* was sired by an even greater one, *Ch. Groveview Sirius*, whose illustrious grandsires were *Ch. Felstead High Flyer, Ch. Felstead Flashaway, Ch. Rhymney Royalist*, and *Ch. Rhymney Real Star*. That group of stud dogs was in back of all but two of the Welsh Terriers earning champion certificates in 1971. In America alone, *Groveview Jake, Dictator, Goldleaf, Typesetter, Typist, Captivator*, etc. are in current pedigrees. And *Red Palm, Red Rufus* are among those found in Swedish records. Groveview dogs were behind the Merthyr stock as well as the current top Dutch kennel, High Flyer.

Two Groveview dogs will stand out forever in the history of the breed—*Ch. Groveview Sirius* as a dominant top sire, and *Ch. Groveview Jubilee*, handled by Ernie Sharpe and national "Dog of the Year" in 1978. She was purchased by Michael Collings and sold in 1979 after she had been mated to several proven

Ch. Felstead High Flyer.

dogs and failed to produce pups. This is reminiscent of the Harold Snow story. The story goes that Harold Snow bred six bitches to *Dundare David*, the top-producing sire mentioned previously, and to everyone's amusement or amazement, never got a pup!

Michael Collings also bought *Ch. Groveview Minstral of Purston*, which he later sold to breeders in South Africa. A few years later, while living in the States, he purchased two Serenfach bitches from Eric Catherall, and also purchased *Ch. Bowers Jigsaw of Eladeria* (a son of *Ch. Puzzle of Kenstaff*). Once back in the U.K., he bought two Felstead bitches (*Felstead French Fry* and *Pride of Gwenog*), which were the foundation of his Purston Welsh Terriers. His success (to this date) culminated with *Ch. Purston Hit and Miss from Brocolitia* (by a *Jigsaw* son ex the *French Fry* bitch) and *Ch. Leading Lady of Wigmore*, owned by Mrs. Halliwell. Michael and Ginny are once again operating Purston kennels back in the United States, beginning on the right foot by winning the breed at Montgomery and a Group 4 with *Ch. Purston Take Off*, a bitch sold to Mr. and Mrs. Thomas Fraser of Canada.

Mr. J. Thomas started the well-known Rhymney kennels (named for the town where he lived) and one son, Charles, has carried on that line. Rhymney dogs have enjoyed great success in America. Among them were, *Eng.Amer.Ch. Rhymney Royalist* (sire of *Ch. Tawe Sweet Song* and *Ch. Tawe Starlight*, bred by T. Evans) and *Eng.Amer.Ch. Rhymney Recruit*. It is even more astounding that of the eleven champions shown at Westminster in 1968, eight were imports representing Rhymney (including *Royalist* and the two *Tawe* bitches), Felstead, Groveview, Ronvale and Paddywell!

Drys Thomas, another son, is one more example of Welsh Terriers as a family interest. Perhaps it has something to do with living in the Rhondda Valley. After Drys married and started his own kennels in 1958, he took his kennel affix, Philtown, from where they lived, Philipstown. His foundation stock, not surprisingly, came from his father's Rhymney kennels.

His top dogs—*Ch. Philtown Parader, Ch. Philtown Paladin, Ch. Philtown Protocol*, and *Ch. Philtown Paragon*—all produced champions mated to a very limited number of bitches. Good dogs of the past always show up in the pedigrees of today's winners and the Philtown contributions are no exception.

Drys is another believer in bringing along new people to become the breeders of tomorrow. David Williams, currently treasurer of the Welsh Terrier Association is one example.

Drys himself resigned as Welsh Terrier Association Secretary in 1982 after serving thirteen years in that position. His most recent efforts have been to gather international support to defeat the anti-docking laws, which are being spread by animal activists. Due to his Herculean work on television, in writings, and before any club that would listen, the laws are currently being reconsidered or repealed.

When queried as to where the breed stands today, Drys Thomas made many significant comments that reflect the feelings of Welsh Terrier breeders everywhere—that we are going through an era where most of the household names in the breed have passed on, leaving few true breed specialists. He estimates that about seventy percent of today's breeder-exhibitors in the U.K. are quite new to our hobby, which holds true in America as well. Some dramatic wins have come to our breed worldwide in the form of BIS at prestigious events, and fortunately these have not resulted in an increase in the breed's population or popularity—to the point of over population, which is the case in too many breeds today. Rather, the Welsh Terrier's success has only resulted in the breed's recognition as worthy pets, which is all to the good. Today, placing puppies with responsible pet owners has become a prime consideration in breeding dogs.

Like so many today who see newcomers trying to move too quickly to the top of the heap, Drys would like to see more teaching about the breed being done through discussion with the remaining "old-timers." He is setting up such seminars on behalf of Welsh Terrier Association on the premise that one can learn a great deal from experience, but only when that experience has proper guidance. Perhaps it has seemed this way in every generation gap, but today's newcomers are in a great rush to win without learning about the breed!

Deirdre Lester (Brocker) summed it up this way, "We went slower in the past. I do not know whether the dogs were better or worse than they are today. It's difficult to say, as memory plays tricks on you. But first we got our dog, then we went along slowly, learning as we went."

The Welsh Terrier has changed in the past fifty years, but not nearly so much as it did in the previous half-century. Some changes have been for the better and have been retained; others went too far and required (and thankfully received) modification. An example of the first would be mouths. Contrary to Glynn's assertion that undershot mouths in pups would always right themselves, breeders consistently found that they did not! In order to sell stock to the continent, where perfect mouths with full dentition were essential, the problem had to be eliminated and mouths are generally excellent today. (Judges, in fact, are duty-bound to find the exceptions.)

An example of the second premise was the extreme or overdone "Wire Fox look," which, fortunately, was a short-lived fashion. Les Atkinson felt the Wire Fox cross was just what the Welsh Terrier needed to raise its position in the show ring, and he is proved right by the number of Group and BIS wins that came our way after this "modernization." However, for a time the Welsh expression, substance, and, in some instances, the coat were overtaken by the Fox! Perhaps breeders thought if a slight infusion of Wire Fox Terrier had improved the general looks of the Welsh, then Welsh Terriers that even more closely resembled the Wire Fox was the way to go. Suddenly Welsh appeared with Wire traits such as narrower heads, smaller lightweight ears, and narrow fronts. But, as I said, it was a short-lived fad. Thankfully. Any breed suffers when winners are merely examples of extremes that no longer represent true breed type. A very young and aspiring Les Atkinson was once warned by Joe Hitchings that "a good modern one will always beat one of the old fashioned" and perhaps this is still true. Not because the dogs are any better or worse or even that much different, but only because the "we of today" will always consider ourselves to be better, more savvy judges than the "they of yesterday."

On the other hand, Atkinson's observation of *Philtown Protocol* was "a beautiful youngster that should make the grade. Grand neck and shoulders. Good lengthy head—maybe a bit Fox

Terrier-like, but none the worse for that." What was interesting about those remarks was that when the dog arrived in the States where blood boils at the mention of Fox in the same breath as Welsh, *Protocol* was never thought to be lacking true, one hundred percent Welsh Terrier type. The "youngster" easily fulfilled his promising start (see Chapter Six).

The early 1980s was probably the height of the overdone Wire Fox look and I recall seeing several exhibits that could not get out of their own way. Les Atkinson (who died in 1985) considered the movement afoot to be poor and "heads and expression even worse." It didn't take breeders long to get the message, however, and it was only a few years later that Cyril Williams praised the return of the true Welsh Terrier type.

One judge's critique caught my eye because there are many people in the States (and I am one of them) who deplore the American Kennel Club's ruling that allows a six-month-old "baby" to become a champion whilst at the same time acknowledging that every breed standard is written to describe a <u>mature</u> adult specimen. Mr. Des Butler said of a "very nice dog" (who was seven months of age) that "he looked as if he should have been in his playpen."

It is a tribute to those stalwarts who have kept "the whole dog" in their mind's eye that the breed's original attributes have been retained. Again and again over the past twenty-five to thirty years, dedicated breeders, judges, and the top handlers have spoken out on the importance of maintaining correct breed temperament. They have pointed out that the Welsh Terrier is basically a working terrier and as such must be mentally sound and sensible with self-control. These are the same qualities that are wanted in companion animals, which breeders must admit is the destiny of almost every pup in every litter.

Welsh Terrier Association

Although this organization was founded in 1923, it wasn't until 1970 that they produced a yearbook, which was an immediate success. Mr. George Jackson was president and the editorial committee who produced this first edition consisted of Alec James, Gerrard Morris, Mervyn Pickering, Tudor Burnell, and Drys Thomas.

Club yearbooks are a boon to breed historians for the written history, and in particular for the photographs that give us a visual history. In the 1970 book, under a photo of *Ch. Hardway Hot-Pot* (Mrs. B. Napthine and Miss J. Simcock) was the notation that another, *Hardway Hidden Star*, was probably the last sired by *Ch. Sandstorm Saracen*. There is a nice international flavor about the book, too: An article by Frans Heerkens Thyssen (Merthyr). A lovely photo of the very feminine typey bitch, *Ch. Jokyl Sonoma Sweet Chimes*, owned by Olive Jackson before going to the U.S. to do a nice share of winning. And one of *Ch. Bengal Wiredot Welsh Prince* (bred by R. Taylor), owned by Mollie Harmsworth and handled by Ernie Sharpe to win five champion certificates in six shows before also leaving for America. A list of Rhymney champions known on both sides of the Atlantic including *Real Star*, *Royalist*, *Reward*, and *Rambler*. Even a sort of reverse hands-across-the-sea credit to U.K. breeders in a page from Peter and Gaynor Green with a dog of their breeding, *Ch. Twin Ponds Plaid Cymru* (by *Ch. Felstead True Form* ex *Groveview Golden Gleam*). "Ianto" was top Welsh in the States that year.

The Cedewain kennels of W.A.E. Egerton are well-repre-

Ch. Twin Ponds Plaid Cymru, bred and handled by Peter Green for Mrs. Alker. "Ianto" was breed winner of the N.Y. Specialty and Westminster in 1970, '71, '72, and '73!

Ch. Cedewain Cavalier purchased by Henri Dolne of Liege, Belgium.

sented with a list of dogs and wins, and a striking dog, *Ch. Cedewain Cavalier*, proudly owned by Henri Dolne of Belgium. A lovely head and neck, good set-on. Granted, one cannot see it all from photos, but from what can be seen, this is a dog that could easily win anywhere today, which is to say that he supersedes that modern-versus-old-fashioned conflict. After twenty-five years in Wire Fox Terriers, Bill Egerton got into Welsh Terriers about 1950 with great success. *Ch. Cedewain Cymro* was BIS at the Cardiff Championship show in 1954, and was bred back to his dam, *Cedewain Ceiniog* before going to Harold Florsheim (Harham) in the U.S.

The extensive list of Felstead stock exported to the Bilgers (Reglib Kennels) of California shows their determination to stay with the stamp they liked. Another overseas kennel with the same view was the Dutchman, Jan Albers (High Flyer), who in one year imported five dogs from Felstead and Groveview. And as we've seen, Drys Thomas's *Philtown Protocol*, that "young dog just beginning his show career," continued it with exceptional success and also as a top producer (over fifteen champions) in the States along with his Rhymney relatives.

What a shocker, however, to compare stud fees! In 1970 the fee for all the top stud dogs in the U.K. ranged from four to six

Ch. Felstead Fullflight of Reglib, imported by Mr. and Mrs. Frank Bilger of California

guineas. Compare this—at any rate of exchange past or present—to the Coltan (USA) listing of $125, an average stud fee in the U.S. at that time. Stud fees are rarely mentioned these days in touting a dog. Perhaps they are negotiable—or just too frightening! A normal range today in the States is $500 to $750. Cyril Williams (Caiach) once told me he frequently did not take money for a stud service. If he liked the bitch and felt the mating would benefit the breed, there was no fee. But if he did not approve of the bitch or the mating, no amount of money could buy the services of one of his stud dogs. Like many people involved in what is referred to as the "moving art" of trimming show dogs, Mr. Williams was a noted sculptor of all breeds of dogs, and of cattle.

1980s

The first day of June 1980 saw the first Open Show to be held by the Welsh Terrier Association. It was held at Frensham Manor, the home of George and Olive Jackson (Jokyl) where many Welsh Terrier Association shows were held over the years. This one was judged by Beryl Blower and by all accounts, was an enormous success. A lovely lunch on a perfect summer's day, a beautiful venue, numerous trophies and special prizes all made it an auspicious beginning for an annual event. There were thirty-nine dogs making eighty-eight entries, with BIS going to Mr. Jenkins and Miss Nock's *Ch. Bowers Princess*, handled by Ray Davies.

This was also the year all shows in Sweden were put on

hold from January 1st to April 30th due to an outbreak of the parvo virus. Despite this late start, Lars Adeheimer had a good year with *Ch. Adens Mackay of the Orchestra*. Five of Sweden's top twenty bore the Aden prefix and six more were sired by Aden dogs. Per Thorsen also did some very nice winning with his import, *Ch. Groveview Red Rufus*.

The following year, due in great part to the efforts of Cyril Williams and Des Butler, the Welsh Terrier Club was allowed by The Kennel Club to award championship certificates—95 years after the club was founded. Mrs. Margaret Thomas, the president, judged this first event.

The bitch, *Ch. Puzzle of Kenstaff* (breed by R. Ogles, and owned by Mr. Jenkins and Miss Nock) was handled by Andrew Hunt to "Top Welsh Terrier" for 1981 and '82. She took the breed at Crufts and BIS at the National Terrier Specialty and was still going strong in 1983. Not too far behind her was *Ch. Scrumpy of Turith* bred by Mrs. F. Hughes and handled by Ray Davies for Gerard Remy of France. Mrs. Hughes' bitch, *Ch. Bzylizy Busybody*, was the runner-up bitch to *Puzzle*.

AROUND THE WORLD WITH WELSH

Germany

I am grateful to the late Rolfe Wernicke who knew the importance of the written word and left us a small, but pertinent, history of the Welsh Terrier in Germany after the Berlin Wall came down. The breed was in rather sad shape as a show dog. At the World Show in 1990, held in Czechoslovakia, Welsh Terriers came from Russia, Poland, and East Germany, as well as Czechoslovakia. However, the dogs from Italy, Holland, West Germany, and the U.K. drew much interest from people in the East since they were the first show dogs they had seen. Imports were not permitted and Welsh Terriers were only allowed to be bred for hunting purposes. The dogs had to pass tests of their skills, which,

Ch. Welsh Lady von Rowedo, from Rolf Wernicke's kennels.

overall, was not a bad thing but didn't do much to improve those qualities perceived essential for the show ring. It is amazing that despite these obstacles, there were about thirty breeders who stayed with the breed and, judging from Rolfe's photos, the dogs being shown were not nearly so lacking in show quality as one might have expected.

As chairman of the Welsh Terrier Klub of West Germany, Rolfe organized the first meeting with those in the East and sixty people showed up. He even took a contingent of East German breeders to Wales. (When in doubt, go to the source!) When we met at Montgomery shortly before he died, Rolfe spoke of his slide presentation of the breed, which was sponsored by the Klub. He was pleased that it had made quite a hit.

Lore Eggerking (Bauernhohle) imported *Ch. Felstead Fair View* in 1980 and received nine BIS awards, thus confirming Emlyn Snow's eye for the dog, which he feels was one of the "best of Felstead."

Von der Bismarckquelle

Here we have still another family involved in terriers—the Axel Mohrkes. Again it goes back to Axel's father who was a breeder of Wire and Smooth Fox Terriers. Elke and Axel obtained their kennel prefix in 1954. Their daughters, Corola, Corinna, and Claudia are all involved in the dogs, but perhaps Corola most of all and certainly she is best known to Americans due to the time she has spent with kennels here.

The unusual aspect of Bismarckquelle is its size. Few kennels today run as many dogs, and fewer still would run as many together as is done here—twenty to thirty at a time in a huge run! There is no doubt that sound temperament is as important to the Mohrkes as is a sound and beautiful show dog. Many of their dogs also have working titles.

Welsh Terriers come under the KfT (Klub fur Terrier), which uses a Zuchtwart system, or breeding system, involving a nightmare of paperwork. A litter must be reported within three days, visited, then visited again a few weeks later, and piles of papers filled out before the pups can be registered. (Fox Terriers have their own club, of which Axel Mohrke has been chairman for many years, and which is recognized by the Hunting and Working Dogs Association.)

Both the Mohrkes judge, as well they should, having been in dogs for so many years and getting their hands on so many specimens of the three breeds in their kennels. In evaluating their own puppies they look first for body. The pup must have a good front and a powerful (and broad) hindquarters. Heads and ears may change "style," but these points will remain, as will the temperament.

Von der Bismarckquelle dogs are known all over the world and have made obvious contributions to many Welsh Terrier lines in America. Some of the best known of these imports are: *Ch. Para v.d. Bismarckquelle* brought over by Bruce Schwartz (Bruhil) of California; *Int.Ch. Nathan v.d. Bismarckquelle* imported by Kathleen Reges, also from California; and *Ch. Patt v.d. Bismarckquelle*, who is now part of the stud force at the Leamans (Hapitails) of New Jersey. All have a stamp of soundness and substance and are worthy additions to the U.S. bloodlines.

Because they are adamant regarding the fact that terriers were bred to hunt, Carola and her father feel it is possible to breed beautiful dogs that are also able to work. Corola shows dogs, has worked in kennels in Europe and America, and one day will inherit the pleasures and responsibilities of the renowned von der

Bismarckquelle kennels.

Holland

De Nederlandsch Welsh Terrier Club, the first Welsh Terrier club on the European continent, was founded in Holland in 1939 in the proverbial "five minutes" before war broke out. It currently boasts more than 200 members.

Frans Heerkens-Thyssen of Aerdenhout started his famed Merthyr kennels in 1931 with foundation stock from the leading Welsh Terrier kennels in Wales: Groveview, Cedewain, and Felstead. He sent out numerous champions worldwide. Most notable in the States were *Ch. Merthyr's Show Master* and *Int.Ch. Murthyn's Crackshot*, the sire of eleven U.S. champions in the '70s and breed winner at Montgomery. *Ch. Merthyr's Hyperian*, a son of *Crackshot*, went to Mrs. Norma Apprahamian's Chaos kennels in Virginia and did almost as well as his sire in siring champions. *Ch. Merthyr's Maestro* and *Ch. Merthyr's Superman* were two more who sired a list of American champions.

Mr. Thyssen judged the Welsh Terrier Club of America Floating Specialty in Illinois, which lead to one amusing incident. After he had gone over each dog on the table, he lifted the dog and put it on the ground. The exhibitors were overcome by this bit of Old World European courtesy. Thyssen shared the joke later that evening: While the exhibitors thought he was being polite, he was actually assessing the ribcage and the weight of each dog! In breeding Welsh Terriers, Thyssen inveighed against three things: a dog that is shy, a dog that is low set, and a dog lacking a good black nose.

Jan Albers' High Flyer prefix is another well-known around the world. *Ch. High Flyer's Welsh Princess*, *Ch. High Flyer's Galaxy*, and *Ch. High Flyer's Show Girl* were just three of the successful dogs from this kennel to do well in America. In 1978 *Ch. High Flyer's Top Star* took the breed at Westminster and was part of the trio of breed winners for the year, all bitches.

More recent breeders on the scene are the Janssens (Penrhyn) whose *Ch. Penrhyn Miss Mazoola* was a leading Welsh in the Netherlands in 1992.

Sweden

The first Welsh Terriers to enter Sweden went from Walter Glynn's Brynhir kennels to Mrs. E. Cassel in 1912. In more recent years, the breed has become quite popular. The year 1982 saw two imports as top winners—*Ch. Philtown Performer*, and Per Thorsen was still showing and winning with *Int.Scand.Ch. Groveview Red Rufus*. The top Welsh Terrier at that time was *Ch. Toreador's See You Later* bred by Barbra Wiren. The Swedish Welsh Terrier Club held the first Welsh Terrier championship show outside the U.K. in 1983, which was judged by Mrs. Deirdre Lester (Brocker).

Lars Adeheimer (Aden) is one of the best-known breeders of Welsh in Sweden and is another exporter of good ones.

Per Thorsen (Snowdonia) is now showing the great-great offspring from the *Red Rufus* dog and has added some Felstead imports with success in the ring and the whelping box. In 1995, *Snowdonia Daily Mirror* made the Top Ten list in Denmark.

Another kennel producing some nice Welsh is the Dimwitch kennel of Lennart and Anki Nordlund. Their *Ch. Dimwitch Vining Witch* took the breed under the Danish breeder-judge, Ingrid Borchorst, at their club show in 1992. Under English breeder-judge, Alexandra Witmond, BIS went to *Ch. Toreador's Nathalie* and Best Dog in Show to *Dimwitch Fire Demon*.

The Swedish Club has a newsletter, "Welshen," which covers all of Scandinavia. A topic of great interest, of course, has been the docking ban that went into effect in 1990 and is due to be lifted (at this writing) on all varieties of German Pointers and requests to lift it are being considered from other breed clubs. Those members who are working to lift the ban deserve much credit for tackling what initially seemed like insurmountable odds.

Ch. Scrumpy of Turith was top dog in 1983 with 12 CCs in the U.K. before joining Gerard Remy in France and adding championships in Belgium, France, Luxembourg, and World Champion in Madrdid.

France

Gerard Remy (La Fontaine de L'Erable) acquired *Ch. Scrumpy of Turith*, the top-winning Welsh in the U.K. in 1982 and went on to earn championship titles in Belgium, France, Luxembourg, and World Champion in Madrid.

The Michalskis (De La Fontaine Melusine) imported *Serenfach Dan Cracker* with similar success in gaining titles.

Ch. Serenfach Dan Cracker as a promising puppy, with breeder Eric Catherall.

And here winning on the Continent for new owners Adeline and Dominique Michalski (De La Fontaine Melusine).

Belgium

Henri Dolne imported the handsome dog, *Ch. Cedewain Cavalier*, and must have been well-satisfied with his acquisition, because he soon added *Cedewain Cronyn* to his kennels.

Italy

Two kennels in Italy have done well over the years with Welsh: Ara Pacis, owned by Massimo Rocchi and Adamo Iotti, and Attiluccio, owned by Antonio di Trapani with stock that came from Brocker, Geralt, and Paddywell.

Ch. Geralt Red Dragon, bred by J. Jones "Gerallt" of Lampeter, Wales, was top dog in 1983 and continued his career in Italy with Massimo Rocchi and Antonio Di-Trapani.

Denmark

The best known kennel in Denmark is that of Ingrid and Carl Borchorst. The top Welsh in 1991 was *Ch. Borchorst Alberta*, who was also the Number Two Terrier. Of the top ten in 1995, six were sired by Borchorst dogs (*No Doubt* and *Gulliver*) and the Number One was the bitch, *Borchorst Hoedown*.

The El-Fri-Ba kennels of the Nielsens are proving they are on the right track. In 1992 with *Ch. Purston Stop the Show* and *Ch. Baron von der Bismarckquelle* and in 1995 with their home-bred *El-Fri-Ba Midnight Passion* and *Midnight Patriot*.

Another Purston import, this time a bitch and from Purston's home base in the U.S., *Purston American Maid* is doing well with certificates in Germany and Denmark for her new owners, A. Nielsen and B. Madsen.

Finland

The number of Welsh Terriers peaked in the 1960s with annual registrations of about sixty dogs. Stock had been imported from great Britain, Sweden, and Denmark with Ms. Gritta Ringwall (Black Spot) and Mrs. Britta Vaahterlinna (Briddle) having a great influence on the breed. By the end of the 1970s, the registrations were slipping, but a few dedicated breeders, such as Dorotea Riipinen (Ripcoy) and Mrs. Kirsti Lundstedt (Kittyhouse), continued to breed and import good ones. *Ch. Katiewell Fire Cracker* was one that did well.

The Finnish Welsh Terrier Club was established in 1975 and currently has about sixty members. The past twenty years have seen selective importing of dogs from top European kennels. Ms. Irmeli Salasmaa (Dixie Sound) has bred several champions, including the Group winner, *Ch. Dixie Sound Dangerous Dix*. One of Ms. Sari Mäkelä's top dogs in the ring and at stud is *Multi.Ch. Vicway Live and Die*, and the top Welsh in 1997 and World Winner in 1998 is his son, *Ch. Vicway Live Free or Die*. Mr. Jouni Perttula (Bartos) lays claim to having bred the first Finnish Welsh to gain a U.S. championship—*Ch. Bartos Big Time*.

Agility is very popular here among Welsh Terrier owners. *Fin.Ch. Ava Dixie Sound Foghorn-in-Fact* placed third in European Championships and currently two Vicway dogs, *Live Free or Die* and *Vicway Dirty Harry*, are doing the most winning in agility.

Australia

Welsh Terriers are virtually a rare breed in Australia, but two people are currently working to change that: Keith Lovell, who has judged in most parts of the world, and his wife, Trish, who had Wires and Airedales. They have now dedicated Darewe kennels, in Victoria, to the Welsh Terrier.

Between 1961 and 1974 three different people each owned one male. In 1978 Mr. and Mrs. Tuckett (Llanrust) bred two litters, and three in 1979 by *Ch. Erme Dancing Kite*. Then in 1982, M.J.

Corderoy regis-
tered a litter by *Ch.
Roseview Cracker-
jack of Brocker*,
and in 1991 Mr. E.
Higgs (Mynydd)
registered three lit-
ters sired by *Gerallt
Welsh Guard* ex
Pendevour Passkey
and *Ucheldir Dar-
oganes*. He repeat-
ed these breedings
the following year,
but no show
records could be
found.

*Eng.Swed.Dan.Nor.Int.Australian Ch. Adens Fit for
Fight, bred by Lars and Inga Adeheimer in Sweden, has
an enviable pedigree, going back to Groveview Red Rum,
Felstead Trade Secret, and Philtown Performer.
"Freddie" (whelped in 1984) was a multiple Group and
BIS winner in Australia and is now retired at Keith
Lovell's.*

David Barclay is the sole breeder and exhibitor (in a coun-
try the size of Australia!) who has teamed up with the Lovells. In
1992 they had all imports, including the well-traveled dog, *Ch.
Aden's Fit For Fight*, who had his championships in England,
Sweden, Denmark, Norway, and Australian, with multiple Group
wins and one BIS in Australia. They'd also imported *Aden's Lazy
Oskar*, *Ch. Aden's Never-To-Be-Forgotten*, *Ch. Aden's Made In
Sweden* and *Ch. Aden's Knight's Queen*.

In 1995 and 1996 the Number One Welsh was "Benni," the

*David Barclay and Keith Lovell
have set records for Welsh Terriers
in Australia with "Benni," their
import from Sweden with multiple
BIS and Group wins.
Austalian.Swed.Ch. Welsas Hey
I'm Hot News, bred by Anki and
Lennart Nordlund, shown here winning a BIS, handled by Barclay.*

Swedish-Australian *Ch. Welsas Hey I'm Hot News*, a three-year-old bred by Almgren Elsa and campaigned in Sweden by Anki and Lennart Nordlund (Dimwitch). Benny is now owned by Lovell and Barclay. This dog is by *Int.Ch. Vanitas New Generation* ex *Ch. Purston Hot As Hell*. Benny had two all-breed Bests in Show to his credit—Kyneton Kennel Club and Geelong—in 1996. Things are looking up for the Welsh Down Under!

Canada

The Welsh Terrier Association of Canada was founded in 1973 by Lief and Svea Osterberg (Volfsing), Ron and Nora Hibbert (Bronwynne), Jack and Lorraine Eves (Lorja), Mrs. Mildred Black (Milroy), Dr. Rendyl Godwin (Renwood), Mrs. Diana Johnson (Medonte), Ted and Charlotte Nott (Trabil), Rudy and Linda Joss, and Tilman and Janet Martin. Six more members came aboard the following year and they were soon up to thirty members. Booster shows were held, a newsletter published, and at the Terrier Breeders Association in 1973, a Welsh, *Ch. Wil-Wag's Singapore Sling* bred by Ross and Barb Pirrie, was Best in Show. Wil-Wag Welsh ranked number one in 1966, '67, '68, '69, and '70. The original members were also a simply fun group. One year they hired a bus, had seats removed to make room for crates, and arrived en masse for Montgomery weekend. There was no overseas visitors tent in those days, but the Welsh contingent did have a Canadian hospitality bus!

There were also some good imports in the early years, among them were *Ch. Felstead Forceful*, *Ch. Jokyl Karlstar Commodore*, *Ch. Windonwell Wide Awake*, *Ch. Groveview Ember*, and *Ch. Brocker Bandit*.

In more recent years, the Frasers have had success with their *Ch. Purston Take Off*, including a Group 4 at Montgomery. Mrs. Lee Steeves (Regalridge) of Nova Scotia brought out *Ch. Regalridge Here Comes Sparkle* to top the breed in 1991 and '92, followed by *Ch. Regalridge Lites Camera Action* in 1994 and his

Eng.Amer.Can.Ch. Purston Take Off with handler R.C. Carusi under the late terrier judge, Dora Lee Wilson. "Wendy" was a multiple BIS winner and Group 4 at Montgomery County in 1992, as well as Top Terrier in Canada in 1993.

daughter, *Ch. Regalridge Ain't She Loverly* in 1995. Lee is in the fortunate position of having access to many East Coast U.S. shows and many of her dogs have dual championships.

Canada has a geographical problem similar to that of Australia—too many hundreds of miles separate the very few breeders and even fewer dog shows! In spite of this kind of isolation, Mrs. Patricia Fleury (Cymro) of Saskatoon has done well in establishing a line, founded on two Bardwyn Welsh—*Ch. Bardwyn Powys o Cymro* and *Ch. Bardwyn Toby o Cymro*. A breeding to *Ch. Nathan von der Bismarckquelle* gave her two notable champions, one of them, *Ch. Cymro's Master of the Hunt*, going Best in Show and Best in Classic. The Classic is an invitational for all dogs who

Ch. Regalridge Here Comes Sparkle was the Number One Welsh in Canada in '89, '90, and '91, and top Canadian-bred bitch all time in point standings. "Sparkle" was also a top producer for Lee Stevens and Ken Curren.

Ch. Regalridge Lites Camera Action, Number One Wlesh in Canada in '92, '94, and '95. and top-winning Welsh in Canada all time in point standings, with the most Bests in Show. All the Regalridge dogs owned by Lee Steeves and Ken Curren are owner-handled.

have won a Group in the previous year. A bitch, *Ch. Cymro Mischievious* was Best Puppy In Show at the Puppy Classic.

Dogs from the States sometimes travel to Canadian shows (especially those on the two coasts), which can take on a love-hate relationship since the Canadian breeder-exhibitors have so few chances to make up champions and the "imports" are often top-winning dogs with top U.S. handlers. On the plus side, for some it is a learning experience in handling and grooming; for others it is at least an opportunity to get their hands on dogs other than their own.

Their club is in good shape now with an excellent newsletter resurrected by Pat Fleury to keep the spread-out membership informed and held together. Quite a few people from both sides of the boundary have membership in both U.S. and Canadian Clubs.

Breeder-owner handled by Pat Fleury, Ch. Cymro's Master of the Hunt is one of Canada's top Welsh in the ring and the sire of numerous champions.

CHAPTER EIGHT

PART I: BREEDING

"The winter will ask what we did in the summer."
—Old Welsh Gypsy saying

This will not be a "how-to" of breeding and whelping since there are several excellent books devoted to the subject, namely *The Standard Book of Dog Breeding—A New Look* by Dr. Alvin Grossman, and *Successful Dog Breeding* by Walkowicz & Wilcox, DVM. What follows is merely a commentary on the subject, with a few tips specifically pertaining to Welsh Terriers.

Welsh Terrier breeders have for many years coasted along on a wave of euphoria regarding the health of our dogs, and the ease with which they breed, conceive, and whelp, producing healthy pups with stable temperaments. Compared to numerous other breeds we are still riding that wave. But due to our small gene pool and to the increase in novice breeders and, simultaneously, the decrease in larger lifetime linebreeding kennels, no one should be complacent about our past and present good fortune.

The quality and variety of dog foods now covering every stage of growth, dietary problem, or gourmet preference, have generally improved the health of all purebred dogs. Veterinary care has escalated, especially in the areas of research and specialization, which has led to the identification of diseases, disorders, and abnormalities that were unknown fifty years ago. Along with those findings, have come more tests, cures and preventatives. Every discovery is heralded via the dog magazines, newsletters, seminars, symposia, and computer chat-rooms, but in spite of our ability to recognize more defects, the overall health of the Welsh Terrier still comes out ahead when judged against every other breed.

Keep in mind that *all* breeds have the *potential* for any of the genetic defects found in any *one* breed. The future of our dogs always has and always will lie in the present, in the hands of responsible breeders who would not breed any dog or bitch known to carry a genetic (physical or behavioral) defect.

The Breeders' Code of Ethics

In 1974, Jack Kimmel (Tujays) suggested a code of ethics for the entire Welsh Terrier Club of America membership. That basic idea did not take hold, his idea finally became a reality in 1998. A copy of the breeder's code of ethics can be found in the Appendix.

Begin with the Bitch

Ask anyone who has been successful in breeding quality dogs over an extended period of time where to begin and you'll be told, "Always start with the best-bred bitch you can afford." Look carefully between the lines here: "The best-bred." Not the prettiest, not the winningest, not the most expensive. No. The best-bred bitch is from an established line that consistently produces healthy, sound, typey offspring with correct temperaments. The best-bred bitch is one whose siblings, sire, and dam are of good quality, free of genetic defects, and whose sire, dam, and grandparents were producers of quality get. *That's* the bitch you're looking for! The only problem with that advice today is that there are so few "established lines" in which to find her.

Linebreeding

Linebreeding is a long-term endeavor and it pays in many ways to start off by buying judiciously into an established one. An exceptional stud dog or bitch (one that produces consistent type and quality) is used over and over again. That name will appear on both

A theoretical pedigree showing the development of linebreeding.

```
                                              Stuff & Such
                              Holiday Such
                                              Holiday
               Holiday Supreme
                                              Winners Supreme
                              Supreme Enough
                                              Sure Enough
        Gene Surprise
                                              Hot Stuff
                              Dear Stuff
                                              Liza Dear
               Super Dear
                                              Winners Supreme
                              Super Sure Enough
                                              Sure Enough


                                              Holiday Such
                              Holiday Supreme
                                              Supreme Enough
               Gene Surprise
                                              Best Bet
                              Super Dear
                                              Winners Bet
        Gena Gena
                                              Best Bet
                              Winners Supreme
                                              Winners Bet
               Super Sure Enough
                                              Holiday Such
                              Sure Enough
                                              Supreme Enough
```

sides of the pedigree. A dog and a bitch that "nick" (produce out-standing pups) will also appear on the pedigree several times. Linebreeding is the cautious, continuous development of what becomes the "stamp" of the line—and always heading toward that elusive, "perfect" specimen. The kennel Licken Run had it, as did Groveview, and so for many years have Felstead, High Flyer, and more recently, Purston. You can look at a class of dogs in the ring and pick out the dogs from a specific kennel by their "stamp" or signature, be it head, color, substance, or size.

Inbreeding

Inbreeding is often confused with linebreeding. In fact, father-to-daughter, or mother-to-son is considered by some to be inbreeding, by others to be linebreeding. However, the breeding of siblings or half-siblings is definitely inbreeding and is done for one of two reasons: either to concentrate the genes of a superior dog or, more commonly, to expose problem recessive genes. Faulty recessive genes doubled-up by inbreeding become obvious, whereas in outcrossing they can remain silent and unseen in the individuals carrying them (to say nothing of passing them on). The get of such an experimental inbreeding are neutered, or, in many cases are put down. *Inbreeding will not, and cannot, <u>create</u> abnormalities.* This is a persistent old wives' tale.

The responsibility for spreading both the good and bad within the breed lies primarily with the stud dog because, whereas the bitch may have four or five litters in a lifetime, the stud dog may service that many bitches in a month. One gorgeous (phenotype) stud dog carrying genetic flaws (his genotype) can permeate a large segment of the breeding stock in no time at all with recessive genes when the gene pool of a breed is limited, as ours is. He may be used extensively because he's magnificent to behold or has numerous Bests in Show, but if he carries recessive genes for glaucoma, Legge-Perthes, etc., he will cause long-term damage to the breed's gene pool. Obviously, you want typey specimens for breeding and you're going to want that magnificent stud dog. However, a decent dog with some slight flaw in beauty (a tad long in body, not quite enough neck, etc.) but healthy, sound, and with a good temperament, and who is free of *genetic* defects, is far and away a worthier stud dog than his phenotypically more handsome but genetically impaired counterpart.

Outcross

Outcrossing is the breeding of a totally unrelated dog and bitch. There may be a connection somewhere generations back, but only if the outcross is from one *line* to another *line* can you hazard a guess at the resulting offspring. A totally unrelated outcross is a hope-for-the-best breeding. Many small breeders back themselves into a corner in keeping, say, a stud dog that can't be used on resident bitches or vice versa. It's easy to see that the large kennels have a definite advantage in working with all three methods! Every outcross waters down the gene pool, just as linebreeding strengthens it.

"Paper" Breeding

A big mistake made by the novice breeder today is the reasoning behind taking their bitch to a "winner." The neophyte thinks that the name of a big winner on a pedigree will sell puppies—and possibly it may when selling to pet buyers. The more serious mistake, however, lies in thinking that somehow the "Big Name" will pave the way to instant stardom for the breeder. It most certainly won't; we all must pay our dues.

Unless you have gone over the dogs yourself, or at least know them by sight and by what they've produced, a pedigree is merely a list of names. Pedigrees are more useful to the breeder in trying to trace a specific fault or attribute, a health problem or other single thing you are attempting to pinpoint. The answer to "Where did this horrible coat come from?" may well be found in the pedigree, but *only* if you know the dogs, not just the names.

These family trees are indispensable to historians in tracking down a certain dog or breeder or for compiling statistics. However, beware of breeding "on paper." It's a fun exercise in the midst of a blizzard when no bitch is due in season for six months,

A pedigree leaning toward "winners."

                                    Ch. Zacharias, CD
                        Ch.Sorreisa's Six And A Tanner
                                    Ch. Groveview Allgo
            Ch. Anasazi Trail Boss
                                    Ch. Tujay's Touchdown
                        Ch.Windsong Helter Skelter
                                    Ch. Chayna Laird's Lady

                                    Int. Ch. Bengal Wiredot Welsh Prince
                        Ch.Norlake's Bachelor
                                    Janterrs Regal Norlake
            Ch. Moore Tommy's Teensi Bowag
                                    Ch. Penzance Polaris
                        Bowag's Pocahontas
                                    Schwer's Lady of the Lake

but merely that. Pedigrees are also a great source of names for your next litter.

If you can't get your hands on the stud dog's offspring yourself, ask someone other than the breeder or owner about the dog, someone whose opinion you value for a candid appraisal. And take into account the bitches that produced the various offspring. Just don't rely on the bit of paper—even if all the "Ch"s are in red ink. Look at it "genetically." Each dog carries fifty percent of the genes from each parent, twenty-five percent from each grandparent and twelve and a half percent from each great-grandparent. It's not worth considering anything further back UNLESS there has been tight linebreeding and one sire or dam well known to you appears consistently. Here the pedigrees are of some help, because the more outcrosses you see, the less chance that the dog or bitch will breed true to its own conformation.

The Final Analysis

While the evaluation of type, soundness, and temperament

is important, of even more concern is which come from the sire, and which from the dam. And since we are discussing Welsh Terriers, not Toy Poodles, the ultimate question is: are all the dogs in question—sire, dam and get—capable of performing the breed's intended function? That is, do they have the form, stamina, temperament, and intelligence that enables the Welsh Terrier to go to ground or to spend a day hunting above ground with handlers and other dogs.

The Welsh Terrier Club of America's Constitution is very specific about this: "The objects of the Club shall be: (a) to encourage and promote quality in the breeding of pure-bred Welsh Terriers <u>and to do all possible to bring their natural working qualities to perfection</u>" (emphasis mine). The emphasis here is definitely on function. Over time, the majority of Welsh Terriers became either show dogs or pets, but the current trend is back to bringing out our dogs' intelligence and "natural working qualities." To do all possible to bring them to perfection is the challenge. When I think of breeding for form and/or function, I am reminded of a line from the Welsh poet, Gwyn Thomas, "The beauty is in the walking. We are betrayed by destinations." Breeding solely for show dogs is a dream sport.

Is there anything cuter than puppies? These two look like they're doing some early Brace Class Training.

Genetics

There are a lot of considerations in breeding, but today, with our greatly expanded knowledge of genes and chromosomes, much of the guesswork has been removed. The old saying, "Breed the best to the best and hope for the best" is only partially true (at best). It's what you consider, or are willing to accept, as "best" in any given area that will produce superior, satisfactory, or mediocre results. Much of the planning of a breeding is, like judging, in the eye of the beholder. Right or wrong, breeders, like everyone else, sometimes fall for a handsome dog. Beware the trap!

Keep the *whole* dog in mind, what you can readily see and what you can't. Breeding for any specific trait will most assuredly backfire. For example, breed a small bitch to a large dog, while hoping for the best, or all medium-sized offspring, and you will get both small and tall in the litter. The chances of getting all "middlings" are remote in the extreme. All pups will inherit half their genes from each parent. And if you should luck out and get one pup of perfect size, it, too, will carry genes for both large and small. It takes many generations of careful linebreeding to get consistency in specifics.

In a show bitch, femininity is most desirable. The slightly finer-boned bitch, with a slightly more refined head and body, while still of Welsh substance, is preferred in the show ring because it looks distinctly feminine next to the male. But what is referred to as the "peasant type" of bitch often makes the better brood bitch simply because she is sturdier and bigger-boned, and with this build will probably carry her pups more easily and have an easier time whelping than her somewhat more refined counterpart. She will not necessarily pass on her more robust look to all her offspring. The preferred stud dog is totally masculine, often referred to as "stallion-like." Our breed standard calls for substance and that doesn't come from refined stock.

Temperament is dependent upon several things. Part is hereditary (and not through a single gene, but from a complex combination of genes); part is environmental, which includes the dam's capabilities as mother and disciplinarian, gentle handling from day one, and the socialization of young pups with people and other dogs.

Frozen Semen

The use of frozen or fresh-chilled semen might be called, "how to succeed without really tying." One of the first Welsh Terrier litters from frozen semen were five pups whelped in 1989. The procedure from collection to insemination to AKC registration has been simplified somewhat. The AKC has also approved the use of imported frozen semen, but here the paperwork, import/export expense, delays at customs, the services of a qualified veterinarian, and timing it all with a bitch's estrus are almost insurmountable obstacles. However, considering how many Welsh Terriers are imported, it seems a pity not to take advantage of this not-so-terribly innovative procedure. (It's been around for use in cattle and zoo animals for many decades.)

Breeders in the States have not taken advantage of frozen or fresh-chilled semen as widely as one might have expected, given the great distances bitches must be shipped, the weather prohibitions, and the vagaries of airline schedules. And the added fact that bitches tend to "settle" better at home than in transit or mid-air. According to International Canine Genetics, Inc. (ICG), the success rate of fertilization with either frozen or fresh-chilled semen is on a par with that of natural breedings. It would seem wiser to use the "right" stud dog for a bitch via this method than to settle for a less desirable alternative based only on his geographic proximity.

Mating

Welsh Terrier bitches are equally divided into those that come in season (estrus) at six months and those that wait until nine or ten months of age. Thereafter, they either hold to every six months or continue on that nine- or ten-month cycle. Even a bitch that comes in season as late as a year old, should not be bred her first season.

Newcomers, anxious to accomplish the breeding, often make the mistake of trying to mate the bitch too early in her season. In talking to breeders worldwide, the consensus seems to be to breed later rather than sooner—the twelfth to sixteenth day, for example, rather than the ninth. However, we no longer need to guess, since there are test kits that will indicate the optimum moment. I am definitely in agreement with not hurrying a breeding. I had one bitch who, if you were still counting, was in her thirtieth day. She was mistakenly turned out with a stud dog and nine weeks later produced six lovely pups.

False pregnancies occur occasionally and are more of a nuisance than a worry because the bitch may lactate, "mother" toys, etc. The exact cause is unknown but could possibly be some sort of hormonal imbalance. In any case, the outcome is as much a mental affliction as a physical one, and nothing to be unduly concerned about. In other words, do not rush to the "hormone" cabinet. Silent heats, where there is no discharge or other outward signs of estrus, are occasionally encountered in Welsh. One or two such heats are often followed by a perfectly normal one.

Natural and herbal remedies, some similar to old wives' tales, abound and I once went along with feeding a bitch raspberry leaves from the day she was bred. The idea was it would ease the whelping and promised that all the pups would be born as fresh and aromatic as the raspberry patch. Needless to say, the whelping was normal and all the pups smelled as amniotic as every other newborn.

Welsh Terriers are free whelpers, meaning that most bitches do not require caesarean sections or other outside assistance to deliver their pups. Problems may occasionally occur, but there are no breed-specific problems, such as are encountered in many toy breeds, for example. An average litter runs anywhere from five to eight puppies, with their average weights ranging from six and a half to eight ounces. In the case of a whelping problem, veterinarians will invariably blame any difficulty on the fact that the pup is "so large." It is difficult to realize that eight ounces is normal for every one of six or seven pups out of a bitch, who herself weighs only eighteen to twenty pounds. Compared to Airedales, at fifty pounds with pups at ten ounces, it is indeed remarkable. The situation is compounded by the fact that veterinarians (at least in the U.S.) have very little practical training in whelping puppies. It's why we prize so highly that person we reverently refer to as a "breeder's vet."

The Stud Dog

Stud dogs can be divided into three categories.

1. The one that comes on like a gangbuster and needs to be restrained lest he flatten the bitch.
2. The reluctant, stud-dud with low self-esteem. Low self-esteem can be caused by using the artificial insemination method for the first matings. This is because for an artificial insemination, the vet or breeder manually stimulates the dog, and collects the semen in a sterile receptacle, which is then inserted into the bitch with a tube or syringe. (There's a good reason they call this "artificial"!) Artificial insemination is the method used when a mating can't take place naturally due to any number of reasons, including too great a distance for the bitch to travel, or after the demise of the stud dog and frozen semen is used. This method is also sometimes misused by an impatient breeder who doesn't care to wait with a stud dog that has forty-five-minute ties.
3. The gentleman who must be allowed time to say hello, sniff ears, etc.

The perfect stud dog is the gentleman who also has a built-in barometer that tells him precisely which day, and which hour, is "right."

Use an experienced stud dog on a virgin bitch and, conversely, a would-be stud dog should first be mated to an experienced bitch. It helps to have at least one of them know what they're doing.

Care of the Breeding Stock

It goes without saying that any dog or bitch in a breeding program must be kept in optimum health. The best of food, adequate exercise, and regular veterinary checkups. Before the bitch comes in season, immunizations should be brought up-to-date; she should be given a thorough vet exam, brucellosis test, and a diet plan to cover the nine weeks of pregnancy.

Antibiotics and certain inoculations, while curing a bitch's infection, can cause problems for nursing pups as they become second-hand recipients of the medication. Keep her healthy!

Brucellosis is a bacterial disease that can cause sterility, abortion, or failure to whelp. Since it is easily transmitted at the time of mating, owners of stud dogs generally now require a brucellosis test before accepting a bitch for breeding. There are many symptoms of the disease, but a dog or bitch may also show no symptoms whatsoever, making it a silent destroyer Once detected, all animals in the kennel must be tested to stop the spread.

Pyometra is a serious uterine infection. Pyometra not only precludes breeding a bitch, it can be fatal if left untreated. The visible symptom is a discharge of thick, bloody, and foul smelling pus from the vulva. Another form of the infection is called "closed-cervix" pyometra because the pus is retained in the uterus. Symptoms for both include lethargy, a loss of appetite, increased thirst, and frequent urination. There may also be vomiting and fever. A pregnant bitch will abort. If caught in time, pyometra can be treated; if not, the infected uterus must be removed.

PART II—PUPPIES

"To whelp" means to bring forth, but in Middle English a "whelp" referred to a saucy or impertinent fellow who was also appropriately called "a puppy." In 1589 the verb "to puppy" came briefly into use, but the verb "to whelp," and "whelp" the noun, continue to be used in reference to birthing bitches and their pups.

From personal observation, I have found that evaluating the whelps as soon as the sack is removed and the pup is still soaking wet, is the optimum (albeit fleeting) moment to see skeletal structure. A few minutes later when the pup is dry, nursing, and has begun to fill out is too late. In those few soaking wet seconds, you can see shoulder layback, length of loin, length of neck, angulation of the quarters, and the Roman nose that promises good length of muzzle. Don't dillydally—another pup may arrive in the meantime—but do try this early assessment. And don't hang your hat on a certain pup to be pick of litter! It's just one way to hone your skills of observation.

Some bitches have a tendency to cut the umbilical cord too close, resulting in a hernia. So, interfere as little as possible with a delivery, but be prepared to cut the cord (leaving an inch or more), to push back the sack from around the head of the pup quickly, and to ease out the afterbirth. I've never had a problem in assisting a Welsh Terrier bitch (even those totally strange to me) but *after* the pups arrive and are nursing can be another matter entirely! It's normal and instinctive, and even has a name—maternal aggression. Be calm, quiet, pleasant, and firm—and use delectable tidbits freely in your approach.

A Puppy Life-Saver

It's not unusual to have one or more of the pups do poorly in the first twenty-four to forty-eight hours. As soon as you suspect a pup is losing ground—not nursing, listless, even lifeless—get out the beef-liver and yogurt. I once printed this recipe in the *AKC Gazette* and have since been asked to repeat it several times. Word of its success came from breeders of everything from Pekes to Great Danes! Make it up while you're waiting for those contractions to start.

Put trimmed, raw beef liver into the food processor until it is pureed (with a spoon, remove any bits or lumps). Refrigerate a small amount and freeze the rest. (Using an ice cube tray will make thawing easier.) Warm about a teaspoon of the liver and stir slightly into an equal amount of plain yogurt at room temperature. Feed it to the pup from your little finger. The first several times, the pup will take very little. (If you have to pry open the mouth, only put a tiny amount on the tongue.) This is *not* a replacement for the bitch's milk, but strictly a supplement. Now give the rest to the dam. That part is very important, as you will soon see. Keep it up every two hours. If the pup is reluctant to nurse, rub a tiny amount of the liver mixture on a teat. Be sure to check the pup for a short tongue, which makes nursing impossible.

Here is the chain of events that invariably takes place to save these fading pups. The yogurt is a natural source of lactobacillus acidophilus (a form of lactic-acid which is an essential ingredient in the bitch's milk). The liver is high in minerals and vitamins. By giving the delicious leftovers to the dam, she also gets a small, top-quality treat and invariably licks the yummy stuff from around the pup's mouth (and wherever else it has landed no matter how careful you try to be), which in turn stimulates the pup. The dam quickly makes the connection and begins to single out that pup as "special" giving it VIP treatment, keeping it close, prodding it to nurse, etc. All of which results in dramatic improvement often within twenty-four to thirty-six hours.

The puppies all need the colostrum (the bitch's first milk) for temporary immunity, so reach for the beef liver-yogurt formula before you start supplementing with a milk substitute. It is said that more newborns die than are saved from the eye-dropper or toy nursing bottles methods of supplemental feeding. Tube feeding (gavage) is the safest way to save an orphaned litter or whelps that for any reason can't nurse.

Newborn Welsh puppies are almost completely black.

Totally Personal Statistics!

Some breeders are very concerned about birth weight and what it portends for the future. Here is a chart to indicate how small a part birth weight can play. It is not a scientific study, but just from my own records of one litter.

Birth	2 Weeks	4 Weeks	6 Weeks	Maturity
(b) 7.5 oz	14 oz	2 lbs 8 oz	4 lbs	16 lbs
(d) 8 oz	1 lbs 8 oz	2 lbs 15 oz	4 lbs 14 oz	25 lbs
(d) 5 oz	1 lbs 1 oz	2 lbs 1 oz	4 lbs	23 lbs
(b) 10 oz	2 lbs	3 lbs 6 oz	5 lbs	20 lbs

The tiny male was a liver/yogurt beneficiary. The big bitch had completely slowed down by five months. But note how they were leveling out by six weeks. There are two stages of growth when a new breeder thinks they have produced the perfect dog. At about seven weeks of age, a Welsh Terrier pup is a "box" (as tall as long) and then again at about twelve weeks of age they hit the magic cube: height twelve inches, length twelve inches and weight twelve pounds. Just all part of a normal growth pattern. At six or seven weeks they are "nice pups." At twelve to sixteen weeks, there may be one or two that "show promise." At a year or more, you can say, with some assurance "that one is a show prospect."

And Puppy Dogs' Tails

Centuries ago in Europe, hunting with dogs was the sport of nobility and it was the nobles themselves who felt a long tail was essential to a good hunting dog and thus placed a huge tax on these hounds. Owners of some of the lowly terriers that controlled vermin (and an occasionally provided a rabbit for the table) couldn't afford the tax so they docked the tails and discovered that it didn't hamper the animals' hunting ability at all. In fact, they found that the short tail had many advantages, one of which was that it provided a convenient "handle" for extricating the dog from the underground habitats of prey.

At this writing, bans on tail docking led by animal activists in various countries are undergoing reconsideration and, in certain cases, complete withdrawal. In 1991 a Council of Docked Breeds was formed to defend the docking option in the U.K. Steadfast work under the guidance of Mr. Drys Thomas (Philtown) has brought the matter factually and truthfully to the public and the powers-that-be. When the ban is indeed lifted in Europe and no longer poses a threat to docked breeds in the rest of the world, we can all thank Drys for gathering countless numbers of signed petitions, making television appearances, radio broadcasts, speaking to clubs, and writing a barrage of articles.

Welsh Terriers' tails are docked, but how it is done involves myriad methods, each with its own advocates to accomplish the very minor surgery. My father used one of the easiest methods, common in his day, which is to bite off the tip and press the tongue against the end of the tail; the pressure and saliva effectively sealed the cut. Not for the squeamish, but maybe someday if you're caught without any sharp instrument other than your teeth, you'll know it is possible.

There are other methods, including using rubber bands, twisting off the tip, or tying a gauze or string tourniquet where you will cut. Given my large hands and whelps' tiny tails, I found all of these methods to be too complicated.

When

Tails are docked (and dewclaws removed) on the third or fourth day, when the tiny vertebrae are still soft and unformed. One important point needs to be stressed: Dock the tails and remove dewclaws on *each* and *every* whelp, regardless of its size, stamina, or rate of progress. The small "trauma" incurred is often the exact stimulus to the system that is needed to get that one on its feet, so to speak. If not done by the third or fourth day, tail docking and dewclaw removal become major surgery and must be postponed until the pup is old enough to tolerate anesthesia.

Veterinarians can create a *cause celebre* out of the surgery, making flaps, putting in stitches, etc., but the most important part of docking tails on Welsh Terriers is simply measuring correctly! If the tails are cut too short, it doesn't really matter what docking method was used. What follows is my personal tried-and-true procedure from start to finish. And it might surprise you to know how many veterinarians I've shown it to who now swear by it for Welsh, Fox, and Lakelands!

The Dam Comes First

Begin, not with the pups, but with the dam. Her pups are only three or four days old and she is naturally apprehensive if you

try to take them away. A nursing bitch doesn't need
stress. Put her outside, or in a crate with her dinner, while you
remove a couple of pups to wherever you'll do the tail docking.
Just be sure to make it as far from that whelping box as you can
manage, and turn up the radio or TV for good measure. When those
two pups have been done and you've checked to be sure there's no
bleeding, return them to the whelping box, remove the rest of the
litter, and return the dam to the first two pups.

The Tools

You won't need much. A small box or basket lined with a
clean white towel over a heating pad or hot water bottle to keep the
pups warm. (A white towel makes it easier to see any bleeding
should it occur.) Cover the box with another towel if the room is
cool.

- A surgical clamp, which is called a "hemostat" with
  straight ends, like the kind you'd use for removing
  hair from the ears, and a locking device on the handles.
- Styptic powder, the same as you use when cutting
  nails.
- A new single-edged razor blade.
- A white towel or sheet on a waist-high surface
  under a good light where the pups can be placed to
  measure tails.

Having a second person is a must. It's a good time for a
trainee or novice breeder to learn, and another pair of warm hands
to comfort each pup can't hurt. Besides, it's nice to have someone
to chat with and to admire your work. After all, even Frankenstein
had his Igor.

Measuring

Hold the puppy's head in one hand and place the puppy on the table with its feet touching the towel or sheet. Slide the fingers of your other hand down from the tip over the tail to hold it in what would be a "show pose." At this point, most whelps object vocally and strenuously, so hold gently but firmly. Squat down until you're eye-level with the pup and move your fingers down from the tip of the tail to a point that is on a horizontal plane with the backskull, even if the legs have given out and the pup is now on its belly. See the illustrations below for measuring.

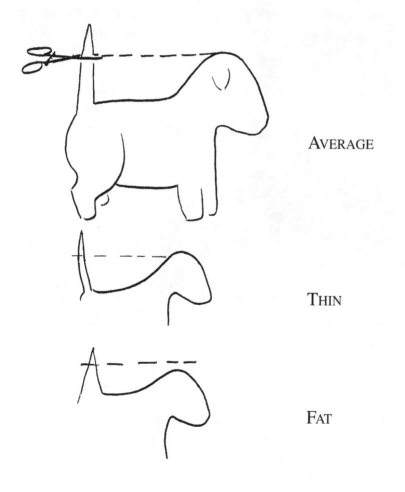

AVERAGE

THIN

FAT

Do __not__ exaggerate the "show pose" in any way. You are not trying to impress a judge. You may <u>wish</u> the pup had a longer neck, but if you extend it now, the result will be an adult Welsh with an average neck and a too-long tail.

An average tail will probably need to have a little less than one-third removed. A whippy, skinny tail will continue to grow more than a short fat one, so you will take a *fraction more* off the skinny one, and a *fraction less* off the fat one. The old adage, "measure twice, cut once" was never more true than in docking tails. If you've never seen it done, visit as many Welsh Terrier breeders as you can to observe and participate. Measuring takes practice, but don't give up. And

Typical Welsh Terrier puppies, at five weeks.

don't despair either when at five weeks of age the tails all look too short—they'll catch up!

Docking

Hold your fingers in the "right" spot and apply the clamp right up against them. (The clamp should be between your fingers and the dog's rump. If your fingers are between the clamp and the dog's rump, you've got it backwards. Remember, the clamp should still be attached to the dog after you've made your cut.) Close the clamp in one steady firm motion. The clamp will probably lock into the first or second ratchet on the handle. At this point you are <u>not</u> cutting the tail, but merely applying a tourniquet that's easy to manage.

Now run the razor blade straight across, against the *upper side* of the clamp, removing the tip of the tail. *Do not remove the clamp yet.* Dab a generous pinch of styptic powder on the cut, and with the clamp still in place, curl the tail down around the pup's rump in a natural position. Hold the clamp steady for about a minute (a minute and one-half for a fat tail), keeping the pup warm and secure in your hands. Then very slowly—to be sure there is no bleeding—begin to release the clamp. There should not be one drop of blood. If there is, dab on more styptic powder and keep an eye on that pup to be sure the bleeding stops.

It is essential to point out a phenomenon that affects the novice or trainee witnessing this for the first time. The scenario (the whole Frankenstein image comes in very handy here) goes like this: The pup screams its head off and struggles mightily as you try to hold it in show pose—and the trainee is ready to faint. You explain what the pup is actually upset about, which is simply being held in this unfamiliar position, and pick up the clamp. At this point the trainee mutters, "Oh, I don't think I can watch." Then there is quiet and the novice, who hasn't even noticed the razor blade, now says, "Okay, let me know when you're going to cut, because I don't want to watch!" or "Gosh, I can't stand the sight of blood." You show them the tip you have already silently removed and the reaction is a wide-eyed "Wow!"

Dewclaws are done next, but see the paragraph below on removing them.

Next!

Put that pup into the prepared warm box and remove the

next one. If you should notice any bleeding as you go along, pinch the tip between your fingers for a moment and
dab on more styptic powder. However, I would remind you again that there is usually no bleeding whatsoever with this procedure. After a couple are done, and there's no bleeding, put them back with the dam and check again after they are all back with her because she may be too vigorous in cleaning them. By this time, most bitches are only interested in counting noses and the pups are only interested in their next meal.

Dewclaws

Most Welsh Terriers have dewclaws on the front legs, and some have them on the rear. These are the small extra toes (complete with nails) that are found on the back of the front legs above the feet, and on the inside of the hind legs below the hocks. Be sure to check for those back ones. It's major surgery if discovered later. Normally they are removed at the same time as tails (tail first, then dewclaws on each pup), but only if you know how. Until you have learned how to do this from someone with excellent credentials, take the pups to your veterinarian the same or next day. And please ask that no stitches be used! I have never heard of a dewclaw on a Welsh Terrier so large that it required stitches.

As with docking tails, never let this minor surgery go beyond the fourth day. After that and it ceases to be minor.

This is one area where the old-timers (i.e. experienced breeders) can do the novice breeders a great service by inviting them to watch tails being done. In teaching new people with a real interest in the breed, much emphasis is placed on grooming, handling, and showing. But once the talk turns to breeding, Tails 101 is a good class with which to begin. Watching a whelping is good for beginners, too, but too often it's a midnight watch. There's a lot more to being "in dogs" than playing with warm puppies. That's just one of the rewards for going through the rest of it.

Culling—Cruelty or Kindness?

One of the toughest decisions for breeders to tackle is the matter of culling. Mother Nature has been successfully using the method for millions of years to refine all living species. Emlyn Snow (Felstead) said that ruthless culling at the beginning is what produced the Welsh Terrier of today and he feels it is now up to our judges in the show ring to have the knowledge and integrity to be ruthless in the placing (or "culling") of our breed. Some find it hard just to accept the *word* because somewhere along the way, culling got a bad rap. The word simply means "to sort out." It's what we pay the judge to do at every dog show, after all—to sort out the best among the entrants. It's what every ethical breeder does with every litter.

Culling a litter at birth does include putting down a defective pup. And all litters must be culled at birth to maintain the health and welfare of our breed. Then at two, three, five, ten weeks, or at any time along the way, a pup with a physical or mental defect should also be put down. (At the vet's. Held in your hands. Tears are okay, too.)

Physical defects include any disabling deformity or any known defect that would preclude *top quality life as a pet*. This does not mean breed standard disqualifications such as white feet or hound-like ears. Such disabling deformities include an abnormal heart or lung, achalasia, or epilepsy. Mental retardation is easy to spot early on; the pup is dull, spacey and is completely ignored or constantly picked upon by its littermates. All these problems exacerbate as the pup matures. No one should be asked to purchase or give foster care to such a defective pet and no responsible breeder wants their kennel name on such a dog. It is the duty of every responsible, ethical breeder to take prompt action to cull defects. This culling is kindness.

There is another type of culling altogether. Apart from sorting out defects, culling is exactly what every breeder does in determining which pup is the pick of litter, which might be a flyer, and

Welsh Terrier bitches are generally good mothers and excellent teachers.

This one's getting a little rough and might be about to get his first lesson!

which ones are definitely not destined for the show ring or breeding program. That is also culling.

All breeders are culling again when they decide how the pups will be registered. Which will it be—with limited (non-breeding) registration or with full breeding rights? That is also culling. Next time someone speaks out against culling, remind them that culling is the major means of safeguarding our breed.

Raising Healthy Puppies

Occasionally I hear of a litter of pups being taken off the bitch at three weeks and I can only wonder what went wrong, or what's the rush. The dam is not just a food machine, she is the teacher of all things canine. As soon as the pups' eyes and ears are open (at about two weeks), they need to be handled gently and spoken to softly to establish a positive association with humans, but for many weeks to come they will be learning all day every day to be dogs. Litter learning is so important that a solitary pup should be put in with a foster litter if at all possible. The challenges that begin as rough and tumble play are lessons for each individual pup, as every action is met with a positive or negative reaction by littermates. As the ultimate disciplinarian, the dam has the final word. Welsh are notably good mothers. She holds no grudge, nor does she nag. The breeder, and then the new owner, take over—we hope—with the same criteria.

By the end of three weeks, the pups are bobbling around like tipsy sailors and exhibiting their short-lived ability to back up at top speed, only to collapse in the attempt to go forward. The first "fearful" stage occurs at about four weeks (and then again at eight), so at five weeks, I introduce them to interaction with me, sitting on the kitchen floor. This lets me evaluate the pups, which pup is cautious, calm, boisterous, confident, sweet, curious, clinging, or independent. (More culling!)

When they are brave enough to leave me and go exploring, it's time to begin teaching them to "come" using "puppy, puppy, puppy" until all have run back. This is an ideal time to begin training pups, because they are still litter-ally minded! After a few days of this, I stand up as they approach and we play follow the leader, ending every play session with this rather silly Mother Goose "puppy, puppy, puppy" come/heeling exercise back to their pen. Praise at this stage is simply your warm and cheery voice.

The first individual lesson my pups learn is to stand on command. There are numerous perks to this: The dog will stack on a

An example of "puppy, puppy, puppy," or the heeling exercise as taught by the dam.

loose lead; a pup that's on a "stand" command can't jump up, and the stand is harder to teach later on. You can get stands with eager faces and wagging tails, starting at about six weeks of age with the most dominant pup. Let him play for a few minutes then call him to you. This time, as he approaches, offer a curd of cottage cheese and say, "stand." By the third try, the pup usually has caught on. Hold your fingers down so he arches his neck nicely—a six-week-old show pose. Pawing or jumping up meets with a closed hand, no treat. Every couple of days, teach another one, until the entire litter will "stand."

If you line them up, the pups invariably look up and down the line to be sure no one is cheating. Puppies that are six to eight weeks old are virtual sponges for education, all done by positive reinforcement. Obviously this is no guarantee of an obedience degree, but the whole point of such an exercise is to encourage very young pups _how to learn_ from people. Then at seven to eight weeks, another "fearful" period emerges. That is why many breeders now hold back on selling pups until they are over it, say at ten weeks.

An outdoor puppy obstacle course teaches such things as agility and playing hide-and-seek, which often entails entering small dark places with caution (a littermate may be hiding in there) but without fear. On a safari in the garden, a seven-week-old pup that came out from under a bush with a mole in her mouth went on to become the first Welsh Terrier to earn a Certificate of Gameness from the American Working Terrier Association. Native skills need exposure for development.

Puppies also need to be with people, although screen children. The right children are great socializers, the wrong ones are a disaster. Welsh Terrier pups accept a collar and leash at eight weeks, especially if at first you follow the pup around, then revert to that "puppy, puppy, puppy" bit for changing direction to go your way.

Early crate training has lifelong benefits—safety in travel by car or plane, and stress-free boarding in kennel or veterinary hospital, for starters.

Crate Training

At about six weeks when the pups are almost weaned, a good den for them is a VariKennel® (the plastic crate) with the door removed. They can pile in for comfort and warmth and will forever have a good feeling about being crated. By eight weeks, they can graduate to two pups per crate with the door closed at night. Before going to its new home, a pup should sleep for several nights alone in a crate.

It is then easy for the new owner to continue using the crate at night, taking the pup outside first thing in the morning to eliminate as the start for housetraining. No pup—especially an active, robust Welsh Terrier—should be confined to a crate again during the day for more than two or three hours. If the pup must be left alone longer than that, an exercise pen with newspapers, a water bowl, toys—and the crate with the door open—are a must for the protection of household furnishings and the longevity of the dog as a family member!

Food

Every breeder has his or her puppy-formulated food of choice and with so many on the market today, most of them excellent, take your choice. Puppies used to be weaned on baby cereal and milk, but the trend today is toward soaked puppy food, since cow's milk can sometimes cause diarrhea. (Come to think of it, some Welsh can't assimilate chicken or turkey, while others thrive on it.) Cottage cheese, plain yogurt, and an occasional cooked egg are good things to add to the pup's food. Some things, such as vegetables, can wait until the pup is 4 or 5 months old. Dogs are particularly fond of tripe which is not available

"Snacking on the run" is one indication of when to begin weaning pups.

as dog food in the U.S. Fish, completely free of bones, is another welcome nutritional change from meat. All new foods should be introduced gradually and in small amounts to prevent digestive upsets.

In *Canine Nutrition—Choosing the Best Food for Your Breed*, which looks at the nutritional needs of dogs based on the food available where they were originally bred, Bill Cusick recommends "foods that are a blend of fish, mutton, poultry, corn, wheat, and potatoes." He also warns against feeding "horse meat, avocado, citrus fruit, or white rice" to Welsh Terriers.

Healthy Puppies

It goes without saying (or should) that any puppy showing any sign of illness should see the veterinarian immediately. *Instantly!* Debilitation is quick in a puppy and there's no time for a let's-wait-and-see attitude.

When the pups are six to eight weeks of age, it's time for a complete veterinary examination. The dam may be checked after the pups are born, or now when they are weaned. Initially the pups enjoy immunity from disease through maternal antibodies provided via the placenta and the mother's milk. Unfortunately, these antibodies are disease-specific and not only protect against certain diseases, but also against the vaccine. The period between the time the maternal antibodies wear off and the pup's own immunity (or the vaccine's) can take over varies from puppy to puppy within the litter. It is called the "window of vulnerability," a critical time to avoid exposing puppies to disease, even the weakened forms of diseases used in vaccines. The problem is, there is no way to ascertain precisely when each pup is undergoing these changes, so we immunize and take the chance of rejection.

Immunizations are seemingly endless. I call them alphabet soup—DHLPP (5-in-1) or DHLPPC, plus a new one or two every year. But they are essential for maintaining healthy stock. The initials stand for Distemper, viral Hepatitis, Leptospirosis, Parainfluenza, Parvovirus and Coronavirus. Veterinarians have established schedules for administering these inoculations over a period of months, usually beginning at eight weeks. Rabies vaccine is usually not given before six months of age, but a year later can be given in one shot that lasts three years. Here is a sample schedule for immunizations:

7–9 weeks	DHLPP + Measles vaccine
10–12 weeks	DHLPP-C
13–15 weeks	DHLPP-C
16–18 weeks	DHLPP
19–21 weeks	Parvovirus & Rabies

Teeth

Our breed standard requires the dogs to have full dentition in a scissor or level bite. Teeth need to be watched closely, first to be sure they all come in, that the bite is correct, and then that they fall out in time to allow the second teeth to come through properly. Missing teeth in the adult mouth is a genetic flaw and only long-term careful breeding will correct the problem.

NORMAL

The puppy, or milk, teeth come in between three and six weeks of age with fourteen (six incisors, two canines, and six pre-molars) in the lower jaw and the same fourteen in the upper. They are replaced by permanent teeth starting at about three months. Teething can go on until the puppy is almost a year old, although it often *seems* much longer. There are forty-two adult teeth. The lower jaw has six incisors, two canines, eight pre-molars, and six molars. The upper jaw has only twenty teeth (there are only four molars).

OVERSHOT

The bite can be seen as early as six or eight weeks, but can change anytime during the first year. To check the

UNDERSHOT

bite, don't look at the incisors. Look at the molars from the side. In a normal jaw, the upper pre-molar is centered in the gap between the lower pre-molars. Overshot will have the upper pre-molar in front, undershot it will be behind. That slight gap leads some people to believe the dog is missing a tooth. It is normal.

Ears

There's nothing you can do about the placement of ears. They are where they are and that's that. But it is possible to improve the fold of the ears if they are set prior to the hardening of the cartilage, or between eight to twelve weeks of age. One way to do this, after cleaning the inside, is to apply surgical glue (or Copydex®) along the lower edge of the flap, fold the ear in the right place, and glue the lower triangle of the flap to the head. The flaps will be rather close together on top of the head. When released they will fall naturally to the sides of the cheeks. Another way is to put a strip of freezer tape, sticky side out, around the head where the ear flaps will be placed. Glue as before, putting the tips on the tape. Then put a second strip of tape, sticky side down, over the first.

But before tackling *any* of this, consult two or three breeders or professional handlers who know exactly where the fold should be and where to put the ear tips—or you could be trading a bad situation for a worse one.

Training and Behavior

Here again, there are so many excellent books devoted to training and behavior modification that I won't go into it at any length here. There are, however, a few things that might be considered breed-specific.

For example, a Welsh Terrier should never be trained or taught by using harsh corrections. Welsh aren't stubborn, as some trainers avow, but are just politely waiting for you to calm down and show them what it is you have in mind. Maybe they're just saying, "Could you repeat that in Welsh, please?" *Show* a puppy what it is you want, give it praise (and a treat for good measure) when it gets it right, and simply start over again if the pup didn't get it. Keep this one in mind: Dogs as we know them have been dogs for thousands of years, but the one you are working with has only been a dog for a matter of weeks! Patience.

Kindergarten Puppy Training is excellent for socializing a pup with dogs and people who are all strangers. Classes are for puppies up to five months of age, but the sooner, the better. It is amazing how few puppies destined for a life on the show circuit are given the opportunity to be puppies, to be silly, to be played with and taught games, not just how to stand on a table, hold a show pose and trot briskly "down and back."

I admit to being unimpressed by Temperament Testing. I've noted very strange results with puppies being tested by someone who did not understand a terrier's basic attitude toward life, and perhaps the same could be said of a terrier person testing hounds. I feel the Welsh Terrier breeder might do better taking the time to learn to evaluate the pups himself. But, for those who swear by the tests, if it helps you understand the dog and helps the dog get off to a better start, so be it.

Two pictures of the same puppy, showing how the black markings recede from 6 to 12 weeks of age.

PART III—HEALTH

We are extremely fortunate that our breed has very, very few health problems. There are even some who believe we don't have any at all. They can be forgiven their optimism since the ones we do have are of the general canine variety and not breed-specific. In other words, there are few inherited health defects in Welsh and those that are congenital or acquired seem to appear with about the same frequency in Welsh as in the majority of other breeds. Genetic defects that do surface should never be dismissed as mere "flukes." If it's in the genes, and shows up in the offspring, the dog or bitch should not be bred again and, in some cases, nor should any of the get. Hereditary health or behavioral disorders need to be ranked much higher on your list of what not to breed than the "beauty points" such as imperfect ear or tail sets. You can always go for the aesthetics after you have established healthy breeding stock.

Achalasia (dilated esophagus) was described by my vet as a two–way stretch girdle that's lost its stretch. The esophagus loses its elasticity, and food cannot pass through to the stomach. The condition may not be fully apparent until solid food is introduced. Some or all of the food remains in the sagging esophagus until it is regurgitated. If the pup does not die of starvation, it may succumb to ingested pneumonia. This is a congenital defect with no known cause or cure. A mild case can be helped by raising the level of the food pan, feeding small meals three or four times a day of totally softened food of a soupy consistency (no dog biscuits) for the life of the dog. But again, there is no cure.

Allergies in Welsh Terriers often occur in connection with man–made fibers, certain grasses or food items (corn, wheat, beef, etc.) Reactions range from a mild rash to horrible open, oozing areas of skin. A predisposition for certain severe allergies is inherited so it's something breeders need to acknowledge

Epilepsy occurs in approximately six percent of all dogs—purebreds and mixed breeds, and it very definitely occurs in Welsh Terriers at that rate or higher. This is true epilepsy, which is an inherited disorder, and is one more reason to stay in touch with your puppy buyers over a period of years. Seizures (or convulsions) with no known cause is called "idiopathic epilepsy" and generally surfaces between one and three years of age. But if both parents are carriers, there can be a very early onset of inherited epilepsy in the puppies at two to three months of age and the puppies should be put down, as there is no cure. As a rule the onset of the disease is between six months and five years, but the first symptoms may only show up at three or four years of age—*after* having been used for breeding, thus passing on the condition silently. Inherited epilepsy is more frequently seen in males than females.

Seizures are the result of what might be called an electric short–circuit in the brain, although they may also be caused by a head injury. If only the behavioral or sensory parts of the dog's brain are affected, it is called a *partial* seizure (petit mal), often seen as sudden aggression, fear, tail–chasing, biting air or "catching flies." In a *generalized* seizure (grand mal) the dog falls onto its side with legs thrashing, becomes rigid, and loses bladder and/or bowel control. The seizure may last from half a minute to three minutes. (The longer it lasts, the more damaging it is.) The dog then gradually "comes back" as if nothing at all had happened. The period between seizures can vary from days to months; the more frequent they are, the more medical attention the dog needs. However, in the period between these attacks, the dog is perfectly normal in every way and the tests given will uncover no abnormalities. (Brain damage can be detected by a simple x–ray.) In the case of Welsh Terriers, because it is a foregone conclusion in our breed that this is inherited epilepsy, the veterinarian may skip the expensive laboratory tests if the owner is willing to undertake the treatment and check–ups necessary for control. But again—there is no cure.

Any convulsion should be reported to the veterinarian immediately and once diagnosed, the breeder of the afflicted dog should be informed promptly and fully. Epilepsy may be identified with brain tumors, head injuries, or liver disease, which are often difficult or impossible to treat successfully. Given that, idiopathic epilepsy may seem preferable. With continuing medication, epileptic dogs can live long lives. However, not every pet owner can cope with the care of an epileptic dog.

Heart Murmurs are often diagnosed in young pups. The "lub–dub" beat has another sound in the middle. It is so common in puppies that doctors actually call them "normal heart murmurs." A new pet owner may need reassurance, however.

Thyroid abnormalities have been blamed for so many problems lately, from coat to conception, that many veterinary researchers claim the whole subject has been blown way out of proportion. New tests, replacing the old T3 and T4, are more accurate, which should make the apprehensive more comfortable. Thyroid changes are typically seen in bitches during estrus or pregnancy.

Parasites are either internal (worms) or external (fleas, ticks, lice, etc.). The brood bitch should be kept free of worms and this includes a complete worming prior to her coming in season. It is not something to put off until after she's been bred! Roundworm infestation can lie dormant, be activated by pregnancy and the worms can even invade the whelps in utero. It is not unusual for six– to eight–week–old puppies that appear round and fat to be loaded with roundworms. Rely on your veterinarian's newest and safest medications, not on an old–time remedy. The safety factor is important.

Lyme disease is the newest parasitic kid on the block. It is spread by deer ticks, which are hosted by white–tail deer and white–foot mice. The ticks are extremely tiny and hard to detect. The use of dips and tick killers made with IGR (Insect Growth Regulator) are essential in areas where these ticks prevail.

Symptoms of Lyme disease in people are a red rash (impossible to see on our dogs), flu–like symptoms (ditto), and fever and pain or swelling of joints. *That* is what you can spot in the dog. It may be first one leg, then another. Treatment is available, but even more important, there is now a vaccine that requires only an annual booster with no additional test. There have been many reported cases of dogs getting Lyme several times even with the vaccine, although in these cases the episodes were mild and responded quickly to antibiotic treatment.

Hip dysplasia is a common skeletal defect in dogs, generally found in large breeds. No one yet knows the cause, but it is considered to be inherited, with nutrition and environment also playing a part. The femoral head does not fit into the hip socket and this slippage worsens in time. Initial symptoms are similar to arthritis and corrective surgery is the only solution. No dog or bitch diagnosed with hip dysplasia should be used for breeding, nor should its dam or sire. Be thankful it is very rare in our breed.

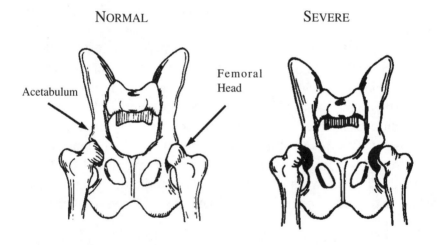

NORMAL   SEVERE

Acetabulum   Femoral Head

Eyes

Apart from round yellow eyes, which are aesthetically objectionable and quite difficult to eliminate from a breeding program, the most frequent eye problems in Welsh Terriers are juvenile cataracts (generally treatable now if caught early) and glaucoma, which is more serious.

Glaucoma is a very serious, painful condition that often causes blindness. Primary glaucoma, in which the eye's drainage is blocked is most common and is inherited. Only a veterinary ophthalmologist can pinpoint the difference between this and secondary glaucoma, which is defined by an increase in pressure in the eye and can be caused by any one of a number of abnormalities. Differentiating between the two is critical because the course of treatment is almost opposite and an error could actually cause blindness. If it is detected early enough, treatment, from oral drugs to surgery, is available and successful. Reports of glaucoma in Welsh Terriers has been on the rise, which may only reflect more accurate diagnosis and preventive care. Any dog or bitch suspected of being a carrier must be removed from a breeding program.

Juvenile **cataracts** are also on the rise, which might also be the result of better diagnostics and general health care. Several methods of treatment are available. Blindness in a young dog is particularly disturbing to a pet owner, so again, stock that is suspect should not be used for breeding.

Spaying or Neutering

It is sometimes difficult to convince pet owners that the animal will not get fat and lazy after being neutered. These are actually the result of over–eating and under–exercising. One argument for spaying is that the rate of mammary cancer is *two hundred* times greater in an entire bitch than one that's been spayed. The incidence of cancer is almost eliminated entirely if spayed just prior to her first heat.

The same odds hold for testicular cancer when the male is neutered at an early age (prior to one year). Researchers believe strongly that sexual maturity is tied in with the development of these cancer cells.

Speaking of Fat

This is a personal diet plan for a chubby Welsh Terrier that I have passed on to other breeders, and has met with great success for some thirty–five years. Obviously, it should only be used on an otherwise healthy dog. It is particularly useful for taking off unwanted weight on a bitch that will be bred.

First Day: Offer no food whatsoever for twenty–four hours. Water should always be available.

Second Day: One cup coarsely chopped lettuce mixed with one tablespoon cottage cheese and one hard–cooked egg, chopped.

Third Day: One–half the normal dinner.

Fourth Day: Repeat Day Two.

Fifth Day: Three–quarters of the normal dinner.

Repeat Days Two and Five until the weight is down to normal. Then continue on Day Five until an ideal weight has been maintained for several months. (You may never go back to a "full" meal!) Increase exercise slowly.

CHAPTER NINE

GROOMING THE WELSH TERRIER

The Welsh Terrier is a broken-haired dog, that is, he has both an outer wire coat and a soft undercoat. The wire outer coat is dense, harsh, and waterproof. It serves to protect the dog from brush, bites, and similar hazards of his natural workplace. The undercoat is soft dense hair that insulates the dog against both heat and cold. It also forms a soft barrier to protect the skin from all that wire and collected debris. This is the only acceptable coat. A soft woolly outercoat is a fault as is the absence of undercoat. A light grayish undercoat beneath the black jacket is a curse on a show dog as it tends to give the jacket a cast of "foreign" color. It is unfortunate that so few breeders are even attempting to maintain the rich red-brown the breed should have on legs and head. The ubiquitous use of chalk or hair dye on show dogs, in spite of the AKC's ruling against it, has apparently diminished the breeders' need or desire to breed for the correct vibrant color. Yet, the very use of these artificial products indicates a distinct preference for the correct colors by both breeders and judges! A conundrum indeed.

Fashion

Fashions in grooming come and go. The earliest pictures of Welsh Terriers are of dogs with very little in the way of furnishings. Then came chin whiskers and front legs groomed as columns. Gradually the foreface was completely filled out, and then came the goatee. We shall have to wait to see what is next from the groomer's tack box. Gerald R. Marriott (honorary secretary of the Welsh Terrier Club) became involved in the breed in the 1890s because of their character and working ability. Some forty years later he voiced his concern with the coats. "I sometimes wonder if we are proceeding on quite the right lines . . . Welsh Terriers are shown in a much less natural condition than they used to be. Coats have suffered as a result, and it is rare now to find a coat that is really 'hard, very close and abundant' which is what the standard has always insisted upon. I do not like to see a Welsh Terrier with bald cheeks or shoulders, and possibly a lot of dead hair on his ribs to hide or draw attention to flat sides."

There was a complete lack of furnishings back in the 1890s. About that time, one would occasionally see a "single coated" Welsh. This was a coat almost identical to that of the Smooth Fox Terrier, not what is referred to today as a "single coat," i.e. wire without an undercoat. But breeders of the day were able to overcome the problem of a single coat and it is never seen today.

Freeman Lloyd, on the other hand, had an obsessive dislike of the beard on a Welsh. "The fluff on the foreface," he called it. At Westminster, the story goes, a prospective buyer questioned an Englishman as to why the Welsh Terrier had all that hair on his face. The answer was, "That's for the rats to hold onto. As long as they hold on, they won't be biting the dog!"

Until the 1950s, heads were groomed to a true rectangle. It wasn't until the end of that decade that the "goatee" was added. It would seem a rather obvious ploy to elongate an otherwise too-short head, but no doubt one dog so groomed did a lot of winning, and this bit of unnecessary hair became fashionable on all Welsh in the show ring regardless of head length

Also up until the 1950s, hindquarters were clean and closely trimmed. There was no way to hide poor angulation, high hocks or weak muscling. By the mid-1950s front legs had blossomed forth in furnishings and soon the hindquarters were matched in a quantity of hair being trimmed—sculpted—to create an illusion of perfection.

Much of these grooming "improvements" (it is always debatable whether or not they are) originated as deceptions for the show ring. By leaving more hair to work with, expert groomers were able to reconstruct the outline and look of substance so that it more closely resembled what's called for by the breed standard. In other words, "faking it." Judges with good hands can still find the dog beneath the falsifications.

The breed is often touted as one that does not shed, which is true up to a point. The hair does not seasonally fall out in clumps, but the hairs do die after a growth of about two inches and are constantly being replaced by new ones. The tips of the new growth are deeper-colored, which is why a properly groomed dog is more attractive in color than one with an old washed-out coat. If the dog is not brushed thoroughly once a week, it will become a matted mess of dead hair, dirt, fleas, and ticks. So we can say that given a thorough brushing once a week, plus hand stripping or clipping four times a year, the Welsh Terrier is, from the tidy housekeeper's point of view, a non-shedding dog.

Terminology

Terrier grooming has a limited but unique language, so before explaining how to do it, here are definitions of some of the grooming terms.

Stripping – Pulling out a few hairs at a time with a stripping knife or thumb and forefinger to remove dead or excess hair and to shape the dog to look neat and attractive .

Plucking – The same as stripping, except that it usually refers only to pulling done with the fingers.

Trimming – This is the precise final stripping or plucking that produces a professional-looking finished dog. Many can strip, but it takes an artist's eye to trim a terrier to perfection.

Blending – The transition from fuzzy foreface to clean backskull, from furry legs into close-stripped shoulder, or from any one length of coat to another in such a way that the eye cannot detect where one ends and the other begins.

Grown out – a dog in this condition is in rough coat (shaggy).

Jacket – On a Welsh it refers to the black coat that extends from neck to tail.

Furnishings – The "fuzzy" tan parts. The hair on legs and muzzle that is left longer, is thick and wiry with sparse undercoat.

Anyone who has never stripped a terrier coat is certain that it is a painful process for the dog. It isn't when done correctly. However, to overcome queasy feelings, it is often easier to begin with thumb and forefinger instead of reaching for the stripping knife. For one thing, it slows down the procedure which is all to the good. It keeps you on the right track of lifting (by the tips) only a few hairs at a time and of pulling quickly and firmly with a stiff wrist so you begin to work in a rhythm Knives in the hands of beginners can leave holes, scrape the skin (thus making it the painful procedure you are trying to avoid) and the dog will rightly protest all future attempts to groom him.

Tools of the Trade

A **grooming table** provides you with the right size, shape, and height to groom comfortably. The clamp-on post with a noose will hold the dog steady and leave both your hands free. By all means, avoid "stringing up" the dog. He should be comfortable and the noose merely a means of control—like a collar and leash. *Never ever leave a dog (especially a puppy) alone on a grooming table even for one minute!*

Stripping knives come in three basic blades: fine for the close work on ears and head, and medium and coarse for stripping the jacket and quarters where the hair is left longer and grows thicker. They are made for right or lefthanded use, so be sure to get the one you need. Also be sure the handle fits comfortably in your hand. But that's not to say you won't get callouses! In fact, the sooner callouses form on your fingers, the easier it will be to groom. Regardless of the size or make, all stripping knives have sharp blades. Incorrectly used, they can scrape you or the dog.

A **metal comb**, commonly called a "greyhound comb," is seven inches long with narrow teeth at one end, wider-spaced teeth at the other.

A **slicker brush** is a small brush with wire bristles and a wooden handle. Get the one labeled "soft" and even so be aware that it can scratch—both you and the dog! Use gently, only through a thick coat, and not down to the skin.

A **palm brush**. This is the one you won't be able to live without! It is an oval, rubber-backed brush with blunted wire bristles, and fits in the palm of your hand. It removes unwanted undercoat, dead wire, stimulates growth of furnishings, sets up furnishings for trimming, and on and on!

A **hound glove** is a horsehair or sisal (the wire version is not recommended) mitt that fits over the hand for smoothing out and training the coat.

Nail clippers come in two basic types—guillotine or scissors. Which one you use is merely a personal preference. And you'll need Kwik-Stop®, a blood-clotting powder. Even the professionals occasionally cut a black nail too short because it's so hard to see the quick.

Use **scissors** or **trimming shears** on those few hairs you just can't pull. They're used more extensively in pet grooming, rather than grooming for show, as are thinning shears. When buying these, go for quality.

Grooming the Puppy

The first growth of hair on a puppy is apt to be fluff which is stripped out using the fingers. It is easily removed. A good time to do it is after the pup has been exhausted in play, or has been fed and is a bit drowsy. In tender areas, such as the loin or stomach, take up a very few hairs at a time. The fluffy puppy coat must be removed so the new wire one will grow in properly. If you don't remove it, the wire will grow through and over the fluff giving the dog what is called a "lifted" jacket. Even if the pup's coat is flat, it still has to come out!

This first stripping is done when the pups are about seven or eight weeks old. It is the only time you can groom with the pup in your lap in front of the TV. By ten weeks, it's time for grooming table training, keeping the sessions very short—fifteen minutes for starters.

There is another method currently used by many breeders and that is to use clippers to remove the puppy coat. Not all breeders are capable of using clippers on an eight- to ten-week-old puppy, nor are all pups of that age able to tolerate the sound and feel of electric clippers. But of more importance, this first clipping seems to have no adverse affect on the next coat coming in because the pup is not clipped down to skin.

Occasionally in a litter there is a "flat-coated" pup, meaning it looks almost smooth rather than fluffy. This generally results in an adult dog with deeper color and a flat, tight, hard wire coat. That's the good part. The bad news is that they usually either lack furnishings or the furnishings are so crisp that they must be kept in oil or they will break off.

Ears must have all the hair removed from inside. Hair left in the ears can be irritating, causing the pup to keep them raised, even prick, and hair left on the outside of the flap adds weight that can cause ears to droop and look "houndy."

Hair in the ear canal must be removed so as not to collect an excess of wax and dirt. Dip your fingers in French chalk or baby powder to get more traction in pulling out these hairs. Grasp the tips of two or three hairs and pull firmly. Because these hairs are based in a soft waxy surface, they come out easily—much to the surprise of the neophyte who is sure this will hurt. Gently wipe out the ear to remove excess wax or dirt.

The Pet Trim (Clippers)

Most professional groomers are taught a single "terrier trim," which turns every breed, including the Welsh, into Mini-Schnauzers. But given this chart and the accompanying directions they can produce a recognizable "Welsh" Welsh. So can the pet owner. The Oster A-5 is an excellent clipper and you will need blades #7, #8-1/2, #10 and #15. Thinning shears for *blending* and barber trimming shears for *scissoring*.

In the beginning it's easy to lose patience. You're trying to turn out a handsome dog and at the same time you're training the dog to stand patiently on the grooming table and have every inch of its anatomy handled.

Learning to use the clippers takes time. The most common mistake is to bear down as if trying to take off the entire amount in one swoop. If you do this, the blade will jam. Feed the coat into the clipper gently until you get the hang of it.

Body – Begin by clipping the neck and body (see Figure 1, next page) with a #7 or #5 blade in the direction of arrows, which is the direction the hair grows, down the sides, up the front of the tail and around back of upper thighs, all *with* the lay of coat. Blend leg hair (furnishings) into clipped area with thinning shears. Do NOT leave "chaps" on the rear legs. See Figure 2.

Scissor the top of hock short.

Clip the front and side of neck with a #10 or #8-1/2 blade in the direction of arrows, going down to elbows in front.

Hindquarters – Clip back of tail and around rectum with #8-1/2 blade. See Figure 2. Blend into the clipped area with thinning shears.

Head – Clip the head in the direction of arrows (against lay of hair) with a #10 blade from the corner of the eye to corner of the mouth, the entire cheek, and top of head and throat. See Figure 3.

Clip the ears, inside and out, with a #15 blade *with* lay of

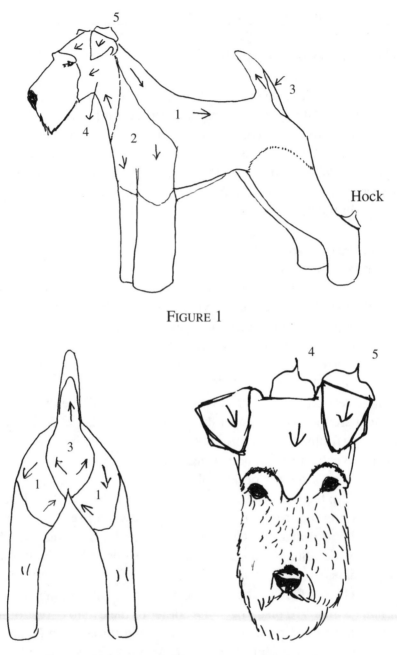

FIGURE 1

Hock

FIGURE 2

FIGURE 3

hair. See Figure 3.

Face – Brush face furnishings thoroughly, comb forward, and using scissors blend the eyebrows into the clipped area. The eyebrows are semi-pointed on the inner side and blend into the cheek on the outer edge. They are much shorter than a Mini-Schnauzer or Wire Fox and not as sharply pointed. Scissor the area between the brows so they are separated.

Scissor face furnishings to form a neat rectangle, as shown in Figure 3. Do not hollow out under the eyes, nor take too much off the bridge of nose.

Legs and Feet – Scissor the back of the elbows short and between the pads or clip between the pads of the feet with a #10 blade. Scissor around feet so they look round when standing. Brush out leg furnishings and scissor to look like cylinders.

Belly – Clip the belly with #10 or #15 blade (including the penis sheath on a dog). Leave a little chest hair, scissoring to neaten up, following outline of ribs.

Finish – by brushing entire dog with a flat bristle brush (*not* wire) to remove all the loose hairs.

Hand Stripping the Welsh Terrier

This has often been referred to as "moving sculpture" because the hair keeps growing and the dog keeps moving! Jimmy Butler, one of the top professional handlers, said it took only two things to prepare a terrier for the show ring—a good eye and a lot of hard work.

You have bought all the clippers, scissors, shears, blades, combs, and brushes, and what is it that you begin with? Your thumb and forefinger. It is the easiest way to learn the basic rhythm of stripping. Here are the two basic steps:

1. Only lift a few hairs at a time, pushing the tips up with your thumb against your index finger.

2. Pull in the direction the hair grows, with a stiff wrist, and a steady firm pull.

When you become adept at this and dare to pick up a knife, you will continue to lift a few hairs, with your thumb, but now against the knife which replaces your forefinger. The wrist is stiff so you won't "curl" the hairs as you pull. (Also so you don't scrape the dog's skin or cut the hairs.) Lift hair up. Pull back and down.

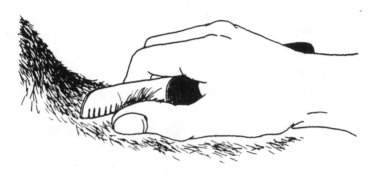

DIAGRAM A

Let's begin. Put the dog on the table and gently brush out the entire dog with a soft slicker brush. Work out any mats with the aid of the end tooth of the comb, separating the hairs with your fingers as you go. Lightly brush leg furnishings *up* with the slicker (Diagram B), and then out with a palm brush. Next, comb straight down—gently! (See Diagram C.) The front legs will become round columns; back legs have bends and curves

DIAGRAM B

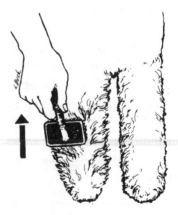

Now you can start to strip. Use your other hand on the far side of the knife to push the skin gently but firmly away (or at times to hold it in place) as you pull hair toward you. Ideally, the entire hard coat should be removed in one session. It's not an ideal world, so a heavy-coated dog may take a couple of days (with breaks as needed by you and the dog). If you find a new coat coming in beneath the one you're strip-

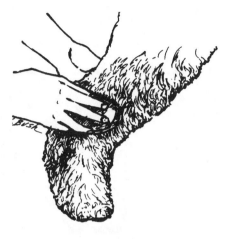

DIAGRAM C

ping off, *leave it!* As you gain expertise, you'll use that incoming growth to "roll" the coat, which is how some dogs can remain in the show ring in top condition for months.

Start with the head, which is undoubtedly the most difficult part of the dog because you have to keep turning and lifting it to get at the hair, which grows in every possible direction. Hold the muzzle gently and you're more likely to get his cooperation. The following instructions are taken with permission from articles by Fox Terrier breeder, Arden M. Ross, which originally appeared in *Terrier Type*.

Standing in front of your dog, start by comb-ing the eyebrows and all the muzzle hair *forward.* Now move to one side of the dog's head. If you're right-handed, the left side is generally easiest, so it should be done first. Then tackle the right side which will be clumsier at first. Strip from just in back of the eyebrows all of the top of the skull as far as the occiput (the boney protrusion where the top of the skull joins the top of the neck).

Next, draw an imaginary line from the *outer*

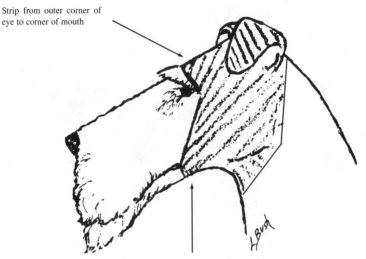

Strip from outer corner of
eye to corner of mouth

and from corner to corner of mouth (underjaw)

DIAGRAM D

corner of the eye to the corner of the dog's mouth.
Strip all the hair from in *back* of this line (toward the
body, not toward the nose) over the cheeks and right
back to where the sides of the head join the neck. As
you work, pull a bit and then comb and separate the
hair—then pull a bit more, etc. Be sure to keep the
long muzzle hair separate from the hair to be pulled
by combing it and the eyebrows forward.

Now draw another imaginary line from the
corner of the mouth *under* the lower jaw to the corner of the mouth on the other side. Strip from this
line *back* to where the throat joins the neck.

Then strip the ears and muzzle and eyebrows with the fingers. This is where you need excellent photographs, diagrams, an
artist's eye—and lots of help! A few wrong pulls and the expression will be all wrong! Keep combing the hair forward and now it

is more important than ever to lift one or two hairs by the tips before pulling. It's the only time you'll just use fingers, not your wrist or arm. Mrs. Ross describes it as the same motion as pulling a thread through a needle.

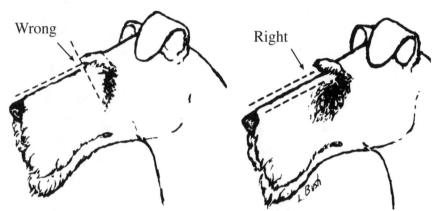

"...the plane of this area is NOT verticle (as on the left) to the horizontal plane of the bridge of the nose..."

DIAGRAM E

Eyebrows

Eyebrows on a Welsh are not fancy. They are longest over the inner corner of the eyes (on either side of the bridge of the nose) and disappear entirely by the time they reach the outer corner. The area directly under and in front of the eyes must _not_ be hollowed out! Comb and look and comb again (or use a palm brush) before pulling. The "fill" under the eye makes or breaks the dog's expression. It's a fair bet that almost everyone trimming their first Welsh, will hollow out under the eyes and dish out the side of the muzzle! Be forewarned because it can take ages to grow back.

On the top of the muzzle from between the eyes to the end of the nose, the line must be level. Still standing in front of the dog, brush the hair forward, eyeball it from all sides, and pick a hair or two at a time. Fluff the hair and begin again.

A rectangle viewed from any angle...

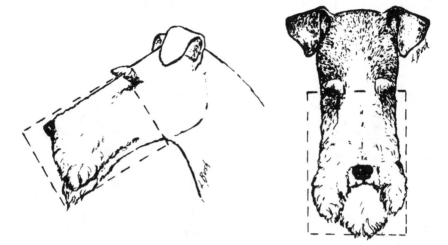

DIAGRAM F

Foreface

The foreface is a rectangle viewed from any angle, so the line from the outer corner of the eye to the end of the muzzle (viewed from above) is straight, as is the entire muzzle viewed from each side. Each dog is an individual and small changes in grooming will be needed to bring out his best look. Trim the whiskers the same way—keeping the rectangle, with or without the "goatee."

This, too, from Ross (see Diagram G):

"Here is a fairly workable pattern. When working on the head, leave the area underneath the under jaw and throat (adjacent to and including the beard) until last. Work it into the upper throat. Then do the top of the neck adjoining the back skull, and the sides of the neck in back of and beneath the ears. Now strip the top of the neck all the way down to the withers and both sides of the neck down to the front of the

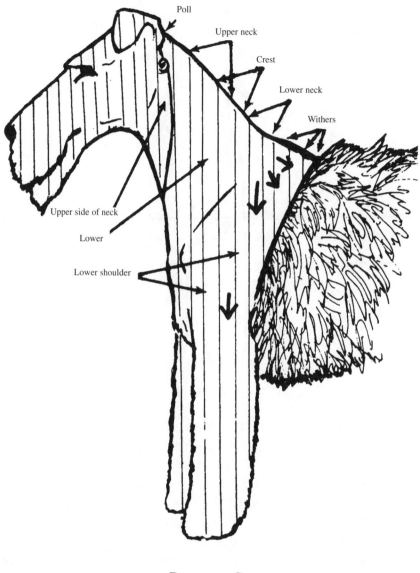

DIAGRAM G

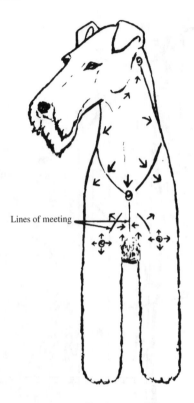

Lines of meeting

DIAGRAM H

shoulders, leaving the lower throat area. Then the shoulders, withers, brisket, and lower throat."

Front legs are next. Viewed from the front (Diagrams H), the outside line is straight (don't create a "valley" at the elbow). We can't go into all the tricks of making a poor front look better, or sparse furnishings look profuse, but suffice it to say the front legs are round columns right down to the ground (Diagram I). Brush, comb, and pick, pick, pick. This is "finger" area. Easy does it.

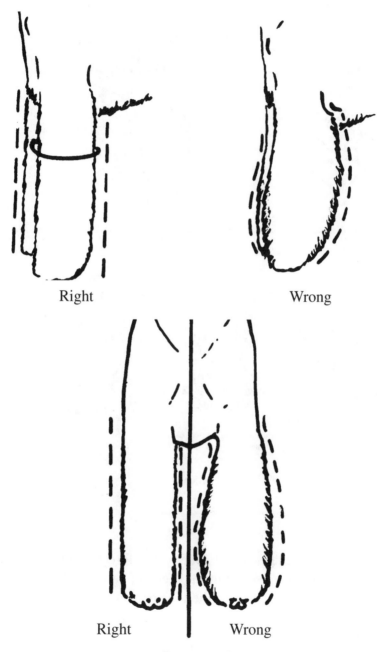

Right · Wrong

Right · Wrong

DIAGRAM I

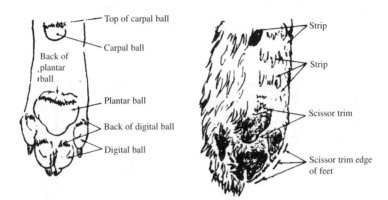

...the object is to remove all the long, bunchy hair from between the Plantar and Digital balls, and from around the bottom edges...

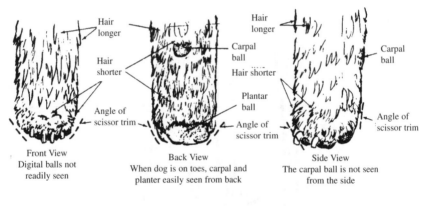

DIAGRAM J

Feet

  Cut the toenails on all four feet before trimming the feet. Now trim around the bottom of the feet and between the pads with scissors. Do not trim between the toes or you'll ruin the desirable "standing on tiptoe" look. Remember that your dog's feet turn at the wrist *backwards.*

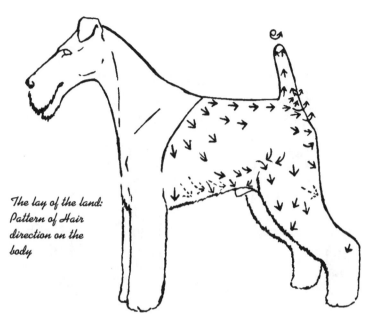

The lay of the land:
Pattern of Hair
direction on the
body

DIAGRAM K

More Stripping

The front is now gorgeous, and we can get on with the rest of the dog, so pick up the knife again. All hair continues to be stripped in the direction it grows. See Diagram K.

Below the hip, at the top of the hindquarters, begin to blend the hair into the longer furnishings. In trimming the hair on the chest, work from the loin forward to between the dog's front legs. Much of this hair is pulled straight down toward the floor. How much you leave will depend upon the dog's natural attributes (depth of chest, spring of rib, etc.) and the illusion you need to create by leaving a bit more here or there.

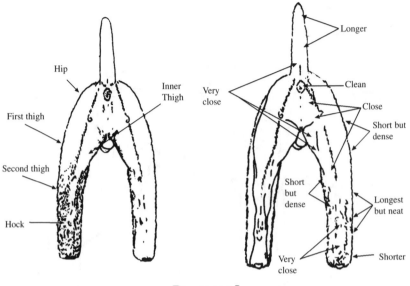

DIAGRAM L

Backside

Standing in back of the dog, you're about to tackle the second-most difficult part (after the head) because the hairs here grow in every conceivable direction. Hold the tail firmly to keep the skin firm and start at the area around the scrotum, working *up* to the anus. These are *very* tender areas and your dog is going to have to learn to stand still because the hair is trimmed very, very close.

Mrs. Ross doesn't give this small trick—it's mine. I have found that rubbing a dollop of peanut butter on the grooming post helps to keep the dog interested in something other than what you are doing. If your dog doesn't care for peanut butter, try tuna fish.

Blending

As you can see from Diagram M, there are several "meeting places" in the hindquarters that must be blended. Shaping the hindquarters again depends upon the actual structure of the dog you are working on. The "look" you want (and the tricky part) is the top of the hock, which is trimmed close on top and blended into the

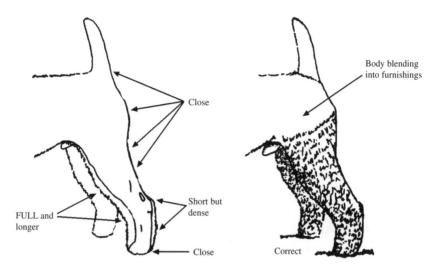

DIAGRAM M

back and sides of the hock. Keep viewing the hindquarters from the side as you work.

Don't panic if the dog is all holes, bumps, and hollows the first few sessions. You will learn something about terrier trimming every time you put a dog on the table, because no two dogs are exactly the same.

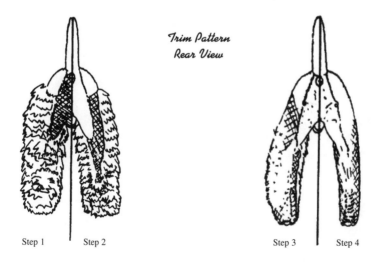

CHAPTER TEN

AROUND THE RINGS

When dogs were first judged in a show ring, it was just that: judging dogs. For conformation, soundness and type, form and function, or, in other words, judging was perceived to be the evaluation of breeding stock. The true "terrier men" were in the British Isles and we in the States were fortunate that in time some of them arrived on our shores. These men were legends; they had an eye for the breed and it has been said that no "mere dog person" at that time would have dreamt of applying to judge Terriers.

Priorities change and over the years, at least in the United States, more and more emphasis has been placed on "show" than on "dog." Part of the blame for this must rest squarely with those who are more interested in winning than primarily in preserving the quality and welfare of the breed. Robert Killick (Kadabra) of North Wales who is well-acquainted with our shows, feels that in the U.S. exhibitors show more to win, whereas in the U.K. they still show primarily to compare, to learn, and to exhibit their skill as breeders. To some extent the switch in emphasis is due to the enormous increase in the numbers of shows, professional handlers and the extremely few judges today who are true terrier men. Most are breeders of unrelated breeds, or past handlers of other breeds. One cannot blame the latter for seeking showiness and artistry in presentation to make up for their lack of breed knowledge, but making Top Winners of dogs for those reasons can soon turn any breed into nothing more than show dogs. American Cocker Spaniels are just one example. According to their standard, "excessive coat" is to be penalized, and yet many cockers have so much coat that they would be completely useless in the field as an upland bird dog. With all that coat, the dog would become tangled in the underbrush!

Judges need to continually remind themselves that it is their job to evaluate the dog for those basic breed-specific properties that will be passed on to the next generation of Welsh Terriers. No puppy is capable of inheriting the hairdressing skills of his sire's groomer, nor the exhibiting skills of his dam's handler. A well-known international judge, David Roche of Australia, commented that professional handlers make some of the worst judges because they have learned to manipulate judges, dogs, and other handlers, and that the judging pool should come from the breeders who have dedicated their lives to it. An excellent idea, but in our breed the problem is obvious. Those lifelong breeders are an endangered species.

William Kendrick, one of our native terrier men, felt that our ratings systems for Top Dog or Bitch had nothing to do with quality. Due to the number of shows in this country, the figures merely indicated how well certain dogs traveled by car and plane!

Form and Function

There are one or two semantic stumbling blocks regarding conformation that judges and breeders run into: The "straight back" and the "level topline." Another is the short humerus or upper arm, which we'll tackle in a moment. A dog's true "back" consists only of those four vertebrae running from the withers to the loin. Purists also know the "topline" includes the arch of neck, which precludes a "level" line. A dog with pronounced withers and/or a slightly arched loin could have a straight *back* but definitely not a level *topline*. In spite of these specifics, most of us commonly refer to the distance from behind the withers to the tail as the dog's "back." In Welsh Terriers, that line should be straight or level, but our standard *does not* call for a short back, which many uninformed breeders and judges feel is prerequisite to all else. "The loin is strong and and moderately short"—*loin*, not the back.

From "The Welsh Terrier in Profile"—the annotated standard of the WTCA.

"Straight Front" means that the upper arm is a shortened bone, and the dog stands correctly with brisket and front legs in a straight line. Good reach is determined by a properly laid-back shoulder. The more upright the shoulder, the shorter the reach will be. Correct drive comes from well-organized quarters, strong hock joints, and strong flexing of the foot. Reach in front should equal drive behind. "Terrier Trot" is a gait used by the straight-fronted terrier, which gives the picture of an alert and out-going dog moving on its toes.

A correctly-made Welsh is short-coupled (i.e., has a moderately short loin) which makes him look almost square as opposed to the longer Irish Terrier with his typical "racy" look. From a functional standpoint, a very short back would inhibit the dog's ability to go-to-ground, to dig, or even to be a serviceable above-ground hunter of ground-burrowing prey. The back must be flexible for such work and a short back is a rigid one. Short-coupled, but not short-backed. "Extremes are not to be tolerated," say the terrier experts.

The upper arm (humerus) is not only shorter on the Welsh Terrier than on dogs with forechest, but is almost upright. This is what gives the "fish-hook" front, or lack of forechest. This structure limits the reach of the front legs at a trot, but also allows the dog when digging to lower its keel by permitting the elbows to move forward and back above the brisket line. All structural experts agree that you cannot have a shortened, almost upright forearm, *and* a short body, *and* a forty-five degree shoulder! In Welsh Terriers about thirty-two degrees from vertical is as "well laid back" as you can get.

Welsh, like the other five long-legged Terriers, have straight front legs and feet made to throw earth out beneath their hindquarters when digging, whereas short-legged terriers with turned-out feet throw dirt to either side. All aspects of "soundness" must be judged in relation to the dog's function. You can't make an apple pie out of oranges.

Ch. Kirkwood Top Brass shown at perfect trot, with correct extension in front and drive behind. Note that in moving forward, the hind foot does not come down in the spot just vacated by the front foot. This is due to the shortened upper arm (humerus). When the ulna is equal in length to the humerus, you "see" a dog that is termed "short on leg."

The terrier trot is accomplished by all four feet being carried both forward and backward very close to the ground (it's called "daisy clipping") and very little flexing of the front pasterns at the wrist. In fact, the front foot is not flexed high enough for the hind foot on the same side to slip beneath it (as it does in other breeds). There is a small space between where the front foot lifts and the rear foot lands. The judge can only view this movement from the side, not the down and back. Only from the side view is it possible to see if the body is too long, or too short, the legs too short, if the dog lacks angulation or is over-angulated, or if all the forward movement is coming from rear drive (often caused by handlers who lift the dog's front.).

Moved at the correct trotting speed, the Welsh will travel with front legs parallel. Faster, and the feet will naturally converge. Movement is a true test of conformation and to assess it accurately, judges should also insist on loose leads.

The eyes are "well set in the skull." Again, form follows function. Deep-set eyes are better protected from flying dirt in a den.

Type

"Type" in the show ring often seems to revolve around a current fad or fancy grooming. You have only to look at the photographs of our dogs through the years to confirm this. People say they prefer "the old fashioned type" or "the modern type." But form and function must go hand-in-hand while adhering to the breed standard, lest down the road we find ourselves with a totally different dog.

Type is first of all what the eye perceives, but is a combination of both the elusive and the material. Everything about the dog—the "look," the expression, the attitude—must say, "Welsh Terrier." And putting your hands on the dog must tell you that the conformation of this terrier is definitely Welsh.

Sparring

Judges are asked to spar our Welsh Terriers. This is a system (controlled by the judge and the handlers, of course) of bringing two dogs at a time out of the lineup to let them look at each other and make the most of themselves. One-upmanship, if you like. However, all dogs have something called a "flight space" or an imaginary line behind which they feel safe. Invaded, it becomes a "fight" space. The desirable qualities in a Welsh Terrier as stated in our standard are "Alert, aware, spirited" but "friendly and shows self-control." Sparring, or facing off, merely lets the judge see the dogs put forth these qualities when they are not being held together by the handler, to see an unaided tail, natural expression, and use of ears, to see what each dog makes of itself and how it responds to one of its own kind.

A good show dog is said to "ask for it." Sparring often changes a disinterested attitude. A "deadhead" may be just bored, but if that's what the judge sees, that's what he must judge and it is not what's wanted in a Welsh Terrier. Nor is a noisy, argumentative specimen. Our breed is sensible and shows self-control.

Richard Chashoudian, a former breeder and handler and now a judge, said, "Terriers need to spar on their own without bait or looking at their handlers. The Welsh Terrier should exhibit character and guts. I want to see him standing strong on his own."

These are the only reasons for sparring. The dogs should never be allowed (or shoved by handlers) to get so close as to invade another's safety zone and cause a growl, snap or snarl. Perhaps if dogs were not over-handled, there would be no need to use this method of viewing them. Cyril Williams, judging at Montgomery, encountered the phenomenon of a ring full of dogs with all handlers down on their knees, holding the dogs fore and aft like immovable monuments. Loud and clear, he said, "Ladies and gentlemen, now that you have all said your prayers, you may rise and remain standing so I can see your dogs."

OTHER RINGS, OTHER EVENTS

Junior Showmanship

In 1932 Leonard Brumby Sr., a professional handler, started children's handling classes, primarily to involve the offspring of breeder-exhibitors in the same sport as their parents (and to keep them busy at dogs shows with an activity of their own). It is no longer the casual event for kids that it was then. It is now a designated, pre-entered part of the dog show, with every youngster required to have an AKC Junior Handler Number. Classes are divided by age and ability. Novice Junior Class is for boys and girls aged ten years but under fourteen who have not already won three first prizes. Open Junior Class takes in those who have won three firsts. Novice Senior Class is for ages fourteen to eighteen who have not won three firsts, and Open Seniors for those who have.

The dog is not judged, only the way the junior follows the judge's instructions, handles the dog and indicates some knowledge of the breed he is showing. Being neatly dressed and respectful to the judge are tacit requirements.

Please be upstanding!

Winning is the name of the game and the kids are very competitive. The parents are sometimes more so! However, the stakes get higher and higher. At certain designated shows, the Best Open Senior receives a prize plus an all-expense paid trip for the winner and a chaperone to the National Invitational finals. The winner of that gets an all-expense paid trip to Crufts! Is it any wonder why some parents can get so competitive? The British have a similar system with Westminster as the goal. Welsh Terrier Club of America offers an annual award for the top Junior Handler of a Welsh Terrier. Many of our current terrier handlers and judges have come up through these ranks.

There have never been a great many juniors handling Welsh Terriers, but recently there have been two of note. Jonathan Cortez of California won a trip to Westminster with *Showdown of Misty Morn*. He did not win that one, but was commended for good sportsmanship, professional appearance and skill in handling a terrier. His plans for the future include veterinary medicine. Another top junior was Beverly Wright-Osment, daughter of Pamela Price and Kenneth Wright-Osment (Shorlyne), who put off starting university when offered a job training and caring for the five Cairn Terriers appearing as "Toto" in "The Wizard of Oz on Ice" touring ice show.

Obedience

Obedience tests (as they were originally called) first appeared in the 1939 Welsh Terrier Club of America Yearbook in an article by Mr. Richard Riggs (Manorville), who encouraged members to get involved in this activity that had just come under the auspices of the AKC. He laments that only two Welsh Terriers had gained titles when so many were in the show ring. The first Welsh Terrier to earn a CD (and later a CDX) was *Windsor of Shanarock* in 1939. Mr. and Mrs. Harry J. Lowenbach did yeoman work in the early years by demonstrating the competence of the breed in advanced classes. They had five Welsh earning Companion Dog Excellent and Utility Dog Tracking titles in 1940 and '41. The first dual-titled Welsh Terrier with an advanced degree was the bitch *Ch. Gaye Malley, CDX* in 1941. And it wasn't until 1968 that a male, *Ch. Lee's Charles of Camelot, CDX* caught up with her. He was owned by Mr. and Mrs. Bruce Melloy, long-time Welsh Terrier

Club of America members. The obedience workers were proving that beauty and brains are compatible components of a Welsh Terrier

By 1955 obedience was catching on in earnest, and Mr. Arthur Jensen, owner and trainer of *Winalesby Justa Bita Pepper, UD* wrote a knowledgeable article on the Welsh in obedience. He certainly understood our breed, saying that the Welsh "quickly realizes he has crowd appeal" and that a "good performance brings applause and other preferred attention." In the early 1960s Mrs. Prescott Gustafson had an Obedience Brace in the ring. *Strathglass Storm, CD* and *Strathglass Tide Rip, UD* delighted the crowds.

One outstanding dog deserves mention here. For five years, from 1960 to '65, *Timothy of Lleyn, UD,* handled by Neva Corboff, won the Birr Trophy, twice with perfect scores of 200 in 1961, and four years later when he was eight years old scored a nearly perfect 199.5 at Golden Gate Kennel Club. More and more champion Welsh were earning a Companion Dog title in obedience, and with AKC registrations topping 1000 for the first (and only) time, it was rewarding for the breeders of the

The "almost obedient" Welsh Terrier. Original painting by Pam Posey Tanzey

day to know that their dogs were realizing their potential in pursuits other than the show ring.

The Birr Trophy was awarded for the next five years to another West Coast dog, Dr. John Vinson's *Sir Truffles O'Topanga, UD.* Dr. Vinson, a veterinarian, had rescued the dog from a local dog pound and began obedience training to restore the dog's self-confidence. (That, he surely did!)

In 1971, Mrs. Barbara Jacoby's *Tuppence Jones, CDX* dog, whose charisma and talent encouraged many Welsh Terrier owners and breeders to become involved in obedience training, won honorable mention. Mrs. Jacoby and *Tup* teamed up to make the AKC obedience video, "200 Plus," which she freely admitted was accomplished with lots of liver and retakes! Good he was, but perfect he was not! Mrs. Jacoby was a well-known trainer and a much admired obedience trial judge.

Theljon's True Grit, breeder-owner handled by Thelma Cottell, earned his Utility Dog title with a score of 197.5. Mrs. Cottell obedience trained several of Mrs. Colt's house dogs, including the latter's favorite, "Jimmy."

In the 1980s Gisele Kuehl, in Canada, put titles on two of her Welsh, *Ch. Kelmike's Two For One, CDX, CG* and *Ch. Secwyn's Ceilidh, CD.* Both of these dogs had champion sires and dams.

It would be hard to find a Welsh with more titles than the dog bred by Charlene Czarnecki and trained by co-owner Kathy Humphrey. Are you ready? *Am.Can.BDA.Bah.Dr.Vens.SA.Mex.PR Ch. of Americas; Int. Ch. Czar's Bring on the Music, TT, CG, CD.* Czar dogs have excelled in obedience work. (No kidding!)

In 1995 there were two Welsh Terrier Club of America obedience awards: the Cascade Lane Trophy for highest individual obedience score, and the Xxtra Trophy for highest scoring champion. The Esty Glen Trophy was awarded for the most versatile Welsh Terrier, incorporating a variety of the newer activities in which the breed was becoming involved.

Kip Pedersen's Welsh, *Kip's Ticket to Bardsele* contributed another breed first. *"Ticket"* is the first Welsh Terrier to earn an

Obedience Trial Champion title (OTCH). He also was third in the Top Dog division of the all-breed World Series event in July 1996.

Today, the "come-heel-sit-down-stay" exercises are accepted as essential for all pets and their owners. Going beyond that into jumps, retrieves, scent discrimination, etc., is definitely not for every Welsh Terrier, or its owner. Part of the problem in training Welsh for routine performance is the fact that our breed functions on several levels—scent, sound, and sight—making it extremely easy for the dog to be distracted. Add to that the fact that once a Welsh is underground facing vermin, be it fox, badger, woodchuck or rat, he works on his own. He has no need for a handler to tell him what to do next. (Although, he may, on occasion, need a rescuer to dig him out of a tight spot!)

Trainers err in labeling all terriers stubborn. It is more likely that their intelligence and independence interferes with performing a solitary action by rote. Once they have demonstrated they can do what you've asked, they see nothing to be gained in repeating it over and over again. Most of us would agree they do have a point. Of course, this is also what makes them innovative, class cut-ups or just bored, all things frowned upon by trainers who prefer to train retrievers. I've always held that you can *teach* a Welsh, but don't try to *train* him.

Working, Go-to-Ground, and Earthdog Trials

"The objects of the Club shall be: to encourage and promote quality in the breeding of pure-bred Welsh Terriers **and to do all possible to bring their natural working qualities to perfection."** (From the Welsh Terrier Club of America Constitution and By-Laws).

It is interesting to note that nothing is said about *showing*, but only the *breeding* of quality, yet when it comes to the function of the breed, the object is plain; even going so far as to request *perfection* in natural working qualities. After a lapse of many years, people involved in the breed are getting back to the basics—into the fields.

No matter what you call natural work, *this* is where our dogs come alive! Even a Welsh Terrier that has snoozed for years in a city apartment, immediately knows why he was born when taken to his first "dig." A show dog, bored with the once-around, down-and-back routine, can work at a trial one day and walk in the show ring the next day ready to let the world see he is a *working* Welsh Terrier. I've done it and I've watched others in the breed ring whose dogs were turned on by doing what they were bred to do.

Freeman Lloyd wrote the following in a 1937 issue of the *Gazette,* some thirty-five years before his prayers were answered.

> The agriculturist's terriers and ferrets were not the least of his belongings; very likely they were absolute requirements in his field of economics [catching rabbits to eat and to sell] and partially sustained the upkeep of his family. A sorry business it is then to record that in America the working terrier is practically an unknown creature. His profession, calling, or what have you, seemingly has been forgotten.

> To remedy this more or less alarming state of things, it might be that field trials for terriers would at least bring back the old sporting spirit that is latent in the terrier; moreover, it is certain t h a t the dog would welcome this opportunity of again coming into his own. Hunting trials for terriers are popular in Ireland. These are "hunting" rather than going-to-ground trials. Rabbits don't bite back and a show terrier is safe from injury or disfigurement. The Welsh Terrier remains the correct size that the working terrier should be when used for going to a fox in his earth or for hunting and catching rabbit.

Lloyd also commented on conformation, wanting more strength in the Welshman's jowls: "Narrow skulls personify that quality the showman delights in seeing, but effeminacy may not be looked for beyond the shoulders in the make-up of vermin-worrying dogs."

Defining "Work"

The definition of a "working terrier" seems to depend on who is doing the defining. To some, it refers to any terrier terminator of rats or rabbits. To the 1930s authority, Captain Jocelyn M. Lucas, M.C., a working terrier is one that will go to ground after fox, badger, or otter. Pat Adams Lent, in *Sport With Terriers* (1973), held that a "working terrier" hunts his quarry underground and a terrier that hunts above-ground is a "sporting terrier." Others refer to the above-ground terriers as "hunting terriers." Take your pick, Welsh Terriers will enthusiastically undertake the job with little interest in what you call it.

Pat Lent formed the American Working Terriers Association (AWTA) to provide trials for the working terriers in a man-made

An AWTA Trial in Sebastopol, California. Note how well all thes working dogs are.

"earth" as well as encouraging owners to hunt with their dogs naturally in fields—above or below ground. American Working Terriers Association issues a Certificate of Gameness (CG) for work in an artificial earth, a Working Certificate for dogs that have qualified by facing quarry underground, and Hunting Certificates for dogs that have hunted above ground with their handlers or that kill vermin such as woodchuck, for example, in barns. Natural hunts, by the way, are exhilarating, but are not just a walk in the woods! Learn from the experts and you'll know to carry a shovel, a bag to carry off dead rabbits, woodchucks, rats, etc., and a first-aid kit. An electronic transmitter on the collar is the modern version of the "gingles" or bells used 200 years ago to

SEQUENCE FOR EARTHDOG TRIALS

1. Enters earth on the run!

2. Reaches and "worries" the quarry for allotted time.

3. *Owner helps dog out of den.*

4. *Dog says otherwise!*

5. *Ready to go back.*

Thanks to the Southern California earthdog enthusiasts for this sequence!

alarm the fox and to locate the terrier underground.

The first Welsh Terrier to earn a Certificate of Gameness from AWTA was *Ch. Bardwyn Penny Wise*, owned by Mary Seck, in 1975. Of the first six Welsh to earn that title, four were owned and handled by Mary Seck! Two also had CDX degrees and one a UD. *Ch. Raykiln Raquel, UD, CG* was the first Welsh to have all three titles.

It wasn't until 1993 that Betsy Adams handled the second Welsh for such honors and went one step further to earn a tracking degree with *Ch. Sunspryte Xxtra Xxcitement, UDT, CG.* Great achievements!

The AKC got into the act in 1994 with Earthdog Trials, based on the American Working Terriers Association's original format of a timed go-to-ground in artificial earths with specific rules for each of the three regular classes. There is also an Introduction to Quarry for which no award is given. The three classes are Junior Earthdog, Senior Earthdog, and Master Earthdog.

At the first AKC Earthdog Trial, held in California, *Ch. Calawyn's Gala Serrana* (Serra) earned a leg on her Senior Earthdog, the first Welsh Terrier—or any breed—to do so. Serra is owned by Jim Tebbetts who, along with Diane Amendola, also shared a "first" in that they were the first AKC-licensed judges of this new event. Both are Welsh Terrier Club of America members.

Serra the day she made history by being the first Welsh Terrier to earn the Master Earthdog title.

John Boyd's *Harri Mordwywyr* was the first Welsh Terrier to earn a Senior Earthdog title. The first male to earn a Junior Earthdog title in Texas was *Secwyn Rhobo the Destroyer* owned by Ethelene Bucy. And the first title won on the East Coast was a Junior Earthdog by *Ch. Rubicon's Sugar Bear, SE, CG, CGC, TPT* owned by Cathy Saito. *Bear* won an Award of Merit at Montgomery in 1995 and six months later drew his first woodchuck on a natural hunt.

Trials have become very popular on the West Coast, less so in the East where they are primarily sponsored by breed clubs. The Welsh Terrier Club of America, will sponsor its first AKC Trial in October 1998 in Crosswicks, New Jersey. Dachshunds, bred to go to ground, are definitely included in these trials, for without their numbers the terrier breeds could not support the events. In 1994 only 230 dogs participated and the following year the numbers shot up to 2,347! In 1995, 235 dogs earned the Junior Earthdog (eight were Welsh) and eighteen earned the Senior Earthdog. Serra made Welsh Terrier history for a second time in 1997 when she earned the highest award for the AKC Earthdog Trials and became a Master Earthdog. In addition to being the first dog of any breed to earn a leg on her Senior Earthdog title, she was also the first Welsh bitch to finish that title. Bred by Lucille Migliano, she was sired by *Ch. Rushwyn's Blackhawk* out of *Ch. Gregmar's Calawyn*.

Su-Tops Hi Ho Terra retrieving a duck. Never underestimate our Welsh Terriers!

Arthur Frederick Jones wrote, ". . . this forthright little dog is eager to give a good account of himself. *Going to ground or rounding up livestock* he will discharge his duties satisfactorily or die in the attempt." I know of only one Welsh that undertook "rounding up livestock"—*Su-Tops Hi Ho Terra, CG,* and her owner, Sue Weiss, has it on video! That little bitch was a natural hunter, doing water retrieves, working upland game, as well as tracking.

Agility

The first agility demonstration took place at Crufts in 1978. Pioneered by Peter Lewis, it spread through Europe like proverbial wildfire. Two years later agility was given the official nod from The Kennel Club. In the States it has taken longer. The U.S. Dog Agility Association was formed in 1986 and did all the ground-work of setting the rules and stirring up enthusiasm for the

Puppies trying to figure out the Weave Poles—this way or that way?

sport, although the dogs needed no encouragement to stir their enthusiasm! The North American Agility Council (NAAC) is another group offering competition primarily in the Northwest. *Mopa's Firefly of Pembrey, CD, JE,* owned by Lynell Dewey was the first Welsh to win a NAAC title. The AKC officially sanctioned agility trials in 1994, but to date no Welsh has earned a title, although many are involved in the sport non-competitively.

Agility is really a dog's idea of heaven. Jumps and tunnels

(both open and closed), ladders, (called a "Dog Walk"), climbing over an A-frame, wriggling through Weave Poles, and even a moment to rest in the Pause Box. It is based loosely on horse show jumping, but with more obstacles and more excitement.

It begins with basic obedience since you must be able to communicate properly with your dog. Then you move into agility classes where the dog's repertoire is slowly built up one exercise at a time. Finally, you are ready to take this show on the road. Spectators at competitive events applaud and cheer and the dogs revel in it.

Tracking

There are many performance events that Welsh Terriers can do and do well, so today's Welsh Terrier owner has no real excuse for sitting home doing nothing.

Tracking seems deceptively easy on your first try. But by the time you are following forty feet behind a Welsh Terrier in a harness through cornfields and cow pastures, you begin to understand the worth of that Tracking Dog or Tracking Dog Excellent title! In the ten years from 1980 (when the Tracking Dog Excellent originated) to 1990 twenty-five terriers did earn a Tracking Dog Excellent title. In 1988 a Tracking Dog Excellent was earned by Darlene Jewell's *Susitna's Naughty Nell* in Alaska where Welsh

Tracking is natural for Welsh. Like all terriers, they hunt by scent, sight, and sound. (The latter two attributes can actually interfere with the first.)

Terriers are a "rare" breed. There is a new goal now—variable surface tracking.

Therapy

It has been known for a long time that stroking, petting, and talking to a dog has great therapeutic value, but it is only in recent years that dogs have become fixtures in nursing homes and hospitals, bringing warmth and smiles to patients.

An old bitch of mine, *Ch. Bardwyn Bittersweet*, CG, went regularly to nursing homes and developed what we called her "nursing home trot" tiptoeing silently down corridors and into the patients' rooms. Every person who has made these visits with a Welsh Terrier has dozens of heart-warming tales to tell. A personal "best" was when a ninety-five-year-old woman, sitting in the sun, called out, "Is that *really* a Welsh Terrier?" She was born in North Wales and raised with a Welsh Terrier. We talked about Wales for half an hour—with the dog on her lap. The Welsh are the right size and temperament for the work and are friendly, sensible, outgoing, and quiet.

Zippy, in her Easter bonnet, shares a moment of deep contemplation with a patient.

Derry Coe (Covail) has been participating with her Welsh for many years in The Children's Hospital Prescription Pet Program where the dogs bring a bit of joy and comfort to terminally-ill children. Her stories are numerous, but one of her dogs played an unusual public relations role. The hospital was up for a monetary grant and *Alpine* took the Foundation's representative on his rounds. After the

"Welsh tour," the hospital won Top Award for Excellence in Colorado, which consisted of a glass trophy (filled with dog biscuits) plus a $10,000 grant for creativity in giving support to the children. *Alpine* worked to the age of fifteen and a plaque on the hospital wall acknowledges her work. It just goes to show how persuasive a Welsh Terrier can be given the opportunity.

Obviously the dog must have good manners for this job, and although it is not time-consuming, it *is* draining. All owners agree the dogs are exhausted at the end of the hour or two of therapy visits. There are organizations, such as Therapy Dogs International (TDI), that offer training, tests, and so forth, and most of the all-breed dog clubs also provide this service locally. You need only volunteer. Therapy Dogs International's canine ambassador is *Zippy*, owned by Eva Shaw who took her on a book tour because TDI dogs are allowed to fly in the cabin! *Zippy* works mostly with Alzheimer patients.

Like many therapy dogs, when invited, *Zippy* jumps up on beds or into wheelchairs to be petted, and also performs numerous tricks, which are so enjoyed by the bedridden. She's a multi-talented Welsh doing a big job for humanity.

Eva occasionally gets credit, too.

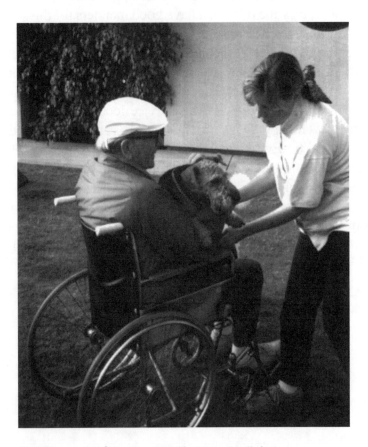

Eva Shaw makes Zippy comfortable in a patient's lap.

CHAPTER ELEVEN

WELSH TERRIER CLUB OF AMERICA
RESCUE

As mentioned in Chapter Nine, the Glyndwr Welsh Terrier Club had for some time been involved in rescuing Welsh Terriers, primarily to encourage breeders to take full responsibility for any dog they had sold, and not just for an arbitrary guarantee period, but for the life of the dog. When the concept of a national rescue program appeared in the Welsh Terrier Club of America newsletter, contributions were received almost at once. At a general meeting held in Chicago in June 1984, the idea was discussed, a committee formed and by October that year, WTCARES was underway, chaired by Barbara Hall. Barbara made the point that the committee actually consisted of *every* club member, every Welsh Terrier breeder, owner, and breed devotee. It was made a priority for the entire membership to participate in the "re-homing" of Welsh Terriers in need. By the end of the first year, several Welsh Terriers had been rescued and placed in a new home.

Unfortunately, some members thought of "rescue" only in terms of finding a lost dog on the street, or retrieving one from the local dog pound. The intent of WTCARES is to take in every Welsh in need—for whatever reason—and to find it a permanent home. At that time we were in the initial throes of such things as corporate moves, no-pets-allowed condominium living, retirement homes, nursing homes, etc., and we were seeing numerous reasons why a much-loved dog could not be kept. Many breeders began to add a line to their sales contract stating that they would take the dog back (or even requesting that it be brought back) *at any time* if the person could not keep it. Responsible breeding begins with breeding healthy, quality specimens of the breed; this unconditional return policy is the "other side" of responsible breeding.

Rob Savage and Jean Vondriska of Illinois took over the committee in 1986 and by the end of 1988 there was over a thousand dollars in the rescue fund. Elizabeth Leaman (Hapitails) headed it in 1989 and the following year Ward and Carolyn Morris of Atlanta, Georgia, took over, reorganized the paper work involved (including a small pamphlet explaining what rescue was all about), and appointed members geographically as contacts in their areas. Rescues have jumped from "several" or "a few" to over thirty a year.

All dogs that are rescued are given interim foster care, evaluated for temperament, previous training, personality and of course checked by a veterinarian and given whatever health care is needed. Anyone looking to adopt a Welsh Terrier is sent information on rescue and must fill out a detailed application. They are spoken to by phone and wherever feasible are visited by a member. Everything possible is done to put the right dog into the right family. The average wait for a rescue dog can be as much as a year. People who indicate any interest in rescuing a puppy are given the names of breeders to contact.

Carolyn Morris has traveled when needed to help with rescues from puppy-mill situations, some of which have been horror stories but always with satisfactory endings. A WTCARES scrapbook is bulging with photos and notes sent by new Welsh families. These people also make generous donations and the funds for rescue, despite increasing expenses for veterinary care, air fare, etc., is in excess of $5,000. In 1996, at Welsh Terrier Club of America's Montgomery Specialty, the Morrises were presented in the ring with a plaque for their years of dedicated work in rescuing our Welsh Terriers in need.

Very few Welsh Terriers are found in pet shops, due in part to the fact that they are not a popular breed and thus are not profitable for the retailer. It is also due to a current trend for the giant "supermarket" type pet shops which do not sell livestock. Only thirty-five of the more than 500 commercial breeders in the United States breed dogs of any kind, which is a comforting statistic for our breed. The other ninety-three percent of commercial breeders breed fish and birds. Puppy mills proliferate in poor farm areas, are difficult to locate, and even more difficult to put out of business since they change names and locale overnight. Commercial kennels, however, are not all "puppy mills." In fact the WTCARES dogs that have originally come from commercial kennels to date, while ranging from bad to deplorable if judged against the standard, have all had remarkably good temperaments. This might be credited to the Welsh Terrier's version of *carpe diem!* Opportunists all!

It has been difficult in some cases to persuade breeders to work with WTCARES due to a misconception that rescuing or re-homing dogs would usurp their sale of puppies. All the rescue service asks is that breeders take back dogs of their own breeding and then contact committee members to help find new homes. Breeders can contribute two very important things to the system: First, they are more apt to have facilities to provide temporary care, and secondly, if the dog must be put down, they are better able to cope realistically with the situation. The worst thing a breeder can do is to tell a pet owner to have their dog euthanized if they no longer want or can care for it. The average pet owner who must part with the dog is too emotionally involved to have to cope with euthanasia. If distance makes returning the dog a problem, another breeder or Welsh Terrier Club of America member can be contacted to take over.

In our conflict with animal activists who would deprive us of *all* pets, and who harp on pet animal overpopulation (although most is due to feral cats), breeders *must* be responsible for what they breed—for life. If they are not, they put themselves in the position of being nothing more than "puppy sellers." Responsible hobby breeders take note, it applies to all the puppies you breed: "Home is the place that when you go there, they have to take you in."

SPECIAL CARE

During all that time when we are not conscious of Taffy's advancing old age, the dog trusts that we will notice, that we will understand and give the needed care. Some Welsh at fifteen years of age are still agile, healthy and have all their faculties about them. When they do go, we always feel it was "sudden" perhaps because *we* were not prepared. But most of our dogs by the age of twelve or thirteen are beginning to show signs of aging. They don't respond as quickly as they did yesterday because they fail to hear us. Or their sight is beginning to fade, or minor aches cause discomfort. Regardless of his chronological age, the longer he lives, the more our care of him resembles the care we gave him as a puppy. If he might not see the danger, or hear your call, he has to be back on the lead for safety outdoors. Leaping off furniture can mean broken bones. There will be more trips outside, more long (and snoring) naps.

When the time comes, and it will, think of your dog, not yourself. If your veterinarian suggests euthanasia, or you know in your heart that's what is ahead, don't shut your mind to this final act of kindness. Judith Wax, an author and editor, wrote of her own dog, a Bedlington Terrier, ". . . there was even dignity in Alfie's departure. And someone (me) who loved him dearly, if a little irrationally, held him until it was over."

Filling the Void

There are two things to do when your pet or house dog dies, no matter what its age. First, *grieve*. Human beings the world over have cried, written heart-rending poems, and created beautiful music upon the loss of their canine companion. It's not noble or brave to hold back the tears. You've lost your best friend. You're entitled to some self-indulgence. By the way, it is perfectly normal to "step over" the dog, or to "see" him by the door or in his spot after he's gone. Children learn an important lesson in the life-and-death scenario by seeing that you care. Soon you'll be remembering all the funny, strange, endearing, and crazy things this particular dog did that made him special.

I said there were two things to do. The second one is *wait*. Wait until the tears and the ghosts are out of the house before bringing in another dog. The next one will not be, and cannot be, a replacement. You can't "replace" one dog with another. Let the new one come in on its own four feet and be its own individual "person." Don't start off looking for similarities, and don't try to compare an old dog who knew you like the back of his paw with a bouncing puppy who has everything to learn and must depend upon you to teach him.

What stands out about the Welsh Terrier is the fact that time after time I meet people whose parents had a Welsh, who then grew up with a succession of three or four more. There is a devotion to our breed unlike that of any other. Is it any wonder that the Welsh Terrier, with his innate tenacity, would find a way to work himself into our hearts and there make his home? The Welsh Terrier leads the way, and we are glad to share the journey.

An original drawing by Diane H. Orange.

CHAPTER TWELVE

TODAY AND TOMORROW

We have recalled the names of the distant past, those who got the breed started in its native land and those in the United States who led us in the right direction—the de Coppets (Windermere), Maurice Pollak (Marlu), Ross Proctor (Brookwood), the Edward Clarks (Halcyon), Hugh Chisholm (Strathglass). There are also those in the more recent past, some of whom are very much still with us, but no longer breeding—"Ernie" Alker (Twin Ponds), Anne Colt (Coltan), the Wimers (Pool Forge), the Bilgers (Reglib), Kimmel and Edwards (Tujays), the Marshes (Gregmar), Nell Hudson (Penzance), Bill Etter (Licken Run), the McClungs (Wenmar). All these people, and so many others, have provided us with both a past and a future in the breed.

Jack Kimmel showing Ch. Tujay's Tia Maria under top terrier man, William Kendrick.

The present names have changed. Among them—Collings (Purston), Leaman (Hapitails), Beattie (Sunspryte), Prehn (Ledge Rock), Coe (Covail),

Briggs (Briggsdale), Czarnecki (Czar), O'Neal (Anasazi), Williams (La Sierra), and Baumgardner (Kirkwood). We trust they will carry on the legacy for those who come after them by maintaining the high goals of the past in sportsmanship, in adhering to the breed standard as originally perceived for conformation, and in never losing sight of the intelligence, friendly temperament, and the natural working ability of the Welsh Terrier.

Jim Edwards leads a virtual living pedigree of Ch. Penzance Polaris's California offspring under Fox Terrier breeder-judge, Evelyn Silvernail.

The Leamans imported several good dogs, among them Ch. Purston Give' Em Hell, Ch. Serenfach David, and Ch. Patt v.d. Bismarckquelle, who is pictured at left. Here, Patt is being handled by Richard Powell, taking BOB under noted terrier man, Richard Chashoudian.

Montgomery—The Last Ten Years or So

Welsh Terrier Club of America's affinity for the Montgomery County Kennel Club Terrier Show may be due to the roots of Montgomery County Kennel Club having been in the Welsh-named Gwynedd Valley Kennel Club, and the fact that many of its year-round workers who pull off this premier show have been Welsh Terrier breeders—Carlotta Howard, Dorothy and Bill Wimer and Bill Etter, to name a few.

Ch. Briggsdale Rowdy Rusty, handled by Christopher Nance, was a 1992 multiple BIS winner, bred and co-owned by Dick & Glenna Briggs and Peter Zablocki.

In 1987 Norbert Savage's dog, *Ch. Colwyn Auspicious Choice*, was the sire of both the Winners Dog—*Helgar's Wundrland Wild Card,* bred by Helen Lambert—and of Winners Bitch—*Bear Hill's Ms Jingle,* bred by Dr. Leon Lussier. Best of Breed that year was the imported bitch, *Ch. Serenfach Dior*, who went on to a Group 3. In 1984 it was *Ch. Anasazi Annie Oakley* who took a Group 2 and a Group 4 the following year. Three more Welsh placed in Groups at this show. In 1988 *Ch. Calkerry's Evening Attire* (bred by Doris Tolone and Clay Coady) was third in Group. (He was also awarded Show Dog of the Year at the Tournament of Champions.) The following year *Ch. Gregmar's Goldspur* was Group 2, and in 1992 the import owned by the Frasers of Canada, *Ch. Purston Take Off* (bred by Michael Collings and handled by R.C. Carusi), placed fourth in the Group.

These statistics point up once again that Welsh Terrier bitches do extremely well in the show ring. Of the six Welsh that placed in Group in the past ten years, four were bitches. And, of course, in 1978 it was the McClungs' bitch, *Ch. Copperboots Wee Blaste*, that took Best in Show honors, the first Welsh to do so since *Dewi of St. Aubrey* did it in 1962. *Ch. Anasazi Annie Oakley*, owned by Jean Heath and William H. Cosby, did a Best of Breed hat trick in 1985, winning the breed all three days at Devon, Hatboro, and Montgomery. She also was Best in Show at the first two and Group 4 at the last. In the Brace Class several have tried, but nary a one has been chosen!

The breed has not been so fortunate with wins at Westminster where the *Goldspur* dog was Group 3 in 1989 and two years later *Ch. Sunspryte Gregmar Shorlyne* also claimed a third.

In 1990 Bruce Schwartz's *Ch. Bruhill's Paradice* from the West Coast was sharing top billing with Carole and Bob Beattie's *Ch. Sunspryte Gregmar's Jewel* from Florida, both Best in Show winners along with *Ch. Wenmar's Copper Pebble*, a *Wee Blaste* daughter.

In 1991 the AKC breed registrations escalated to 896 with 377 litter registrations, seventy champions, and eight obedience title holders. But by 1994 registrations were at the more-normal figure in recent years of 660. Litters in 1994 fell to 277, champions to forty-eight, while obedience titles held at eight. Over the years, it doesn't seem to matter how the individual and litter registrations fluctuate, the ratio is static: for every litter registered, an average of only two and a half dogs are individually registered. One has to wonder what happens to the remaining pups in every litter!

The year 1992 saw *Ch. Sunspryte Gregmar Shorlyne* emerge as the number one Welsh Terrier. Bred by Carole Beattie (Sunspryte) and Hank Marsh (Gregmar), he is co-owned by Pamela Price (Shorlyne) and Marge McClung (Wenmar)—whose kennel prefix didn't get on the dog, since the AKC limits the number of letters to twenty-six, but whose own top stud dog, *Ch. Rushwyn's Black Hawk*, was the sire. The number two dog, also from the

South but shown in the East and Midwest, was *Ch. Cascade Lane's Samson McBee.* After getting one's hands on the multiple-champion, *Ch. Nathan v.d. Bismarckquelle* (bred by Alex Mohrke and owned by Kathy Reges-Carlson), it is difficult to see how judges could resist him! A superior dog, he did have many Group and Best in Show wins, but was denied what would seem to have been his rightful place at the top

Ch. Nathan v.d. Bismarckquelle, handled by Gabriel Rangle.

Kirkwood Top Brass won the 1994 Sweepstakes and his littermate, *Kirkwood Bold as Brass,* was BOS (judged by professional handler and Welsh Terrier breeder, Richard Powell). Both dogs were breeder-owner handled by Ann Baumgardner. *Top Brass,* now owned by Frank Stevens and handled by Gabrielle Rangel, took the breed and Group 3 at Montgomery in 1997.

Ch. Anasazi Trail Boss became Top Producing Sire, breaking the previous record held by *Ch. Penzance Polaris* (who sired thirty-one champion get). *Trail Boss,* known as

Ch. Kirkwood Top Brass, 1997 WTCA Specialty breed winner at MCKC. Judge Lydia Hutchinson, handler Gabrielle Rangel, and WTCA President R.C. Williams.

"Duke," more than doubled it to a new record total of sixty-six champion get. His current "most famous son" is *Ch. Anasazi Billy the Kid.* Duke was just as good in the show ring, with a total of thirty all-breed Bests in Show plus Groups and Specialty Show wins. When he won the Veterans Class at Montgomery in 1988, his owner, Hank Marsh, quipped, "Now we're both Veterans."

Over the past decade we have also benefited enormously from the ease of overseas travel. On this side, we have had as our Specialty Show judges Cyril Williams, Drys Thomas, Eric Catherall, Harry O'Donohugh, Herbert Atkinson, Gerrard Morris from the U.K., and Keith Lovell from Australia. And in reverse, we have sent numerous breeder-judges to their shores, the latest being Bruce Schwartz and Sue Weiss.

Worldwide there is probably less difference in the *dogs* than there is in the dog shows, how the dogs are groomed, and handled (or over-handled as so many comment about the American shows). Also in the way the show is run and in the judging procedure.

Mr. Cyril Williams (Caiach), of Ystrad Mynach, Wales, judged our 1985 WTCA Specialty at Montgomery, putting up Ch. Anasazi Annie Oakley.

Something amusing happened in this period of growth, which suggests a change in what is most important in the dog show. The AKC finally put a halt to allowing dogs' names to be changed, making it easier to maintain accurate records. In the past a dog would be owned by a kennel, or possibly co-owned by a husband and wife, but recently that aspect of registration has expanded to what one European visitor referred to as "dogs being

*Cisseldale Harri Morduyur
("Harry the Sailor" in Welsh),
owned by John & Patty Boyd of
California, proving Welsh
Terriers make very good sailors.*

owned by some kind of cooperative." It is not unusual today to see a show dog listed as being owned by four or more separate, unrelated individuals. There is no AKC limit to the number of owners. The dog's name may be as simple as "Ch. Stoppit" bred by John Smith, but the catalog listing goes on endlessly with the names of these unlimited multiple owners.

Today the Welsh Terrier is in good shape numerically, retaining a low profile while still taking a good share of the top show wins. Fortunately, too, for the breed, many dogs are proving their worth in other activities involving natural work, brains, stamina, and a sensible temperament. We need to keep these things in mind *"lest the breed become just a show dog"* which is a strong warning emanating from our very beginnings. And, updating that warning: lest the ego overtake the breed itself.

Montgomery County Kennel Club 1996

In an unprecedented move, the Montgomery County Kennel Club honored a living member of that club—Bill Etter. An active member of Welsh Terrier Club of America for fifty-four of his ninety-one years, Bill was presented with a plaque commemorating the event and a huge blue banner was strung across our ring also honoring "Mr. Welsh Terrier" as he was known. The day was capped by having the Welsh Terrier, *Ch. Anasazi Billy The Kid*, awarded Best in Show. This was the second time Mr. James Reynolds of Canada judged BIS at Montgomery. In 1978 he also went with the Welsh—*Ch. Copperboots Wee Blaste.* In the Veterans Class, we had a father and son entry for the first time: *Ch. Rushwyn's Blackhawk* and his son *Ch. Sunspryte Gregmar's Shorlyne.* The youngster won the Class, but twelve-year-old *Hawk* was as spry as a puppy and in beautiful condition. Needless to say, a hard class to judge.

We have become used to Sylvia Sidney, the actress, and Bill Cosby's family, attending our shows, but this year also brought out Bob Hope.

Sadly, after such a glorious day of recognition, Bill Etter passed away just two weeks later. Everyone was grateful he had been given such a happy day, widely and warmly shared by the terrier fancy.

European Update

The news in Wales is that more children speak Welsh today than ever before in this century! There are campaigns to keep the language alive (the Welsh Language Act) and to have free Welsh-language nursery schools. (Remember Taliesin's prediction: "Their language they shall keep.") The road signs are in Welsh first, English second. (Thank God for the roundabouts!) In South Wales, where parents don't speak Welsh, bilingualism is a problem for the kids, but it would be a catastrophe to lose such a national identity.

At the 1988 Welsh Terrier Club Championship show, of the sixty-three dogs entered, fifteen were sired by *Ch. Bowers Jigsaw of Eladeria.* Best in Show was *Ch. Felstead Formulate* handled by Ray Davies for Mesdames Remy and Bernaudin of France. In 1995 the top stud dog in the U.K. was *Ch. Solentine Sugar Ray* bred by Wendy Gatto Ronchieri. It was Ms. Gatto's first litter and *Sugar*

Left:
Bill Etter receiving a
commemorative plaque
from WTCA officers and
members of the board.

Right: (left ot right) Freeman Ayers (Welshire)
and Bardi McLennan (Bardwyn) with Bill Etter
on his big day.

Below: It was a day to remember!
Montgomery County KC 1996 was dedicated to
W.H. Etter, and Ch. Anasazi Billy the Kid,
handled by Wood Wornall, was awarded BIS.
Presenting the numerous trophies are (left to
right): Dr. Josephine Deubler, Bill Etter,
James Reynolds from Canada, and Walter
Goodman.

Every specialty should
be such fun!

Ch. Saredon Ray Charles, owned by Judy Averis and Dave Scawthorn, took the breed at the Welsh Terrier Association Championship Show in Usk in 1995 and has added many more big wins since. It's not all silver trophies, however. He's proving his worth as a stud dog, too.

Ray was a solitary pup, proving once again it only takes one good one! He was purchased by Mme. Bernaudin.

In 1994 Crufts' new show site proved the right one for the Welsh Terrier bitch, *Ch. Purston Hit and Miss from Brocolitia*, who went Best in Show. She was bred by Michael Collings, owned by Mrs. A.J. Maughan and handled by the late Frank Kellert.

At the Welsh Terrier Association Championship show at Usk in 1995, Best of Breed was Judy Averis and Dave Scawthorn's *Ch. Saredon Ray Charles* with the Bitch CC going to *Felstead Fine Mist*. The overall top bitch for the year was Mrs. Halliwell's *Ch. Purston Leading Lady at Wigmore*.

In Holland

The High Flyer prefix of Jan Albers is well-known in the States with one bitch in particular, *Ch. High Flyer's Top Star*, who was one of the top three Welsh in 1978, the "year of the bitches."

She was bred to *Ch. Bardwyn Bronze Bertram* before returning to Holland and a direct descendent is currently Albers' top dog—*Ch. High Flyer's Carsillo*. *Ch. High Flyer's Show Girl* was also in the U.S. and a World Winner in 1993 on her return to Holland. Jan Albers is one of a diminishing handful of successful true line-breeders left.

South America

In 1995 *Ch. Ledge Rock's Prince Llewelyn* went to Ecuador, garnered two Bests in Show and finished the year as Number Eight dog (all breeds) in the country. In 1994 the Sandovals of Bogota, Colombia, imported *Col. Ch. Ledge Rock's Welsh Prince* from Ruth Prehn. He was the first Welsh Terrier in Colombia and the following spring, a bitch went down to join him. Terriers, are a sparse group in South America, but with numerous Welsh settlers (from over a century ago) in the region of Patagonia, perhaps our favorite breed will catch their attention.

The Future

We would do well to heed Nell Hudson's admonition of twenty years ago when I served with her on a committee to "translate" some of the breed standard into American-English. She said, "I would like to emphasize that our present standard is identical to the original standard composed in the late 1800s by knowledgeable men who sent their Welsh into the field as well as into the show ring and who enjoyed great success in both areas. Because they were huntsmen and because they were dedicated to one of the oldest of the terrier breeds, they surely knew what qualities to stress in their standard and modeled it accordingly."

All the changes that have taken place over the years to transform the Welsh Terrier from a merely useful dog to an eye-pleasing specimen in the show ring have had to do with his appearance. He remains the same charming companion and capable no-nonsense hunter described by the terrier men who brought him in from the field and farms into the show ring one hundred years ago, and by the recipient who gratefully acknowledged his intrinsic value in that thank you note five hundred years ago.

We've had our ups and a few downs in the breed and are reminded of that old Welsh Gypsy saying: "Winter will tell us what we did in the summer." Only the future can tell us how well, or how badly, we have handled the stewardship of our chosen breed.

Ch. Saredon Forever Young, who won Best in Show at the 1998 Crufts.

APPENDIX

WELSH TERRIER CLUB OF AMERICA
AWARDS, TROPHIES, AND PRIZES

Prizes are the tangible rewards for winning, and wins in the dog fancy are no exception. In 1909 the Welsh Terrier Club of America began a tradition of awarding two major trophies, the Grand Challenge Cup and the Junior Challenge Cup. They have been offered every year since, although the venue eventually changed from Westminster Kennel Club in New York to the Welsh Terrier Club of America Specialty, which is held with the prestigious all–terrier show at the Montgomery County Kennel Club in Pennsylvania. Bases have been added to accommodate the winners" names when space on the cups ran out.

The trophy cups have always been, and still are, awarded to members only. Originally there was a further stipulation that read: "It is for Welsh Terrier dogs or bitches of any age, owned by the exhibitor for at least six months prior to the close of the entries." That qualification was eliminated in 1935 without explanation, but clearly would seem to have had something to do with the number of last–minute imports or the numerous dogs that changed owners rather more frequently than is the case today.

From the beginning, various trophies were offered by the principal kennels (Marlu, Warwell, Halcyon, Windermere, etc.) to acknowledge the most wins in specific AKC classes. They were usually set up to cover a span of two or three years in order to allow exhibitors to accumulate sufficient points. The number and accessibility of shows early in the century was limited Today we have a reverse situation: shows are so numerous in the United States that many either do not draw any Welsh Terrier entry or attract only a few of the top–winning dogs being campaigned.

The Welsh Terrier Club (U.K.) presented Welsh Terrier Club of America with a challenge cup known as The England Cup for the best Welsh Terrier under eighteen months of age bred by exhibitor. The England Cup is competed for at specific shows over a period of five years from 1925 to 1930. The de Coppets eventually claimed this much–admired silver bowl.

Homer Gage Jr. Memorial Trophy

Perhaps no young man has made a more lasting impression on Welsh and Fox Terriers in a shorter time than Homer Gage Jr. Certainly, there is no greater honor than to be awarded the Homer Gage Jr. Memorial Trophy for best American–bred dog or bitch at the same top–rated specialty show where the Challenge Cups are given. However, few recipients today know the full story behind the prize.

Homer Gage Jr. was born November 17, 1895, in Worcester, Massachusetts, the only child of Dr. and Mrs. Homer Gage. He entered Harvard in 1914, but left to join the American Field Ambulance Corps in 1917. On arriving in France, he promptly bought a Belgian Shepherd puppy named Gypsy, which became the mascot of his unit. Gypsy returned to the States with her master and lived to ripe old age. Homer went back to Harvard and then to work for his uncle.

Homer's first show dog was *Ch. Real Welsh of Hafren*, campaigned by Alf Delmont in 1921. About this time, his parents built a modern kennel facility for him and through Mr. George Thomas he acquired the *Eng. Ch. Welsh Scout*. Only one month later, Joseph Booth and his wife came from England to manage the new Welwire Kennels, which eventually housed up to eighty Welsh and Wire Fox Terriers. Homer became an ardent breeder, making many trips to Great Britain, studying pedigrees, learning as much as possible about the art of breeding, and endeavoring to produce in his kennels dogs of the same high quality as were being imported. He became an AKC judge, getting huge entries—a record 133 Wires in February 1924.

Homer Gage and his parents were Welsh Terrier Club of America members when, in September 1925 at the age of twenty-nine, he contracted polio and died after only three days' illness. He left clear instructions to provide for the Booths and for all his dogs and, typical of his true breeder interests, he left a large trust fund to establish the Homer Gage Jr. Memorial Trophy—one for Fox Terriers and one for Welsh Terriers. In his words, "Please offer a trophy through the Welsh Terrier Club of America to be offered, at the same shows as the Grand Challenge Cup and under the same conditions, for the best American Bred Welsh Terrier." Originally presented by Dr. and Mrs. Homer Gage in memory of their son, it is still offered each year and won outright.

Note: In 1926, although the de Coppets won the Grand Challenge Cup with their Ch. Windermere Piper, the name of Homer Gage Jr. with Ch. Wilwin Odds On, appears on the cup. There is no yearbook reference to this duplicity, but perhaps it was the Welsh Terrier Club of America's way of paying tribute to this young man.

The Welwire kennels sustained a devastating fire in 1931, losing both buildings and dogs, but Dr. Gage continued to judge Welsh Terriers until his death in 1938. In 1944 Mrs. Gage was made an Honorary Life Member of Welsh Terrier Club of America.

Breeder's Cup

In 1927 a Breeder's Cup was offered by W. Ross Proctor Jr., for the best Welsh Terrier dog or bitch not over two years of age that was bred by the exhibitor and to be competed for during the years 1927–1930 at Westminster Kennel Club show, the Welsh Terrier Club of America Specialty, Eastern Dog Club Show, and Westbury Kennel Club show and to be awarded to the exhibitor scoring the most wins during that time. There was no Bred by Exhibitor Class, so wins meeting the above requirements came from any class, and at that time the term "bred by exhibitor" meant bred by the owner, not necessarily the handler. Mr. Proctor repeated the award for the years 1930–1934, but the wins were not recorded.

The Welsh Terrier Club of America then offered the Breeder's Cup to be competed for from the fall of 1934 to February 1938 at six shows for best dog or bitch (not a champion) in the Bred by Exhibitor Class.

In 1932 the AKC clamped down on what were termed "special prizes," which put an end to what had been a common practice of handing out prize money in the classes.

The Saga of the Silver Spoons

Sterling silver coffee spoons were first awarded in 1934 as commemorative prizes towards winning the Breeder's Cup. The kennel with the most wins during the three–year period won the cup, and after 1938 it was never mentioned again.

However, sterling silver spoons did surface one more time. They were awarded from 1950 through 1959 with the following rules: "Silver spoons will be offered at all 3–point shows in Bred by Exhibitor Classes—Open to all." Winners from 1952 through 1959 took home a total of 214 spoons! Long–time member, Bill Etter (Licken Run) proudly garnered six spoons in 1954 alone.

Reversing the 1950–59 "open to all" policy, silver spoons (teaspoons this time and no longer defined as "sterling') were offered to "members only" in 1966, with associate members receiving pins instead. This ruling flew in the face of the by–laws which stipulated that associate members had all rights of full membership (including trophies) except for the right to vote (or, apparently, the right to protest).

The odd thing is that with so many spoons awarded, only one or two of these now valuable collectibles have ever turned up in the dog show concessionaires' booths or in antique shops. Since the vast majority of the winners are now dead, one wonders how well over 300 engraved silver spoons could become so totally lost.

Brood Bitch Stakes

The Brood Bitch Stakes were begun in the 1940s and held with the February Specialty. In 1955 there was a record entry of thirty–one bitches judged by Percy Roberts. The winner in this instance was Strathglass Bethesda. There is no record as to why the stakes ended, but either interest dwindled or the Welsh Terrier Club of America could no longer handle the running of it as a non–regular class. They ended in 1960. At a board meeting, the de Coppets tried to initiate a Stud Dog Stakes, but that idea didn't fly.

Obedience—The Birr Trophy

Obedience Tests, as they were then called, began in 1937. There was no club award prior to 1960 when Miss Louise Patterson (Birr Kennels, and founder of the Welsh Terrier Club of the Jemez) presented the Birr Obedience Trophy. It was the first and only prize for obedience at that time, and after Miss Patterson's death in 1970, the Welsh Terrier Club of Jemez continued to donate the trophy in her memory until that regional club disbanded in 1980. The Birr Obedience Trophy continued to be awarded for another five years under the original rules: To the owner whose Welsh Terrier earns the highest single score in the most advanced obedience class in which Welsh Terriers are represented. Open to members and non–members.

Still More Trophies

In 1972 Dr. and Mrs. Eugene Jacoby presented the Tuppence Jones Award "for the highest scoring Welsh Terrier in the U.S. determined by averaging the three highest scores attained in one year. Open only to members and associate members." This last stipulation was later changed and the award was made "open to all."

In 1986 more awards were offered to honor our active Welsh Terriers: the Sunspryte Trophy for Best Working Welsh Terrier, the Cascade Lane Trophy for Highest Individual Score, the Talylln Trophy for Highest Combined Score, and the Esty Glen Trophy for Most Versatile.

By 1995 the "activity" awards had grown to include the Cascade Lane Trophy, the Sunspryte Trophy for "fastest time to the quarry," the Xxtra Trophy for a "champion with the highest score in obedience," and the Esty Glen Trophy for "the most versatile Welsh Terrier." All of these trophies incorporate a variety of AKC activities in which the breed is involved.

Apart from the Challenge Cups and the Homer Gage Jr. Memorial Trophy, the Annual Awards have grown from five in 1930 to twelve in 1950 and to twenty-seven in 1995! Originally, awards were made at the annual meeting, but the club events have now stretched to encompass the entire weekend of the Montgomery Specialty. The annual meeting now takes place separately on

Friday evening after a buffet supper and with the boutique open for business. At the club's annual dinner on the following evening, the awards are displayed and then presented to the winners.

WINNERS

The complete rules for the Challenge Cups appear in Welsh Terrier Club of America yearbooks. In summary these two prize cups are awarded to Best of Breed and Best of Opposite Sex at the Club Specialty held at Montgomery County Kennel Club *only* if all owners of each dog or bitch are club members. The Cups remain the property of the club and currently a gold-plated medallion commemorates the Grand Challenge win, a silver-plated for the Junior Challenge win. Over the years there have been differences in recorded names and the actual engraving on the Cups. New bases have been added to accommodate the almost 100 years of wins.

WTCA Grand Challenge Cup Winners (as Engraved)

1909	B.W.C. Ellison's Ch. Cyron Carboy
1910	B. & G. de Coppet's Windermere Winsome
1911	B. & G. de Coppet's Windermere Winsome
1912	Franklin B. Lord's Ch. Landore Boy
1913	Franklin B. Lord's Longmynd Borderer
1914	Miss Maud Kennedy's Ch. Senny Spinner
1915	B. & G. de Coppet's Dany Craig Masterpiece
1916	B. & G. de Coppet's Windermere Topper
1917	W. Ross Proctor's Ch. Senny Tip Top
1918	B. & G. de Coppet's Ch. Windermere Topper
1919	John N. Stevens' Ch. Carri Eryri
1920	B. & G. de Coppet's Ch. Windermere Topper
1921	W. Ross Proctor's Ch. Brookwood Ringside
1922	W. Ross Proctor's Ch. Brookwood Ringside
1923*	Homer Gage Jr.'s Ch. Welwire Odds On
1924	Dr. & Mrs. Samuel Milbank's Ch. Welsh Emblem
1925	Annandale Kennel's Hafren Cheerioh
1926	Misses de Coppet Ch. Windermere Piper
1927	Halcyon Kennel's Ch. Cock-y-Bondu
1928	Halcyon Kennel's Froth Blower

* AKC records indicate the 1923 BOB was B. & G.de Coppet's Windermere Home Brew

1929	Proctor & Lord's Ch. Maid of Bwlffa
1930	B. & G. de Coppet's Ch. Rowdy Boy
1931	B. & G. de Coppet's Ch. Rowdy Boy
1932	Halcyon Kennel's Ch. Halcyon Play Boy
1933	Scotsward Kennel's Ch. Marrion Mwyn
1934	Scotsward Kennel's Ch. Galen Kola of Scotsward
1935	Scotsward Kennel's Ch. Topnotch Taffy of Scotsward
1936	Aman Ambition of Halcyon
1937	Marlu Farm Kennels Ch. Marlu Marigold
1938	Twin Ponds Kennels Ch. Bodnant Eto
1939	Harold Florsheim's Ch. Towie Thargelia
1940	Halcyon Kennels Ch. Aman Superb of Halcyon
1941	Halcyon Kennels Ch. Hotpot Harriboy of Halcyon
1942	Halcyon Kennels Ch. Hotpot Harriboy of Halcyon
1943	Ch. Flornell Rare-Bit of Twin Pond Kennels
1944	Ch. Flornell Rare-Bit of Twin Pond Kennels
1945	Ch. Twin Pond's Suntan of Twin Pond Kennels
1946	Mrs. E. T. Clark's Halcyon Masterpiece
1947	Mrs. E. T. Clark's Halcyon's Rose-Marie
1948	Mrs. E. P. Alker's Ch. Twin Ponds Belle
1949	Mrs. E. P. Alker's Ch. Twin Ponds Belle
1950	Mr. and Mrs. S. Sloan Colt's Victory Boy
1951	Mrs. E. P. Alker's Toplight Template of Twin Ponds
1952	Mr. Hugh J. Chisholm's Ch. Strathglass Venture's Lucifer
1953	Mr. and Mrs. A. R. Gratton's Strathglass Admirals Baron
1954	Mrs. E. P. Alker's Toplight Template of Twin Ponds
1955	Mr. Hugh J. Chisholm's Ch. Monona's Devil Dancer
1956	Mr. Hugh J. Chisholm's Ch. Licken Run's Panic
1957	Mrs. E. P. Alker's Ch. Syl-Von's Super-Man
1958	Mr. Joseph W. Urmston's Quayside Jolly Roger
1959	Mr. Hugh J. Chisholm's Strathglass Trim Maid
1960	Mrs. Joseph Urmston's Int.Ch. Quayside Jolly Roger
1961	Mr. Harold M. Florsheim's Ch. Licken Run's Top the Rock
1962	Mrs. Edward P. Alker Ch. Caradoc Llwyd of St. Aubrey
1963	Reglib Kennel's Ch. Ernley Felstead Flashfoot of Reglib
1964	Mr. and Mrs. S. Sloan Colt's Ch. Coltan Countess

1965	Pool Forge Kennel's Ch. Pool Forge Fast Freight
1966	Pool Forge Kennel's Ch. Pool Forge Fast Freight
1967	Pool Forge Kennel's Ch. Pool Forge Fast Freight
1968	Mrs. E. P. Alker's Ch. Felstead True Form
1969	Mrs. E. P. Alker's Ch. Felstead True Form
1970	Mrs. E. P. Alker's Ch. Twin Pond Plaid Cymru
1971	VOID
1972	Mrs. Robert V. Clark Jr.'s Ch. Twin Ponds Plaid Cymru
1973	Mrs. Robert V. Clark Jr.'s Ch. Twin Ponds Plaid Cymru
1974	Mr. William Etter's Ch. Licken Run Two Pence Sam
1975	Mr. and Mrs. Sloan Colt's Ch. Groveview Jake
1976	VOID
1977	VOID
1978	VOID
1979	Dr. and Mrs. O.W. McClung Ch. Copperboots Wee Blaste
1980	Dr. and Mrs. O.W. McClung Ch. Copperboots Wee Blaste
1981	D. Cortum & D. Jacob & Dr. & Mrs. McClung's Ch. Johnel's DD of Redondo Beach
1982	Ch. Coltan Coastal
1983	Dr. & Mrs. O.W. McClung's Ch. Snowtaire's Nutmeg Jeds
1984	VOID
1985	VOID
1986	Carole A. Beattie's Ch. Ledge Rock's Benjamin
1987	VOID
1988	J.L. Heath, W. Cosby Jr. & Doris Tolone's Ch. Calkerry Evening Attire
1989	Hank Marsh's Ch. Gregmar's Goldspur
1990	Bruce R. Schwartz's Ch. Bruhil's Paradice
1991	Dr. & Mrs. O.W. McClung & Pamela Price's Ch. Sunspryte Gregmar Shorlyne
1992	Mr. & Mrs. Thomas Fraser's Ch. Purston Take Off
1993	Mr. & Mrs. R. C. Williams Ch. La Sierra's Lucky Lad
1994	Bruce Schwartz's Ch. Anasazi Billy The Kid
1995	D. Guida & C. A. Beattie & J. L. Heath & W. H. Cosby Jr.'s Ch. Cisseldale's Sugar Babe

WTCA Junior Challenge Cup Winners (as Engraved)

1909	B. & G. de Coppet's Ch. Windermere Captive
1910	B. & G. de Coppet's Windermere Chip
1911	F. B. Lord's "Ch. Landore Boy"
1912	B. & G. de Coppet's Windermere Winsome
1913	M. Kennedy's Senny Model
1914	B. & G. de Coppet's Ch. Windermere Winsome
1915	B. & G. de Coppet's Ch. Windermere Winsome
1916	B. & G. de Coppet's Windermere Wistful
1917	W. Ross Proctor's Ch. Bryn Melyn Beauty
1918	John N. Steven's Ch. Cerri Eryri
1919	B. & G. de Coppet's Ch. Windermere Topper
1920	John N. Steven's Ch. Cerri Eryri
1921	Mrs. Malcolm Stevenson's Ch. Bother 'em All
1922	B. & G. de Coppet's Windermere Bother
1923	B. & G. de Coppet's Disturbance
1924	Chappaqua Kennel's What's Wanted
1925	Annandale Kennels Llewellyn Luminous
1926	Annandale Kennel's Excuse Me
1927	Welwire Kennels Ch. Hafren Wizard
1928	B. & G. de Coppet's Windermere Chunkie
1929	Welwire Kennels Defynog Duplicator
1930	Halcyon Kennels Ch. Hulloa of Halcyon
1931	Halcon KennelsDarren Tiddy's Duplicate
1932	Frank Spiekerman's Aman Melody
1933	Halcyon Kennels Ch. Halcyon Play Boy
1934	Halcyon Kennels Ch. Halcyon Play Boy
1935	Marlu Kennels Aman Accurate of Marlu
1936	Marlu Farm Kennels Ch. Aman Accurate of Marlu
1937	Marlu Farm Kennels Ch. Galen Maltose of Marlu
1938	Harham Kennels Ch. Singleton Latest
1939	Halcyon Kennels Aman Crackerjack of Halcyon
1940	Halcyon Kennels Thet Togo of Halcyon
1941	Mr. Harold Florsheim's Ch. Towie Thargelia
1942	Mr. Harold Florsheim's Ch. Towie Thargelia
1943	Halcyon Kennels Ch. Mari Voni of Halcyon
1944	B. & G. de Coppet's Ch. Windermere Bridget
1945	Twin Pond Kennel's Twin Pond's Vera
1946	Twin Pond Kennel's Ch. Twin Pond's Belle
1947	Twin Pond Kennel's Twin Pond's Lend Lease

1948	Coltan Kennels Ch. Halcyon Masterpiece
1949	Strathglass Kennels Ch. Strathglass Venture's Snowden
1950	VOID
1951	Strathglass Kennels Ch. Strathglass Sylva
1952	Coltan Kennels Ch. Dina Del
1953	Strathglass Kennels Strathglass Lucifer's Dyma
1954	Strathglass Kennels Monoma's Devil Dancer
1955	Vaughn R. Sylvester's Syl-von's Super-man
1956	Twin Pond Kennels Ch. Syl-Von's Super-Man
1957	Strathglass Kennels Strathglass Admiral's Gwalia
1958	Coltan Kennels Ch. Patty's Fancy Lady of Dorian
1959	Mr. Harold Florsheim's Ch. Licken Run's Rock and Roll
1960	Twin Pond Kennels Ch. Twin Pond's Madonna
1961	Coltan Kennels' Ch. Coltan Caprice
1962	Coltan Kennels Ch. Coltan Carioca
1963	Mrs. Edward P. Alker's Ch. Dewi of St. Aubrey
1964	Mrs. Nell B. Hudson's Ch. Tawe Telstar
1965	Mrs. Edward P. Alker's Ch. Tawe Superb of Twin Ponds
1966	Ed & Bernice Metcalf's Alokin Achievement
1967	Mrs. Nell B. Hudson's Ch. Tawe Starlight
1968	Mr. John G. Reid's Ch. Licken Run Party Girl
1969	Mrs. Nell B. Hudson's Ch. Tawe Sweet Song
1970	Mrs. Nell B. Hudson's Ch. Tawe Sweet Song
1971	Mrs. Nell B. Hudson's Ch. Tawe Sweet Song
1972	Mrs. Nell B. Hudson's Ch. Jokyl Sonoma Sweet Chimes
1973	Mary E. Leggett's Ch. Tujay's Star Royale
1974	Mrs. Nell B. Hudson's Ch. Jokyl Sonoma Sweet Chimes
1975	Mr. & Mrs. R.B. Masson's Ch. Chayna Laird's Lady
1976	Mr. Peter J. Green's Ch. Swanzee Sky Lord
1977	Coltan Kennels Ch. Coltan Carey
1978	Coltan Kennels Ch. Groveview Jake
1979	VOID
1980	VOID
1981	Coltan Kennels Ch. Coltan Coastal
1982	VOID
1983	E.B. Jenner & N. Apprahamian's Ch. Merthyr's Super Man

1984	Mr. & Mrs. R. Beattie's Ch. Gregmar's San Diego Charger
1985	Mrs. A.R. Howard Jr.'s Ch. Greenfield's Plaid Cymru
1986	Dr. & Mrs. O.W. McClung's Ch. D'D's Devon
1987	Dr. & Mrs. O.W. McClung's Ch. Rushwyn's Black Hawk
1988	VOID
1989	Arlis Gardner's Ch. Windonwell This 'N' That
1990	Harry Kwatny's Ch. High Flyer's Galaxy
1991	VOID
1992	VOID
1993	Mr. & Mrs. Robert Beattie & Ms. Adams' Ch. Sunspryte Xxtra Bejewelled
1994	Kathy Reges-Carlson & Ann H. Baumgardner's Ch. Kirkwood's Comedienne
1995	Bruce Schwartz's Ch. Anasazi Billy The Kid

The Homer Gage Jr. Memorial Trophy

Presented by Dr. and Mrs. Homer Gage for the Best American Bred Welsh Terrier, member owned. To be competed for each year at the WTCA Specialty Show where the Grand Challenge Cup is offered. It is won outright.

1926	Ch. Windermere Piper	Misses de Coppet
1927	Annandale Reik	Annandale Kennels
1928	Windermere Chunkie	Misses de Coppet (stet)
1928	Welsh Ellen	Halcyon Kennels (stet)
1929	Rowdy Boy	Misses de Coppet
1930	Rowdy Boy	Misses de Coppet
1931	Ch. Rowdy Boy	Misses de Coppet
1932	Ch. Rowdy Boy	Misses de Coppet
1933	Ch. Halcyon Play Boy	Halcyon Kennels
1934	Ch. Halcyon Play Boy	Halcyon Kennels
1935	Ch. Halcyon Play Boy	Halcyon Kennels
1936	Ch. Windermere Forrad On	Windermere Kennels
1937	Marlu Rampant	Marlu Farm Kennels
1938	Ch. Marlu Marigold	Marlu Farm Kennels
1939	Ch. Towie Thargelia	Mr. Harold Florsheim
1940	Ch. Halcyon Singleton	Halcyon Kennels
1941	Ch. Bodie's Tom Thumb	Bodie Kennels
1942	Ch. Bodie's Tom Thumb	Bodie Kennels

1943	Twin Ponds Truant	Mrs. Edward P. Alker
1944	Strathglass Bingo's Rexus	Strathglass Kennels
1945	Ch. Twin Ponds Suntan	Mrs. Edward P. Alker
1946	Halcyon Masterpiece	Halcyon Kennels
1947	Twin Ponds Blackout	Mrs. Edward P. Alker
1948	Ch. Twin Ponds Belle	Mrs. Edward P. Alker
1949	Ch. Bodie's Temptation	Bodie Kennels
1950	VOID	
1951	Ch.Syl-Von's Personal Appearance	Vaughn R. Sylvester
1952	Ch.Strathglass Venture's Lucifer	Strathglass Kennels
1953	Syl-Von's Keynoter	Mrs. Thomas W. Bevan
1954	Monona's Devil Dancer	Strathglass Kennels
1955	Ch.Strathglass Admiral's Supreme	Strathglass Kennels
1956	Ch. Beelzebub of Alvin Farm	Mr. & Mrs. Rolfe N. Bolsters
1957	Strathglass Bethesda	Strathglass Kennels
1958	Ch.Pattey's Fancy Lady of Dorian	Mr. & Mrs. S. Sloan Colt
1959	Strathglass Trim Maid	Strathglass Kennels
1960	Windermere Merman	Miss Gertrude de Coppet
1961	Ch. Woodford Coleman	Mr. Frank Ortolani
1962	Ch.Licken Run's Top the Rock	Mr. Harold Florsheim
1963	Ch. Coltan Contessa	Mr. & Mrs. S. Sloan Colt
1964	Ch.Pool Forge Fast Freight	Pool Forge Kennels
1965	Ch. Pool Forge Fast Freight	Pool Forge Kennels
1966	Ch. Pool Forge Fast Freight	Pool Forge Kennels
1967	Ch. Pool Forge Fast Freight	Pool Forge Kennels
1968	Penzance Persephone	Miss Ann Everett
1969	Licken Run's The Admiral	Mr. Wilbert Etter
1970	Ch.Twin Pond's Plaid Cymru	Mrs. Edward P. Alker
1971	Ch.Twin Pond's Plaid Cymru	Mrs. Robert V. Clark Jr.
1972	Ch.Twin Pond's Plaid Cymru	Mrs. Robert V. Clark Jr.
1973	Ch.Twin Pond's Plaid Cymru	Mrs. Robert V. Clark Jr.
1974	Ch.Licken Run's Two Pence Sam	Mr. Wilbert Etter
1975	Ch. Tujay's Touchdown	Bruce Schwartz & J.W. Wornall
1976	Ch. Valoramor's Gala Dulce	John R. K. Tebbetts
1977	Ch. Valoramor's Jolly Rogue	Virginia K. Dickson
1978	Ch. Copperboots Wee Blaste	Dr. & Mrs. O.W. McClung
1979	Ch. Copperboots Wee Blaste	Dr. & Mrs. O.W. McClung
1980	Ch. Coltan Coastal	Mrs. S. Sloan Colt
1981	Ch.Johnel's DD of Redondo Beach	D.Cortum & D.Jacob & Dr. & Mrs O.W. McClung
1982	Ch. Snowtaire's Nutmeg Jeds	O.W. & M.B. McClung

1983	VOID	
1984	VOID	
1985	VOID	
1986	Ch.Ledge Rock's Benjamin	Carole A. Beattie
1987	Ch.Rushwyn's Black Hawk	O.W. & M.B. McClung
1988	Ch.Calkerry Evening Attire	J.L.Heath, W.H. Cosby, & D. Tolone
1989	Ch. Gregmar's Goldspur	Hank Marsh
1990	Ch. Bruhil's Paradice	Bruce Schwartz
1991	Ch.Sunspryte Gregmar's Shorlyne	Dr. & Mrs. O.W. McClung & Pamela Price
1992	Ch.Sunspryte Gregmar's Shorlyne	Dr. & Mrs. O.W. McClung & Pamela Price
1993	Ch. La Sierra's Lucky Lad	R.C. & Karen Williams
1994	Ch. Anasazi Billy The Kid	Bruce Schwartz
1995	Ch.Cisseldale's Sugar Babe	D. Guida, C.A. Beattie & J.L.Heath & W.H. Cosby Jr.

The Sixty-Six Champions Sired by "Duke"

Ch. Gregmar's Vixen of Coppercrest
Ch. Gregmar's Jordyn
Ch. Gregmar's Sunspryte, CG
Ch. Gregmar's Winsom Bewitched
Ch. Gregmar's Montgomery
Ch. Gregmar's Royalcrest RC
Ch. Gregmar's San Diego Charger, CDX, CG
Ch. Gregmar's Synspryte Tribute
Ch. Gregmar's Trendsetter
Ch. Gregmar's Tucson Tontine
Ch. Gregmar's Bandit
Ch. Anasazi Walking Raven
Ch. Anasazi Little Hummingbird
Ch. DD's Rhett Baron
Ch. DD's Johnel Trail Boss
Ch. Calkerry Alexis
Ch. Calkerry Fancy Free
Ch. Gregmar Calkerry Fast Lane
Ch. La Sierra Likely Lass

Ch. Loriden Kalvin Klein
Ch. Loriden Rumor Has It
Ch. Bruhil's Elsje of Melbee
Ch. Bruhil's Maryke
Ch. Glamorgan's Sweet Sue
Ch. Glamorgan's Top Of The Heap
Ch. Gregmar's Olympiad

Ch. La Sierra Mr. Bo Jangles
Ch.Sunspryte'sGregmar Accolate
Ch. La Sierra's Luck Of The Draw
Ch. La Sierra's Lucky Lad
Ch. La Sierra's Up And Coming
Ch. Bowag's Bruce of Moore
Ch. Bronwyn Outrageous
Ch. Calkerry Double Dare
Ch. Desertaire Bombshell
Ch. Mar Mei Belle Starr
Ch. Regency's Sparkler
Ch. Robb's Bonnie's Sparkle

Duke's Pedigree

Ch. Tujays' Yutch

Ch. Tujays' Jason

Premaur's Sparkle Plenty

Ch. Zacharias, CD

Ch. Tujays' Rhett Butler

Tujays' Melanie

Ch. Lady Guinivere of Framar II

Ch. Sorreisa's Six and a Tanner

Eng. Ch. Groveview Valley Lad

Ch. Gunslinger of Groveview

Groveview Miss Penny

Ch. Groveview Allgo

Eng.Ch. Groveview Valley Lad

Pandora of Groveview

Severn Showgirl

Ch. Anasazil Trail Boss

Rhymney Recruit

Ch. Philtown Protocol

Rhymney Peony

Ch. Tujay's Touchdown

Ch. Penzance Polaris

Ch. Tujays' Dubonnet

Tujays' Red Bonnet

Ch. Windsong Helter Skelter

Ch. Quayside Jolly Roger

Ch. Jaclee's Brynn

Morgan Bub's Jolly Patti

Ch. Chayna Laird's Lady

Ch. Penzance Telstar Satellite

Ch. Penzance Nefol Merch

Penzance Personality Plus

Ch. La Sierra Classy Lassie
Ch. Shshown's Wizard of La Sierra
Ch. Bronze Bomber of Dor-Ru
Ch. Dor-Ru Coal Miner's Daughter
Ch. Gregmar's Momento
Ch. DD's Mignonne
Ch. DD's Sir Charles Brown
Ch. Rhondonhaus Renaissance
Ch. Calkerry Carefree
Ch. Calkerry Copper Cruncher
Ch. Bruhil's Paradice
Ch. Wishing Well Main Attraction
Ch. Winsor's Katie Too
Ch. Gregmar's Gossip of La Sierra

Ch. Secwynn Mighty Ms Teak
Ch. La Sierra's Lady Luck
Ch. Woodlanders Mapleafs Forever
Ch. La Sierra's One And Only
Ch. Anasazi Billy The Kid
Ch. Loriden Gucci
Ch. Rhondonhaus Remembrance
Ch. Rhondonhaus Resplendence
Ch. Calkerry Bumper Crop
Ch. Gregmar's Jody
Ch. Bruhil's Paramour
Ch. Wishing Well's Main Event
Ch. Winsor's Tip Topper
Ch. Cascade Ln Rhondonhaus
Andru

Brood Bitches With Six or More Champion Get (to 1995)

Ch. Groveview Typsetter	15
Ch. Gregmar's Gwen	11
Ch. Counselor Wildfire	10
Ch. Valoramor's Gala Dulce	9
Bodie's Top Row	9
Ch. Janterr's Two For One	8
Ch. Barb's Flippant Flirt	7
Ch. Coltan Cherries Jubilee	7
Ch. Deko Deirdre	7
Ch. Janterrs Aur Syndod	7
Jon-El's Autumn Sunburst	7
Ch. Raybrook's Elizabeth Fox	7
Ch. Gatewood Tali's Las Tango	7
Ch. Bardwyn Emily Just Emily	6
Ch. Bernedell First Edition	6
Ch. Counselor Celebration	6
Ch. Daisy Mae of Cascade Lane CDX	6
Groveview Golden Gleam	6
Ch. Jal-Mar's Felstead Kirby	6
Ch. Johnel's D.D. of Redondo Beach	6
Knolland Miss Chaos	6
Ch. Robb's Happy Lady	6
Strathglass Lucifer's Stella	6

Ch. Strathglass Trim Maid 6
Ch. Windsong Helter Skelter 6

Ch. Bodie's Top Row for many years was the top-producing bitch.

Stud Dogs With 20 or More Champion Get (to 1995)

Ch. Anasazi Trail Boss 66
Ch. Ledge Rock's Benjamin 36
Ch. Penzance Polaris 31
Ch. Merthyr's Super Man 31
Ch. Strathglass Bingo's Venture 30
Ch. Rushwyn's Blackhawk 30
Ch. Licken Run's Two Pence Sam 29
Ch. Bardwyn Bronze Bertram 25
Ch. Cascade Lane's Samson McBee 25
Ch. Tujays' Jubilee 23
Ch. Felstead True Form 23
Ch. Colwyn Auspicious Choice 22
Ch. Philtown Protocol 22
Ch. Bengal Wiredot Welsh Prince 21
Ch. Tawe Telstar 21
Ch. Flornell Rare-Bit of Twin Ponds 20

History is in the making and records of stud dogs long since dead will no doubt be increased in future years through the judicious use of frozen semen.

Basic Anatomoy of the Welsh Terrier

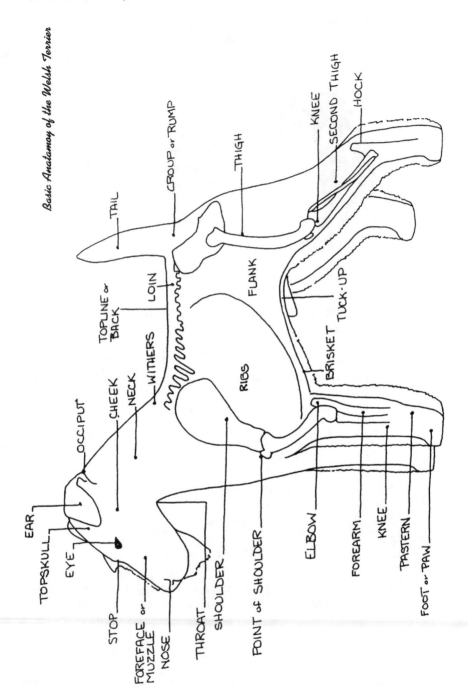

EAR
TOPSKULL
EYE
STOP
FOREFACE or MUZZLE
NOSE
THROAT
SHOULDER
POINT of SHOULDER
ELBOW
FOREARM
KNEE
PASTERN
FOOT or PAW

OCCIPUT
CHEEK
NECK
WITHERS
TOPLINE or BACK
LOIN
TAIL
CROUP or RUMP
THIGH
KNEE
SECOND THIGH
HOCK

RIBS
FLANK
BRISKET
TUCK-UP

WELSH TERRIER CLUB OF AMERICA, INC.
MEMBERSHIP CODE OF ETHICS

As a WTCA member, I will . . .

1. Comply with all American Kennel and Welsh Terrier Club of America rules.

2. Accept and support the constitution and by-laws of the Welsh Terrier Club of America.

3. Be a responsible dog owner and maintain high standards in the care and training of my dog(s).

4. Keep the welfare and health of the dogs and the first criteria in breeding or selling Welsh Terriers.

5. Breed only to improve my dogs to the standard of the breed.

6. Sell dogs with true representation to the purchaser and not use misleading or untruthful statements verbally or in advertising.

7. Sell any dog not of show quality with limited registration and/or a spay/neuter contract.

8. Refuse stud service to any bitch that is not registered with the AKC or a foreign national registry or that is genetically unsound in conformation, health, or temperament. Nor will I use such a dog at stud.

9. Not sell dogs to wholesalers, retailers, or donate dogs to auctions or raffles. Nor will I sell or donate dogs to research unless that research is breed-related and AKC/WTCA approved.

10. Be willing to assist the owner and the WTCARES in the re-placement of all dogs I breed or sell for the life of the dog.

11. Help purchasers with advice and instruction for the life of the dogs and guide novice persons interested in conformation showing, obedience, natural hunts, agility, earthdog trials, and other performance events.

12. Discourage anyone from breeding their dog(s) until they have earned an AKC championship on at least one dog.

13. Make referrals only to those breeders who are believed to adhere to all of the above.

14. Help educate the general public regarding all aspects of the Welsh Terrier.

U.K. BREED STANDARD

1.   The Welsh Terrier is of a gay volatile disposition and is rarely of a shy nature. He is affectionate, obedient, and easily controlled, thus making him an ardently suitable dog for town life. His size and colour render him ideal as a house dog, as the former point is in his favour where accommodation is limited whilst the latter feature precludes the necessity for frequent washing, as in the clips of a white terrier. He is game, fearless, but definitely not of a pugnacious disposition, although at all times able to hold his own when necessary. He is ideally constituted to be a perfect town or country companion. Welsh Terriers are normally hardy and of robust constitution and need no pampering, whilst as working terriers they are second to none, being easily trained to all sorts of game and vermin, to work with gun or ferrets, and are generally found to be capital water dogs.

2.   HEAD and SKULL – Long but proportionate, skull flat and narrow between the ears, but not as narrow as the Wire Fox Terrier, getting slightly narrower towards the eye, free from wrinkle, stop not to defined. The foreface would not "DISH" or fall away quickly, between and below the eyes, where it should be well made up, carrying strength and not chiselled off as seen in a Smooth Fox Terrier. Jaws must be strong and muscular and of good punishing power and depth, but the foreface must not be exaggerated and out of proportion to the skull, as it gives the dog and appearance which is not "WELSH" terrier. An extraordinary long head invariably associated with an oversized or long-backed specimen, which is not wanted and is a fault. The Cheeks should be slightly more muscular than a Wire terrier but an excessive development, usually called "CHEEKY" or thick in head is wrong and uncalled for, and is not becoming a smart, lively terrier as the Welsh terrier should be.

3.   EYES – The eyes should be small, well set in and of a dark colour, expressive and indicating abundant keenness. A round full eye is undesirable.

4.   EARS – The ears should be "V" shaped, small, not too thin, set on fairly high, carried forward and close to the cheek.

5.   MOUTH – Should be as even as possible, with a strong bite.

6.   NECK – The neck should be of moderate length and thickness, slightly arched and sloping gracefully into the shoulders.

7.   BODY – The back should be short and well ribbed up, the loin strong, good depth and moderate width of chest.

8.   The fore-quarters should be long, sloping and well set back.

9.   The hind-quarters should be strong, thighs muscular and of good length, with the hocks well bent, well let down and with ample bone.

10.   LEGS and FEET – The legs should be straight and muscular, possessing ample bone, with upright and powerful pasterns. The feel should be small round and catlike.

11.   The TAIL should be well set on, but not too gaily carried.

12.   COAT – The coat should be wiry, hard, very close and abundant. A single coast is undesirable.

13.   COLOUR – The colour should be BLACK and TAN for preference, or Black, grizzle and Tan, free from black penciling on Toes. Black below the hocks is a disqualification.

14.   SIZE – The height at shoulder should be 15-1/2 inches.

AKC BREED STANDARDS

General Appearance – The Welsh Terrier is a sturdy, compact, rugged dog of medium size with a coarse wire-textured coat. The legs, underbody, and head are tan; the jacket black (or occasionally grizzle). The tail is docked to a length meant to complete the image of a "square dog" approximately as high as he is long. The movement is a terrier trot typical of the long-legged terrier. It is effortless with good reach and drive. The "Welsh Terrier expression" comes from the set, color, and position of the eyes combined with the use of the ears. The Welsh Terrier is friendly, outgoing to people and other dogs, showing spirit and courage.

Size, Proportions, Substance – Males are about the 15 inches at the withers, with an acceptable range between 15 and 15-1/2. Bitches may be proportionally smaller. twenty pounds is considered an average weight, varying a few pounds depending on the height of the dog and the density of bone. Both dog and bitch appear solid and of good substance.

Head – The entire head is rectangular. The eyes are small, dark brown and almond-shaped, well set in the skull. They are placed fairly far apart. The size, shape, color, and position of the eyes give the steady, confident but alert expression that is typical of the Welsh Terrier. The ears are V-shaped, small, but not too thin. The fold is just above the topline of the skull. The ears are carried forward close to the cheek with the tips falling to, or toward, the outside corners of the eyes when the dog is at rest. The ears move slightly up and forward when at attention. Skull – The foreface is strong and powerful, punishing jaws. It is only slightly narrower than the backskull. There is a slight stop. The backskull is of equal length to the foreface. They are on parallel planes in profile. The backskull is smooth and flat9not domed) between the ears. The cheeks are flat and clean (bulging). The muzzle is one-half the length of the entire head from tip of nose to occiput. The foreface in front of the eyes is well made up. The furnishings on the foreface are trimmed to complete without exaggeration the total rectangular outline. The muzzle is strong and squared off, never snipy. the nose is black and squared off. The lips are black and tight. A scissors bite is preferred, but a level bite is acceptable. Either one has complete dentition. The teeth are large and strong, set in powerful, vice-like jaws.

Neck, Topline, Body – The neck is of moderate length and thickness, slightly arched and sloping gracefully into the shoulders. The throat is clean with no excess of skin. The topline is level. The body shows good substance and is well ribbed up. there is good depth of brisket and moderate width of chest. The loin is strong and moderately short. The tall is docked to a length approximately level (on an imaginary line) with the occiput, to complete the square image of the whole dog. The root of the tail is set well up on the back. It is carried upright.

Forequarters – The front is straight. The shoulders are long, sloping and well laid back. the legs are straight and muscular with upright and powerful pasterns. The feet are small, round, and cat like. The pads are thick and black. The nails are strong and black; any dewclaws are removed.

Hindquarters – The hindquarters are strong and muscular with well-developed second thighs and the stifles well bent. The hocks are moderately straight, parallel and short from joint to ground. The feet should be the same as in the forequarters.

Coat – The coat is hard, wiry, and dense with a close-fitting thick jacket. There is a short, soft undercoat. Furnishings on muzzle, legs and quarters are dense and wiry.

Color – The jacket is black, spreading up onto the neck, down onto the tail and into the upper thighs. The legs, quarters, and head are clear tan. The tan is a deep reddish color, with slightly lighter shades acceptable. A grizzle jacket is also acceptable.

Gait – The movement is straight, free and effortless, with good reach in front, strong drive behind, with feet naturally tending to converge toward a median line of travel as speed increases.

Temperament – The Welsh Terrier is a game dog – alert, aware, spirited – but at the same time, is friendly and shows self control. Intelligence and desire to please are evident in his attitude. A specimen exhibiting an overly aggressive attitude, or shyness, should be penalized.

Faults – Any deviation from the foregoing should be considered a fault; the seriousness of the fault depending upon the extent of the deviation.

PHOTO CREDITS

Photographers

Acme
Dave Ashbey
John Ashbey
William Brown
Scott Chamberlain
Dalton
William P. Gilbert
Bernard Kernan
Peter Kirkwood
Joan Ludwig
JoAnn Frier-Murza

Michele Perlmutter
Mikron Photos
Kitten Rodwell
Hiroshi Saito
Henry Schley
Evelyn Shafer
Chuck Tatham
Rudolph W. Tauskey
B. Thurse
Missy Yuhl

Artists & Illustrators

G. Muss-Arnolt
Lori Bush
R. Crowther
Maud Earl
Dorothy Hardcastle
J. F. Lewis

Edwin Megargee
Diane H. Orange
Patricia Peters
Arden Ross
Pam Posey-Tanzey
Arthur Wardle

BIBLIOGRAPHY

AKC's The Complete Dog Book. New York: Macmillan, 1993.

Ash, Edward C. *Dogs: Their History and Development.* London: Hutchinson, 1927.
— Great research, its readability is better than *Dog Encyclopedia*, q.v.

Barrow, George. *Wild Wales.* U.K. and U.S. editions. New York: Putnam, 1901.
— The author travels on foot through Wales at turn of the century.

Bruns, James. *Owney, Mascot of the Railway Mail Service.* Washington, D.C.: The Smithsonian Institution, 1990.
— Adventure piece about a dog that rode the mail trains from 1888 to 1897. Photos seem to indicate he was a Welsh Terrier.

Caius, Dr. Johannes. *De Canibus Brittannicis I.* London, 1729. Translated 1570.
— This is the classic.

Cusick, William. *Canine Nutrition—Choosing the Best Food for <u>Your</u> Breed of Dog.* Wilsonville, OR: Doral Publishing, Inc., 1997.
— General health and nutrition for all dogs, then each breed is examined by what foods were in available to them in the area where they were originally bred. Contains a section on Welsh Terriers.

Fishlock, Trevor. *Wales & The Welsh.* London: Cassell & Company, 1972.
— Anecdotes, history, and the present-day nation of Wales and its people.

Fryman, Elizabeth. How to Raise and Train a Welsh Terrier. Neptune, N.J.: T.F.H. Publishers, 1961.

Gilbert, Edward M. Jr. and Thelma R. Brown. *Structure & Terminology.* New York: Howell Books, 1995.

– How dogs are put together and why.

Glynn, Walter S. *Dogs by Well-Known Authorities*. London, 1906.
    – Contains a chapter on Welsh Terriers.

Greenslade, David. *Welsh Feve*. Wales: D. Brown & Sons, 1983.
    – Welsh people and ethnic activities in the U.S. and Canada.

Grossman, Dr. Alvin. *The Standard Book of Dog Breeding—A New Look*.
    Wilsonville, OR: Doral Publishing, Inc., 1992.
    – Breeding and whelping resource for all breeds.

Horner, Tom. *Terriers of the World*. London: Faber & Faber, 1984.
    – A chapter on Welsh Terriers.

Hubbard, Clifford. *History of the Literature of British Dogs*. Ponterwyd:
    Macmillan, 1949.

Hutchinson, Walter. *Dog Encyclopedia,* vol. III. London: Hutchinson, 1934.
    – Contains numerous wonderful illustrations of Welsh Terriers.

Jesse, Edward, Esq. *Anecdotes of Dogs*. Page 188. London, 1846.

Lee, Rawdon B. *A History of the Modern Dogs of Great Britain & Ireland*. 3
    vols. London: 1893–4.
    – See especially the 1894 volume on Terriers.

Leighton, Robert. *New Book of the Dog*. London: Cassell, 1907.
    – Color plates Chapter XXXIX by Walter S. Glynn on The Welsh
    Terrier.

Marples, Theodore. *Show Dogs*. London, circa 1900.
    – Chapter on Welsh Terriers versus Old English Broken Hair Black
    and Tan.

Marvin, John T. *The Book of All Terrier*. New York: Howell Book House,
    1979.
    – A chapter on Welsh Terriers. Good general terrier history and infor-
    mation.

Maxtee, J. *English and Welsh Terriers*. London, 1908.
    – Breeding, show preparation, training, and management.

Morlais, Thomas I. *The Welsh Terrier (Daeargi Cymraeg) Handbook.*
London: Nicholson & Watson, 1959.
– This is the only full-length book written solely on Welsh Terriers.
(Besides this one of course!)

Ritvo, Harriet. *The Animal Estate.* Harvard University Press, 1987.
– An interesting historical view of how animals took their place in
society.

Ross, Arden M. with illustrations by Lori Bush. *Grooming the Broken Haired
Terrier.* (Originally appeared in *Terrier Type* magazine.)
– This booklet is available from the Airedale Club of America.

Shaw, Vero. *Illustrated Book of the Dog.* London, 1881.
– Color of Airedale, Bedlington, Dandie, Irish, and Fox

The Collins Spurrell Welsh Dictionary - English/Welsh. Glasgow:
HarperCollins, 1991.
– Words, place names, and basic help with pronunciation. Good luck!

Walkowicz, Chris and Bonnie Wilcox, DVM. *Successful Dog Breeding: The
Complete Handbook of Canine Midwifery.* New York: Arco
Publishing, 1985. (Illustrations by Mary Jung.)
– Serious, thought-provoking, informative, and lots of laughs.

Walsh, J. H. "Stonehenge". *The Field.* London, circa 1880.
– "Stonehenge" was Walsh's *nom de plume.* He was *The Kennel* editor and a prolific writer on all breeds of dogs.

—. *The Dogs of the British Isles.* London, 1867.
– History, care of dogs, with a reference to Black and Tan Terrier.

Watson, James. *The Dog Book.* London: Doubleday, 1906.
– Contains a chapter on The Welsh Terrier.

Children's Books

Colby, Jean Poindexter. *Dixie of Dover* New York: Little, Brown & Co.,
1958.
– A boy and his dog. Very "fifties."

Dale, Penny. *Wake Up, Mr. B.!*. London: Walker Books, 1988.
  – Picture book of child's early morning adventures with the dog who
  is either a small Airedale or a large Welsh. We'll assume it's the latter.

de Paola, Tomie. *Jingles the Circus Clown*. New York: Putnam, 1992.
  – Two Welsh pups work in a magical, Christmas circus. Illustrated.
  The author is a WTCA member.

Phillpotts, Beatrice. *Clem and the Runaway Pig*; *Clem and the Dancing Dog*;
  Clem and the Fancy Dress Party; and *Happy Christmas, Clem*.
  (Illustrated by Ingram Pinn.) London: George Weidenfeld &
  Nicolson, Ltd., 1987.
  – This is a series of four children's books featuring Clem, a Welsh
  Terrier, who is reportedly owned by Laura Ashley's son.

GLOSSARY

AKC (American Kennel Club) – An organization that registers approved breeds of dogs and sponsors, sanctions, or licenses dog events. Its equivalent in England The Kennel Club.

AKC Field Representative – AKC's official representative on site at dog shows. Monitors adherence to rules and interprets rules. They evaluate judges, administer judges tests, and answers exhibiters questions.

AKC Gazette – A monthly publication of the American Kennel Club containing articles, statistics about shows and registrations, official, and proposed actions of the Kennel Club.

All Breed Club – A club devoted to the showing and breeding of all breeds of dogs and membership is open to breeders and exhibiters of all breeds. Holds championship shows.

All Breed Show – The most common from of dog show that provides judging for all breeds of dogs. Compare this to a "specialty."

Artificial Insemination – Impregnating a bitch with frozen or extended sperm.

Awkward Phase – Rapid growth period for a puppy that is usually associated with planing out of the head features. Occurs from three to eight months in most breeds.

Back – That portion of the topline starting just behind the withers and ending where the croup and loin join.

Backcrossing – To cross a first generation hybrid with one of the parents.

Baiting – Keeping a dog alert in the ring through the use of liver or a favorite toy.

Balance – Overall fitting of the various parts of the dog to give a picture of symmetry and correct interaction.

BIS – Best in Show. This is the top award in an all breed show.

Bitch – A female dog. Not to be confused with "bitchy," which refers to a human who has gone without sleep for 48 hours while awaiting the birth of puppies.

Bite – Position of upper and lower teeth in relation to each other. Various breed standards call for different kinds of bite often based on function. In Welsh, a scissors bite is preferred.

Bloodline – A specific strain or type within a breed.

BOB – Best of Breed. Best of that breed in an all breed or specialty show. In an all breed show it goes on to compete for higher awards.

BOS – Best of Opposite Sex. If a male wins Best of Breed, then the judge will pick the best of the bitches. The reverse is true if a bitch wins Best of Breed.

BOW – Best of Winners. Defeats other sex winner and captures that sex's points if greater than its own on that day.

Breech – Puppy is born feet first rather than head first. Can cause whelping difficulties.

Breed Ring – Exhibition area where dogs are judged by breed.

Breeder-Owner Handled – When the breeder, who is also the owner, personally shows the dog. See also "handler."

Brucellosis – A sexually transmitted disease or infection.

Caesarean Section – Removing puppies from the womb surgically.

Campaigning a Dog – Seriously exhibiting a champion to compete for top honors in his breed, group, and top-ten all breed honors.

Canine Herpes Virus – An infection in puppies caused by an infected dam. It is a leading cause of puppy mortality.

Canine Parvovirus – Myocardial forms attack only puppies. Severe, often fatal reaction. Cardial form attacks older dogs.

CD – Companion Dog. A title earned in obedience, it is the lowest of four levels of obedience. See also "UDT."

CDX – Companion Dog Excellent. A title earned in obedience, it is the second lowest level of obedience, one step up from CD.

Championship – A title earned by winning 15 points under AKC rules including two major awards of 3, 4, or 5 points under two different judges. See also "points."

Colostrum – Sometimes referred to as the "first milk," it great improves a puppy's immunity and resistance to many viral and bacterial diseases.

Contour – Silhouette or profile, form, or shape.

Conformation – The form and structure of the various parts to fit a standard. When a dog is being judged on conformation, the judge is evaluating him on his physical structure and how it adheres to the standard of the breed.

Crabbing – Moving with body at an angle to the line of travel like a land crab. Also called sidewinding. Also refers to what is heard ringside when entrants lose.

Crate – A metal, plastic or wood kennel (in various sizes). Dogs may sleep and travel in them.

Cropped – Trimming the ears to fit a breed pattern.

Cryptorchid – A male dog with neither testicle descended. Ineligible to compete at AKC breed shows but may enter any AKC performance events.

Dam – Mother of a litter of puppies. Not to be confused with the expletive often used at obedience trials when your Welsh pretends you no longer exist.

Dehydration – Loss of body fluids - may lead to death.

Developmental Phases – Stages through which puppies grow.

Dew Claws – Hardy nails above pastern. Most breeds have them removed. In many breeds they are not present.

Docking – The clipping off of the tail to a prescribed length to meet a breed standard.

Dog Shows – An AKC-sponsored event in which any or all AKC approved varieties of dogs compete in conformation, obedience, and/or junior showmanship.

Eclampsia – An attack of convulsions during or after pregnancy.

Eng.Amer.Ch. – A dog who has won both its English and its American championships.

Estrus – Period of bitch's heat cycle when she is ready to breed.

Exhibiters – People who show their dogs.

Expression – Facial expression or countenance.

Fading Puppy Syndrome – A malnourished puppy due to loss of electrolytes. May lead to death. (See beef liver-yogurt recipe.)

Fallopian Tubes – Conduits for eggs from ovary to uterus.

Fetus – The growing puppy within the womb.

Filial Regression – The tendency of offspring to regress toward mediocrity if controlled breeding is not carried out.

Finishable – A dog who is capable of completing its championship.

Forechest – The point of the thorax that protrudes beyond the point of the shoulder.

Foreface – That part of the muzzle from just below the forehead to the nose.

"From the Classes" – In a dog show, there are the following classes: Puppies 6–9 months, Puppies 9–12 (although in a specialty shows there is also a class for 12–18 months), Novice, American-Bred, Bred-by-Exhibitor, Open, and Champions Only. In specialty shows, there may also be classes for veteran dogs and bitches. When a dog or bitch wins "from the classes," it means that it won not only over the other competitors, but also beat out the champions!

Gaiting – Moving a dog to discern proper movement.

Genetics – The study of the science of heredity.

Genotype – Genetic term meaning the unseen genetic makeup of the dog. The traits carried within a dog likely to be passed on to its descendants.

Gestation – The organic development of the puppy within the uterus.

Get – A dog or bitch's descendants.

Go-to-Ground – When a dog burrows after its prey or enters its underground den. In Earthdog Trials, going-to-ground is a timed event that takes place in a man-made structure (often bales of hay or other structures—sometimes actually built into the ground) with live prey, which is caged so that it can't be harmed.

Groom – To comb, clip or strip, and brush a dog which does not want to be combed, clipped or stripped, and brushed.

Grooming Table – A specially designed (often foldable) table with matting for grooming and training dogs. Not intended as a high-diving board.

Handler – The person, often a paid professional, who shows the dog. Often they not only show the dog, but are also professional trainers as well.

Handlers Guild – An association of Professional Handlers stressing professionalism.

Heat – The time when a bitch comes into season and can be bred. May be once or twice a year for Welsh Terriers.

Heredity – The sum of what a dog inherits from preceding generations.

Hetrozygous – Non dominant for a trait or color. Carries both dominant and recessive genes for a variety of traits.

Homozygous – Dominant for a trait or color. Carries no recessive gene for that characteristic.

Hypothermia – A chilling of the puppies which is likely to cause death. Place the puppy on a towel and use a warm hot water bottle or heating pad set on medium and watch closely. Add another puppy or two on either side of the cold puppy for companionship and additional warmth and stimulation.

Inbreeding – Very close familial breeding. i.e., brother to sister, father to daughter or son to mother. See also "line breeding."

Intl.Ch. – A title won in multiple countries. It sometimes refers to a dog who has won both his American championship and his championship in at least one other country, but not from England. Such a dog would be titled "Eng.Am.Ch."

Judge – A person approved by AKC or UKC to judge various breeds. Your best friend if you win. But often a person who hates you and your dog unfairly and without provocation; one who takes it upon himself to personally ruin your dog's career. See "Satan."

Junior – The preteen and teenage version of showing dogs in conformation at AKC events. The dog is not judged, only the junior showing it.

Labor – The act of whelping puppies.

Lead – Also called a leash.

Lead Training – Teaching the dog to walk and trot properly so as to best exhibit his conformation. Also used for safety.

Line Breeding – Breeding closely within a family of dogs. i.e., grandfather to granddaughter. Similar to "inbreeding" but the breeding is between members not quite so closely related.

Match Show – A dog show that serves as a training ground for young dogs, prospective judges, and members of the dog club holding the show.

Metritis – A uterine infection in the dam that can transmit bacterial infection to an entire litter.

Monorchid – A male dog with only one testicle descended. Ineligible to compete in AKC shows.

Nasal Aspirator – A suction device for sucking mucous from infant puppies nasal passages.

Neonatal – New born.

Neonatal Septecemia – An infection in newborn puppies caused by staphylococcus germs in the dam's vaginal tract.

Obedience – An AKC-sponsored portion of a dog show in which the dog is evaluated by the judge on performance of the required elements for an obedience championship. To achieve an obedience title, a dog must receive three "legs," i.e., qualifying scores.

Outcrossing – The mating of a dog to an unrelated dog with the idea in mind to reinstate vigor and substance or to improve a given feature, physical or temperamental.

Ovulation – The female process of creating eggs for reproduction.

Ovum – An egg ready for sperm to fertilize it.

Parasites – Infestations of lice, ticks or fleas as well as internal infestation of various worms.

Pastern – The dog's shock absorber. Located at the juncture where the paw meets foreleg.

Pedigree – Hierarchical listing of a dog's ancestors. Best used when combined with hands-on knowledge of the dogs. Where to look when assigning blame for undesirable physical traits.

PHA – Professional Handlers Association, which stresses the ethics and training of handlers.

Phenotype – The actual outward appearance that can be physically seen—opposite of genotype.

Placenta – A vascular organ that links the fetus to the dam's uterus. Nourishes and mediates fetal change. After the puppies have been born, it is discharged and is also called "afterbirth."

Points – Awarded by the AKC based on the number of dogs competing by sex and breed. Each part of the country has a different point rating based upon previous years entries. The maximum number of points per show is 5. See also "championship."

Pounding – Results when front stride is shorter than rear. Hindquarter thrust forces front feet to strike the ground before they are fully prepared to absorb shock.

Proestrus – First part of heat cycle.

Proven Sire – Male dog that has enough offspring to judge his potency.

Puppy Septicemia – Bacterial infection caused by a mastitis infection in the dam. Often fatal if not treated immediately.

Purebred – A dog whose sire and dam are of the same breed and whose lineage is unmixed with any other breed.

Recessive – Color or trait that is not dominant and must link up with another recessive for expression.

Reserve Winners – The runner up to the winner. A reserve winner may gain points if the winner is ineligible or is later disqualified.

Ringside Pickup – When a handler takes on a dog on the day of the show rather than having him in his traveling string of dogs.

Ring Stewards – Persons assisting the judge by assembling classes, giving out arm bands, arranging ribbons, and a general helper for the judge.

Sac – Membrane housing puppy within uterus.

Satan – Evil incarnate. Known to take many forms including dog show judges, handlers, exhibitors, or even another dog whose mere presence makes your dog act worse than his true champion self. What you become when you speak badly of other exhibitors/competitors, purposefully harm's another's campaign, or willfully allow your dog to hinder or interfere with other dogs.

Scrotum – Housing for male dogs testicles.

Show Pose – Setting a dog in a position to exhibit its conformation. Also called stacking.

Show Superintendent – The person hired by a show-giving club to manage and run the show.

Sidewinding – See "crabbing."

Sire – Father of a litter.

Specials Dog – A dog or bitch that has competed its championship in the conformation classes and is shown in Best of Breed, Group, and Best in Show.

Specialty Club – A club devoted to fanciers of one specific breed of dog.

Specialty – A show dedicated to only one breed of dog and only dogs of that specific breed may be entered.

Spermatozoa – Motile sperm from male dog.

Stacking – See "show pose."

Stamp – A desirable quality or expression that becomes synonymous with a specific stud dog or line of breeding.

Standard – An official description of the breed developed by a breed's parent club and approved by AKC.

Structural Design – The blueprint from which the originators of a breed sought to create a dog for the task at hand

Symmetry – A pleasing balance of all parts.

Test Breeding – A mating usually of a parent of unknown genotype and one of a known genotype to reveal what characteristics the unknown one will throw.

Tie – The locking together of the dog and bitch during mating caused by the swelling of the Bulbis Glandis just behind the penis bone.

Topline – That portion of the dog's outline from the withers to the set on of the tail.

Type – Characteristics that distinguishes a breed.

UD – Utility Dog. An obedience title, it is the second highest title that can be earned in obedience, higher than CD and CDX.

UDT utility Dog Tracking. This is the highest obedience title that can be earned. The others, in ascending order, are CD, CDX, and UD.

Umbilical cord – A cord that connects the fetus with the placenta attaching at the puppies navel.

Unbroken Line – A pedigree line of continuous producers down to the current sire or dam.

Vaccinations – Shots administered to ward off a plethora of diseases.

Wean – The gradual changing of a puppy from its mother's milk to solid food.

Whelping Box – The place where you you wish to have the litter born and the bitch doesn't. Later used by the nursing bitch and her puppies.

Winners Dog and Bitch – The best from all the competing classes. Wins points toward championship.

Withers – Highest point on the shoulder blades.

WTCA – Welsh Terrier Club of America.

WTCARES – Welsh Terrier Club of America REScue.

INDEX